A REMARKABLE TRUE STORY OF HOPE AND TRIUMPH
AMID THE HORROR OF TEHRAN'S BRUTAL EVIN PRISON

CAPTIVE IN IRAN

MARYAM ROSTAMPOUR & MARZIYEH AMIRIZADEH
WITH JOHN PERRY

For current information on the persecuted church please contact:
THE VOICE OF THE MARTYRS
PO Box 443
Bartlesville, OK 74005
(918) 337-8015
www.persecution.com

TYNDALE
MOMENTUM
AN IMPRINT OF TYNDALE HOUSE PUBLISHERS, INC.

Visit Tyndale online at www.tyndale.com.

Visit Tyndale Momentum online at www.tyndalemomentum.com.

TYNDALE is a registered trademark of Tyndale House Publishers, Inc. *Tyndale Momentum* and the Tyndale Momentum logo are trademarks of Tyndale House Publishers, Inc. Tyndale Momentum is an imprint of Tyndale House Publishers, Inc.

Captive in Iran: A Remarkable True Story of Hope and Triumph amid the Horror of Tehran's Brutal Evin Prison

Designed by Jennifer Ghionzoli

Edited by Dave Lindstedt

Published in association with the literacy agency of Calvin Edwards & Company, 1200 Ashwood Parkway, Suite 140, Atlanta, GA 30338.

Scripture quotations are taken from *The Holy Bible*, English Standard Version® (ESV®), copyright © 2001 by Crossway, a publishing ministry of Good News Publishers. Used by permission. All rights reserved.

Because of the sensitive nature of the stories told about women imprisoned in the Vozara Detention Center and Evin Prison in Iran, many names have been changed to safeguard the privacy and dignity of the individuals involved.

ISBN 978-1-4143-7120-7 (hardcover)

ISBN 978-1-4143-8304-0 (International Trade Paper Edition)

Printed in the United States of America

19	18	17	16	15	14	13
7	6	5	4	3	2	1

To the memory of our dear friend Shirin Alam Hooli, whose courage, kindness, and love live on in the hearts of all who knew her; to the precious women who were with us in Evin during our imprisonment (some of whom have since been released); and to all the women in Evin today still waiting for the justice that only a free nation can give them.

CONTENTS

FOREWORD

RECENTLY I RETURNED from a ministry trip to India, but within thirty-six hours I was on the road again. This time my destination was a women's retreat about ninety minutes from Atlanta, Georgia. I spoke in the evening, and the next morning the director of the retreat came to my cabin with two Iranian women she felt I would be interested in meeting. I was given the American version of their names: Marcie and Miriam.

We chatted for a moment, and then, knowing they were both from a Muslim nation, I asked them each to share how they had come to place their faith in Jesus Christ. I wasn't prepared for the thrilling blessing they began to pour out upon me as they shared their personal journeys of faith. They hadn't been just saved from sin. They hadn't just converted to the Christian religion. They were both in love with Jesus! For the next hour or so, they shared with me why—it was a love forged in the fires of pain and persecution.

Toward the end of our time together, with tears streaming down their lovely faces, they made a comment that haunts me still: They said it had been easier for them to experience God's peace and presence and power inside Evin Prison than on the outside in America. Evin Prison! The prison in Tehran that has a worse reputation than Alcatraz or Angola in the United States. A place that causes even the strongest to shudder. How could that be?

Because I had a plane to catch, there was no time to find out why they would make such a comment. Or to hear some of their experiences inside Evin Prison. Or how they had known God there. Or how their faith had not only survived the experience, but thrived in it! So several weeks later, when I received a letter from them asking for permission to send me the manuscript of their new book for the purpose of writing the foreword, I quickly agreed. I couldn't wait to plunge into the details of their experience. And I was not disappointed.

As I read, I was held spellbound page after page, story after story. But what impacted me most was not the words they used to describe life behind prison walls, but what I read between the lines. I was, and still am, blown away by their boldness, their strength, their steadfastness, and their unwavering declaration of Jesus as the Son of God, the Savior of the world, the risen Lord and King. They lovingly and fearlessly presented Him to broken women who responded with tearful desperation, to manipulative women who tried to use them for their own purposes, to hostile officials and guards who had the power to torture, to judges who could have released them earlier if they had just been willing to compromise their faith.

Inside the dark hell of Evin Prison, Marcie and Miriam turned on the Light! Their love for the least, their kindness to the meanest, their gentleness to the roughest, their willingness to serve in the dirtiest place imaginable is truly a stunningly clear reflection of the Jesus they love, as well as evidence of His presence inside those walls. He didn't just carry them through *somehow*—He carried them through triumphantly!

And I wondered . . . has God brought them here, to America, to share their remarkable stories in order to prepare His people for what's coming? So we will know that our God is faithful and true, wherever we find ourselves? Because we all have our prison experiences, don't we? Prisons of physical pain, of financial ruin, of emotional brokenness, of spousal abuse, of marital betrayal . . .

Captive in Iran has strengthened my faith. Read it, and I believe you will be strengthened in yours, also.

Anne Graham Lotz

CHAPTER 1

NOTHING TO WORRY ABOUT

MARYAM

I arrived home from the dentist to an empty house, and my jaw was throbbing. As I poured a glass of water to take some pain medication, the phone rang. It was my sister, Shirin.

"I'm so glad I caught you at home," she said, her voice anxious. "I had a terrible dream about you last night. I dreamed you had disappeared, and a voice told me you would be in a dark and dreadful place where you would be afraid. Suddenly the sky opened above your head and you were pulled upward by your hair into a beautiful green landscape. Then the voice said, 'This is what is happening to your sister.'"

"Forget about it," I said lightly. "You're getting yourself all worked up over nothing. Everything's fine. Marziyeh and I are going on vacation for two weeks during the New Year's holidays, and you and I can talk again while we're on the road."

The truth was that Marziyeh and I would be traveling, but not on vacation. That was just the story we told our friends and family for their own safety. We would actually be spending the time in other Iranian cities, handing out New Testaments.

To be honest, Shirin's dream bothered me more than I would admit, because I had also recently had a disturbing dream, one in which Marziyeh and I were standing on a hill with a group of boys and girls. A shining old man told a prophecy about each of us. When he looked at Marziyeh and me, he said, "You two will be taken."

With our upcoming trip, and now these two dreams occurring so close together, it was more than a little unsettling.

Whatever God has planned is what will happen.

| | |

I was dozing on the couch when the doorbell rang. I heard Marziyeh's voice in the hallway and some other voices I didn't recognize.

That's odd. Why doesn't she just come in? Maybe she forgot her key.

Peering through the peephole, I saw Marziyeh, another young woman in Islamic dress, and two young men.

"Open the door," the young woman said.

My mouth hurt and my mind was fuzzy from the medication, and I needed time to think.

"You'll have to wait until I change my clothes," I said through the door. For a man who was not a relative to enter the apartment, Islamic law required that I observe the strict dress code prescribed by the Koran.

"Don't worry," the woman answered. "Only I will come inside."

When I opened the door, the woman pushed her way in and immediately escorted me to my room to put on acceptable clothes. When we returned to the living room, Marziyeh was sitting on the couch with her hair properly covered, and the two young men were ransacking our apartment. As we watched in shock and horror, they methodically rummaged through every corner of every room, emptying drawers, cabinets, and closets, and pawing through our books and CDs. They even searched the food pantry in the kitchen.

Of course, they had no search warrant, no written orders of any kind. They were *basiji*, part of the Revolutionary Guard, and they didn't need permission to do anything. Like most *basiji*, these two were young and arrogant, bullies in their late teens or early twenties dressed in ragtag outfits that reflected their semiofficial status, somewhere between government militiamen and common thugs. They wore no uniforms, and because they wanted to blend into the crowd, they didn't even wear *chafiehs*, the black-and-white-checked scarves that some *basiji* wore symbolically as followers of Iran's supreme leader, Ayatollah Ali Khamenei. Their clothes were as dirty as they were.

Marziyeh and I had shared this simple apartment north of central Tehran for the past year. It was a quiet flat on a hill, with a fireplace in the living room, white walls, dark red curtains, and modern furniture covered with bold, dark orange fabric and big poofy pillows. The windows in the two bedrooms looked out onto the beautiful Darkeh Mountains, a popular destination for mountain climbers. From the balcony off the kitchen, we could see the street below and the severe, high walls of a nearby prison.

This apartment was our home, our refuge, and also the meeting place of a secret church of young people and others who risked imprisonment or death to worship Jesus Christ with us in violation of the law. In our bedrooms, we each had a stack of plastic chairs and a supply of Christian New Testaments and other literature. From our base of operations, we were quietly spreading the gospel of Jesus Christ in this sprawling city of more than seven million. Now these strangers had arrived without warning and were ordering us around.

"Sit on the couch," one of the *basiji* snapped, "and don't talk to each other."

He was lanky and nervous, more a boy than a man, with heavy eyebrows, a shock of thick black hair, and a sparse, fuzzy beard. Emboldened by his position and by Islamic law—which places women under the authority of men from age nine, the time girls are considered old enough for marriage—he left no question that we had better cooperate and keep our mouths shut.

The other *basiji*—older and taller, with fair skin and green eyes—who seemed to be in charge, took a more conciliatory approach. "Don't worry, ladies," he said. "Just stay seated and remain calm."

Though the two men were clearly in command, they had to have a female chaperone, according to Islamic law, in order to enter our home, because we were not relatives of theirs. The young woman wore a *chador*, the long, loose, lightweight robe that Muslim women must wear in public or in the presence of men who are not relatives. Underneath, we could see her green uniform. Maybe she was some kind of police officer.

Fortunately, while the *basiji* were searching, Marziyeh and I found an opportunity to hide our cell phones. Our address books, text messages, and photo archives could tie our friends to us and put them in danger. There were pictures on our computer of our missionary trips to India and South Korea. Unfortunately, I hadn't turned off the television before the intruders burst in; our TV was illegal because it had satellite service with programming that was uncensored and therefore a threat to the purity of the Islamic state.

| | |

Marziyeh

As the minutes stretched into an hour and then more, the young police-woman kept a close watch on us as the two men began tossing our belongings into boxes on the living room floor. They had found hundreds of Christian-themed CDs and New Testaments in Farsi, the language of Iran. They noticed Christian messages posted on the refrigerator.

"Have you become a Christian?" the older *basiji*, whose name we learned was Mohammadi, asked Maryam.

"Yes," she answered, her voice strong and confident. "I have been a Christian for eleven years."

He turned to me. "Why did you become a Christian? What bad has our Imam Husein ever done to you?" he demanded, referring to one of our Islamic religious leaders.

"I became a Christian because I met Jesus," I explained. "I didn't turn away from anything. I turned toward Jesus because He came into my heart and called me to Himself."

"So you met Jesus?" Mohammadi asked sarcastically. "What did he look like? Was he black or blond? Did he have a beard?"

I didn't answer. As I watched the systematic destruction of our apartment, I remembered the dreams I'd had that I would one day be in prison, doing battle for my faith. I had told only Maryam and a few other friends about this premonition that I would somehow end up behind bars. "Aren't you afraid of the thought of prison?" they had asked me. "Aren't you afraid of being tortured or raped?" My answer was always the same. "God is my Father, and He would never let these horrible things happen to me. If He did, it would be to fulfill His will in a way I could not understand. It is a mystery, but I will always trust the Lord."

By now it was after 6:00 p.m. and the *basiji* had been ransacking our apartment for more than two hours. Asking permission to leave the couch, Maryam and I brought them New Testaments and CDs they had overlooked, and even helped to count them: 190 New Testaments and 500 CDs.

Refusing to be intimidated, Maryam said, "You must return all of these to us!"

"I'm sure you'll get them back," Mohammadi promised unconvincingly.

Maryam picked up a New Testament and handed it to him. "You should take one of these and read it."

"I have," he insisted. "But I've read the real and true version, not one of these distorted ones."

By that he probably meant that he'd read the so-called Gospel of Barnabas, a false version of Scripture, published in Farsi in the 1700s, that portrays Jesus not as the Son of God and Savior of the world, but as a lesser prophet in line with the Koran's description of Him. Many Muslims think this is a Christian Gospel because they've never had a chance to read the real thing.

He held up another book, *The Confessions of St. Augustine.* "What are you doing with this book?" he demanded.

"You can get it in bookstores all over the country," I replied. "We thought it would be interesting."

As Mohammadi continued poking through our books, I wasn't sure he could even read. If he could, his knowledge of books was sketchy at best—typical of the close-minded, poorly educated people the government had on its payroll by the thousands. He couldn't tell Christian books from the rest. He didn't recognize CDs we had by one of the top music groups in the country.

"The Lord seems to be everywhere in this house," Mohammadi said after a minute.

"You won't find anything but the Lord here," I replied, "because we live with the Lord."

We were on dangerous ground. These people had searched our apartment without a warrant. Now they were likely to arrest us without bringing any charges. Technically, it's not illegal to be a Christian in Iran. However, in practical terms, policemen, Revolutionary Guards, judges, and every other authority in the country interpret the law for themselves and aren't accountable to anyone. These two boys and the young woman with them could charge us with anything, or hold us and not charge us at all. And though being a Christian was not a crime, converting from Islam to another faith and evangelizing on behalf of that faith were considered crimes of apostasy and punishable by death.

While it was true that Maryam and I had been raised in Muslim households and had Islamic names, we had not embraced Islam as children or young adults. In our minds, we had never "converted" from Islam because we'd never really believed in Islam to begin with. We had met each other at an evangelical conference in Turkey, had decided to work together, and had spent the last three years in Tehran quietly sharing the gospel with anyone who was interested. For two of those years, having divided the city into squares on a huge wall map, we had gone out at night between 8:00 p.m. and midnight, visiting one sector at a time. We handed out New Testaments in cafés, gave them to taxi drivers, and left them in cabs, coffee shops, and mailboxes. When we finished a section, we marked it with a cross on our map. In three years altogether, we had given away about twenty thousand New Testaments.

We also traveled outside Tehran, taking Bibles to other cities. We even left some New Testaments inside the temple at Qom, the most sacred holy place in Islam, a place Christians are not even allowed to enter. But what better place to introduce people to the truth of Jesus Christ! Over the years, we had learned to be cautious and to depend on God to protect us wherever we went.

Nonetheless, we had aroused official suspicions. We weren't going to deny our faith or hide it, under any circumstances, but now that the government had its eye on us, our challenge would be staying true to Christ while continuing our ministry without getting caught.

These thoughts and memories raced through my mind as Maryam and

I helped the *basiji* pack up everything they wanted—New Testaments, CDs, our private journals, personal belongings, identity documents, and more. They ordered us to come with them, though we weren't allowed to take any extra clothes or supplies. We had no idea where they were taking us or when we would be home again.

"Should we take winter clothes or summer clothes?" Maryam asked, trying to lighten the mood. There was no answer.

The young woman escorted us out to a small, dingy white car and sat between us in the backseat. The men followed, carrying boxes of our belongings. It was dusk and the wind was getting cold. The street outside our apartment was quiet, but as we drove through the neighborhood, the streets became crowded with holiday shoppers preparing for the Iranian New Year's celebration, which was a little more than two weeks away. Cars jostled for room along the narrow roadways, and the sidewalks were packed to overflowing.

We drove past the prison walls we could see from our kitchen. It was Evin Prison, a notorious compound built during the reign of the Shah to hold those who opposed his regime. Since the Shah's fall from power in 1979, Evin has been used for political prisoners, solitary confinement, and torture of those considered enemies of the Islamic state. We passed its towering red brick walls almost every day. Often we had wondered who was imprisoned there and what their lives were like. Maybe we were about to find out.

Finally we pulled up to the police station in the Gisha neighborhood, a three-story brick building where people came and went all day for motor vehicle documents. As usual, the main entrance was busy. But instead of taking us in through the front door, the *basiji* ordered us out of the car and escorted us to a quiet back alley out of public view, with extra guards at the door. This was the entrance to Base Two, the facility for the security police who deal with crimes against the state.

| | |

Our incredible, frightening journey had started early that morning, March 5, 2009. As Maryam and I were getting ready to go our separate ways to run some errands, I received a mysterious phone call. A polite voice on the line informed me of a problem with my car registration and asked me to go to the Gisha police station before two o'clock to sort it out. I quickly called the former owner of the car to see if he knew of any problem, but he didn't answer his phone. Then I called an attorney friend to ask if I should be concerned.

"No," my friend assured me. "These problems come up all the time. It's nothing to worry about."

Even so, I couldn't help thinking about what had happened a few days earlier when I went to have my passport renewed. One of the forms had asked me to indicate my religion, and I had checked the box for "Christian." When my turn came at the counter, the clerk was indignant.

"How is this possible?" he demanded. "You have an Islamic name. Your parents are Muslims. How can you be a Christian?"

"With the Lord, anything is possible," I said. The clerk shot me a stern look but said nothing more.

I remembered that exchange as I went on my errands and visited my sister, Elena, before arriving at the police station at about 11:30. A guard at the door stopped me.

"What is your business here?" he asked.

"I received a call saying there might be a problem with my car registration," I explained.

"You should not enter here dressed that way."

I was modestly dressed, with my hair completely covered, as required in public, but I was not wearing the Islamic *chador* because I am not a Muslim.

"But I have covered myself," I said.

"I've said what I have to say," the guard replied. "The rest is up to you. But if you come in dressed that way, you will be ignored and no one will help you."

In the interest of getting to the bottom of the documentation mystery, I went back to the apartment and changed, then returned to the police station. By then, the office was closed for lunch and for one of the daily calls to prayer required by Islamic law.

I explained to the guard that I had been told to be at the office no later than 2:00 p.m. The guard insisted the office was closed and that no one could help me now. After several minutes of arguing, I finally convinced him to let me inside, where I explained to the clerk at the counter about the phone call.

"That's impossible," the clerk declared. "I don't think we called you. You must be mistaken." He handed me an address. "Try this office instead."

At that moment, an overweight, middle-aged man in a police uniform walked by. "I am Mr. Haghighat," he said pleasantly. (*Haghighat* is the Farsi word for "truth." Police officials, judges, and other people in the Iranian government don't use their real names. This man's alias would soon prove ironic.) "I think I can help you," he said. "Follow me."

He led me down a hallway to a sparsely furnished room where a husky man with a big, square face covered with heavy black stubble sat waiting at a table. His dark, deep-set eyes seemed too small for his head, and his brow was deeply furrowed with a constant scowl.

To my surprise, the man smiled and said, "You've come to the right place. I am the one who called you this morning. My name is Mr. Rasti." (*Rasti* is another Farsi word meaning "truth.") "Please take a seat," he said. Mr. Haghighat left the room and closed the door behind him, leaving me alone with Mr. Rasti.

"Show me your papers," he said.

I handed over my identification card, driver's license, and vehicle registration. After looking at them for a long moment, Mr. Rasti began asking questions, without looking up.

"Are you married or single?"

"Single."

"Do you live alone or with your parents?"

"I live with a friend."

He asked for my address and some other personal details. Then there was another pause.

"Are you a Christian?"

Aha! This was their purpose all along. The car had nothing to do with it. They've called me in because of my passport application. "Yes, I have been a Christian for eleven years. Why do you ask me now?"

"Do you know the Bible?"

"Yes, of course. I am a Christian and I know the Bible. I have a Bible. Is there a problem with that?"

Mr. Rasti didn't answer; instead, he asked if I had been at a certain restaurant on a specific date. It was a popular restaurant that served customers in traditional style, reclining on couches at tables placed on low platforms. The food and music were traditional as well. Young people packed the place, and plainclothes security police watched it constantly.

"I don't remember," I replied. "I can't even remember what I ate yesterday. I think I know this restaurant, but I don't know if I was there on that date or not."

Mr. Rasti looked up at last, his eyes drilling into mine. "Our security guards saw you and your friend at that restaurant last month, giving away Bibles. They took down your license number, and now we have found you. Did you give Bibles to people in that restaurant?"

"I am a Christian," I repeated, "and I believe in the Bible. If somebody asks me questions about the Bible, I answer them. If somebody asks me for a Bible, I will give them one. It could be that I gave someone a New Testament in that restaurant. Is there a problem with that?"

Mr. Rasti's mood and expression changed completely. He sprang from his chair with a sour expression on his face and shouted, "I'll tell you the problem with that! Guard! Get me two female officers in this room immediately!"

The sudden change of atmosphere was startling, and it frightened me for a moment. Then I remembered the promise I had made to the Lord long ago: *I will never deny You. I trust You to be with me always and overcome my fear.*

Two women in *chador*s and long veils rushed into the room. "You are under arrest," Mr. Rasti said as one of the women fastened handcuffs around my wrists. He left the room and returned with two other men, one young and lanky, the other a little older and fair skinned.

"We have orders to search your apartment," Mr. Rasti declared. "You must go with these two while they conduct the search. What about your roommate—where is she now?"

"At the dentist," I replied.

"At the dentist, or off somewhere handing out Bibles?" Mr. Rasti said with a smirk.

Still in handcuffs, I was hustled into a small white police car with the two young men and a young woman named Zahra, who beamed at me with a superior air. On our way to the apartment, I leaned over to Zahra and whispered, "I am a Christian. You have shackled me for my faith and for no other reason. I am honored to serve Christ this way, and I want you to know I'm not upset with you for what you did." Zahra's smile quickly faded, and she didn't look at me again for the rest of the trip.

| | |

MARYAM

Before going to the dentist, I had spent part of the morning shopping for the upcoming New Year's celebration, braving crowds so dense I could scarcely walk through the streets, where shop windows were piled high with goods. Some of the items, such as painted eggs, were available only around the holidays.

As I made my way through the crowded streets, I thought, *Maybe after I'm done at the dentist I'll buy a couple of traditional New Year's goldfish— a red one for Marziyeh and a black one for myself.*

I had overheard Marziyeh's phone call about the car registration that morning and the call to her lawyer friend asking for advice. The story about the car had sounded suspicious, and I was worried. But I reminded myself, *Whatever God has planned for our lives to fulfill His purpose is what will happen. No person, no regime, has the power to change it.*

After thirty minutes in the dentist's chair, I made a follow-up appointment for a few days later. Still worried about Marziyeh and the mysterious call, I called her cell phone.

"I'm at home," Marziyeh said, "but I'll only be here long enough to change clothes so that the clerk at the police station will help me."

"Wait till I get there," I said. "Something isn't right about this. Let's talk it over and think about what to do."

"You're right that we have to be careful," Marziyeh said, "but I want to get back to the police station and get that taken care of so I can do the rest of my errands. I'll write the address down and leave it for you." Little did I know that Marziyeh was walking into a trap and would return home under arrest. Our faith in God was about to be put to the test.

Only two days earlier, she and I had been talking to each other about Luke, who had become a follower of Jesus at a dangerous time and had followed the apostle Paul faithfully until Paul's martyrdom. Could we be that faithful, that strong? Yes, we could, we agreed. We would go anywhere for Christ—Saudi Arabia, Moscow, wherever the voice of the Lord was threatened the most.

But could we really? Would we truly go anywhere to follow Jesus and do His work? The commitment seemed easy enough when we were talking about it alone in our apartment. Now we were under arrest and in police custody, and the prospect was a far more serious matter. From the look on Marziyeh's face, I could tell she felt the same way I did: trying to appear confident on the outside, but petrified with fright on the inside. My already queasy stomach had turned to knots and my mouth was suddenly as dry as the Dasht-e Lut desert, but an electric surge of adrenaline pulsed through my veins.

Fighting my rising panic, I knew we were weak and not brave. Even Peter, Jesus' closest friend, had denied the Lord when facing danger. Would we deny Christ to save ourselves? If we failed as Peter had failed, how could we ever forgive ourselves? I prayed for the Lord to keep us strong. We could be brave and resist only in His strength, not our own. Without Christ we were nothing. With Him, we were covered in His strength and protection.

These thoughts comforted me as Marziyeh and I were escorted through the same crowded building where she had been by herself just a few hours earlier. The men who had searched our apartment led us up a flight of stairs to a small office with bare walls, a big desk with a window behind it, and four chairs. What appeared to be confiscated property was piled on the desk and all over the floor. We sat down and watched as they brought in everything they had taken from us and stacked it on the desk with all the rest.

"Sit still and don't talk to each other," a female guard ordered.

We did as we were told. Then we heard footsteps in the hallway.

CHAPTER 2

THE GUILTY GIRLS

Marziyeh

Mr. Rasti walked into the room. He glanced at us with his dark little eyes and began picking through the pile of our belongings on the desk. He held a New Testament up to the light and then rummaged through a stack of CDs. Suddenly he frowned. He looked up at the officer named Mohammadi.

"Have you collected all the evidence?" he asked sternly. Mohammadi and his partner shifted their weight and nodded.

"Didn't they have a laptop?"

Mohammadi started, his eyes opening wide. Sheepishly he said, "I'm sorry. I thought we had it. We must have left it at their house."

"Take one of the guilty girls and go back for it. Immediately."

Here we had been in custody for only a few minutes, yet we were already "the guilty girls." Still wearing handcuffs, and with her jaw throbbing now that the pain medication had worn off, Maryam went with Mohammadi and the young policewoman to retrieve the laptop.

I stayed in the room with a guard, handcuffed. I hadn't had anything to eat or drink since morning and started shaking with weakness. I asked for water, determined to show I was exhausted, not afraid. Mr. Rasti left the room briefly and then returned, settling behind the desk with a stern expression.

"You will tell me the truth from now on," he snapped.

"I have always told the truth," I answered sharply. "But you have not! You lied to me about the car this morning to bring me here. I told you I've been a Christian for eleven years. I've handed out New Testaments at the restaurant you mentioned. I could have denied everything, but I answered honestly. And now you order me to tell the truth *from now on*?" I could feel my voice rising.

"I was obliged to lie to you," Mr. Rasti explained.

"You ransacked my apartment without a warrant," I continued. "Without any authority whatsoever. Is that right? Is that the law?"

"We have a warrant," Mr. Rasti insisted. "It's right here."

He thrust a piece of paper across the desk. In the quick moment I had to glance at it, I could see it was something completely unrelated to our case. Someone had scribbled a notation in the lower margin about searching our house, and added a signature and a stamp.

"That is not a legal warrant," I said. "It's nothing. It's a fake."

Taken aback by my resistance, Mr. Rasti took a moment to regain his composure. "In an urgent situation, we can get permission over the phone," he said. "We don't have time to type it!" Obviously upset, he jumped to his feet and left the room.

When Maryam and her guards returned with the laptop, we were taken to a small room off a beautiful little inner courtyard. They put us in chairs on opposite walls so we couldn't talk to each other, and told us to wait.

Three young women guards started talking among themselves. "They have become Christians!" one of them said. "We discovered a bunch of Bibles and other Christian propaganda in their apartment. They're in deep trouble. And because they're still here, I probably won't have time for my afternoon nap!"

"What made you become a Christian?" one of the women asked Maryam angrily. "Don't you know that makes you *kafar*?" she added, using the Islamic word for "infidel."

Another woman was reading aloud from the Koran. She looked up from the page and said, "I want to know why you became a Christian. We believe in Jesus too."

Though Maryam was obviously exhausted and no doubt hungry and still in pain, she briefly explained the Christian belief that Jesus is the Savior of humankind. "He was not just a prophet, as the Koran claims. He was God in the flesh, who accepted the sins of the world. He was crucified to pay the price we should have paid for our transgressions. Three days after His death, He rose from the dead and ascended to heaven to be with God the Father."

The woman with the Koran said in a loud voice, "According to the Koran, you are *kafar*! Jesus was never crucified. He escaped beforehand. He came as a prophet, not a savior, and anyone who believes he is the son of God is *kafar* and will be sentenced to death! I feel very sorry for you."

The female guards all started talking at once, laughing at our claims and the idea that we would sit in jail to uphold such ridiculous beliefs.

Another guard came to the door and called my name. "Come with me," she ordered. I followed her upstairs and back into Mr. Rasti's office.

"Have a seat," Mr. Rasti said. I sat in front of his desk, still piled high with our New Testaments and CDs. The handcuffs hurt my wrists and I was very hungry by now, but I said a quick, silent prayer and was determined to stay calm.

"How long did you say you have been a Christian?" he began.

"Eleven years."

"And how did you convert to your religion?"

"From the Spirit of Christ entering my heart, and from reading the Bible and other books."

"Do you have a relationship with any churches in Iran?"

"No."

"How many Christians do you know?"

The truth was, I knew of many other Christians. But if I admitted that to this man, he would demand their names and addresses. Their safety, freedom, families, and even their lives would suddenly be in danger—and Maryam and I would be completely unable to warn them. I would never lie about my faith in Christ, no matter what the cost. But I had to protect innocent people from whatever Maryam and I were about to undergo.

"None except for Maryam."

"Where did you convert to Christianity?"

"In Turkey." Again, this wasn't exactly true. I had been baptized in Turkey seven years after becoming a Christian in Iran. But I knew that if I admitted to becoming a Christian in Iran, it would raise enough questions to get a lot more people in trouble. "Turkey is where Maryam and I met each other."

"Did you go to church in Turkey?"

"I lived there for a year, and sometimes I went to church."

"Why did you go to church?"

"To pray and to get in touch with other Iranians in Turkey."

"How many people did you give Bibles to?"

"To my friends there who asked questions, and anybody I thought would like to know about my faith in Christ."

"Have you given away Bibles when you travel?"

"I always carry some New Testaments with me, and if people ask, I will give them one."

There were more questions: Why did I live in my own apartment and not with my parents? How much money did I make? How did we get Bibles into the country? Who were the people in the pictures on our laptop? Finally, Mr. Rasti shoved a stack of papers across the desk.

"Sign," he ordered.

I didn't have a chance to read them and was too tired to argue. After I signed, a guard took me back to the room where Maryam waited and took Maryam upstairs for her interrogation by Mr. Rasti.

| | |

MARYAM

After I was seated in Mr. Rasti's office, he began with the same litany of questions I later learned he had asked Marziyeh.

"How long have you been a Christian?"

"Eleven years."

"Are your parents also Christians?"

"No."

"Why do you believe in Jesus? Does this mean you're no longer a Muslim?"

"I believe in Jesus because His Spirit came into my heart," I explained. "I know He is the Son of God, and He is my Savior."

"Who invited you to become a Christian?"

"Nobody. I studied the Bible. Jesus Himself revealed His truth to me."

"What Christians are you connected to, besides your roommate?"

"Nobody."

"Who gave you all the Bibles and CDs and other religious material?"

"Nobody. They are my property. I personally brought them to Iran."

"Did you speak to anyone about Jesus after you converted?"

"Yes. Family, friends, anyone who asked."

"Did you give them Bibles or CDs?"

"Yes, if they asked."

"According to Miss Marziyeh Amirizadeh, the two of you have been out today in your car distributing Bibles. Do you deny this?"

What a ridiculous trick. This is a common interrogation method: tell a lie about what the other person said on the chance the suspect will admit something she wouldn't otherwise, because she's duped into thinking the authorities already know about it. Marziyeh and I knew each other too well and trusted each other too much for this trick to work.

"No, we weren't handing out Bibles. I was at the dentist."

"Your friend has confessed that the two of you went to various cities in northern Iran to distribute Bibles."

"She said that?"

"Yes," Mr. Rasti insisted, glowering. "I have it all written down right here." He motioned to some papers in front of him.

"It didn't happen," I replied.

"Do you know it is illegal to speak about Jesus or give away Bibles?"

"No," I said. "I didn't know that talking about God could be an offense."

"How many people have you talked to about Jesus since you converted to Christianity?"

Untold thousands, I thought to myself. But I didn't say it out loud.

"Maybe ten or twelve people a year, and I handed out about the same number of New Testaments."

There were questions where I could avoid saying anything that would harm others, and not tell a lie. But this question could lead down a trail of more questions and tragedy for others, and I would not say anything that would put people in danger. Though neither of us would lie about our personal faith, we also would not betray our friends. Although I didn't know it at the time, I had just made the same choice that Marziyeh had made during her interrogation.

"Why do you do this?" Mr. Rasti demanded harshly. "Why do you want to separate the youth from their faith and beliefs?"

"That has never been my objective," I said. "I've never tried to separate anyone from their beliefs. If they have questions, I answer them. If they want to know more, I tell them, because I want them to know the truth about the Lord's love and about Jesus, their Savior."

"Don't you believe in the prophet of Islam, the leadership of the imams, and the fact that Islam is the most complete religion?"

"No, I don't. The Bible says that Jesus Christ is the first and last Savior of the human race. Jesus says, 'No one comes to the Father except through me.'"[1]

"You have been misled!" Mr. Rasti said, frowning. "There are no such words in the true Bible. Jesus has promised that the last prophet will come after him, and that prophet is Mohammed. You have been brainwashed by a distorted version of the Bible. You should read the correct version, which is for sale in bookshops all over Iran."

"Mr. Rasti," I said, "I did not come to believe in Jesus because of any book, other people's opinions, recommendations of the church, or my own research. Jesus spoke to me in my heart. I experienced Him, felt Him, and my spirit touched Him and knows He is alive. Before I believed, before I ever set foot in a church, I heard His voice calling me and I answered."

Mr. Rasti motioned to a stack of notes he had made during the interrogation, with the questions in red and answers in black. "Put your signature and fingerprint beside every answer," he instructed.

"But I haven't read any of them," I replied.

Mr. Rasti drew himself up in a huff. "I would not risk destroying my life after death to write down lies on this paper! I assure you I'm an honest man."

By now, it was after 11:00 p.m. I had been interrogated for more than two hours. I had been at the police station since late afternoon and was too exhausted and too sore from my dental appointment to argue. I did as instructed, then was taken back to the office where Marziyeh waited. We still weren't allowed to speak, but we knew each other so well that we could communicate silently.

Are you okay? Marziyeh asked with her eyes.

Yes, I assured her.

It was nearly midnight when another guard came in and said, "You will remain in custody. I will take you to the detention center."

Prisoners were not housed at the police station. We had to go across town in order to be locked up. We were ushered into a room to do the necessary paperwork. A bored and sleepy-looking soldier sat behind the counter.

"What is the charge against you?" he asked, reaching for a form.

"Christianity," we said together.

"Advertising and promoting Christianity," added our guard as she hand-cuffed us to each other.

For some reason, being cuffed together struck us as funny and we started laughing. Marziyeh raised up our hands and said, "We are proud of these handcuffs because we're wearing them on account of our faith in Jesus Christ!"

"I have faith in Jesus too," the soldier said, "but I would never try to convert someone else to my beliefs. You're not in custody for believing in Jesus; you're in custody for promoting Him to others."

We got into another dirty little white car and were driven to the Vozara Detention Center. Inside, an officer asked our guard what we were charged with. "Advertising and promoting Christianity in Iran," he answered.

The officer let out a chuckle. "Is there really any such charge as that?" Our guard said nothing. Another officer, rough looking and overweight, seemed to be in charge. After reading over our paperwork, he started asking the same questions we'd been answering all day: How long have you been Christians? Do you live alone? And on and on.

"Is Christianity an offense?" I demanded.

"That's what we've been charged with," Marziyeh added.

"No," the man in charge insisted, "you are not charged with being Christians. Most probably yours will be a political case. If the court can prove you've been supported by someone from the outside in promoting Christianity, the charge will be spying."

We were led down a long flight of stairs into a basement, through a series of steel doors, and past a small room with a red carpet and an oil heater. The floor was littered with junk food. "Is this where we're staying?" I asked Marziyeh. It was our first time inside any sort of jail. We had no idea that what we had seen was a break room for the staff, nothing like the rooms where prisoners lived.

We were escorted into a room where two sleepy, grumpy female guards waited for us. "Hand over all your belongings," one of them ordered. We gave them our wristwatches and everything else we had. "Now take off all your clothes. Underwear, too." We were then subjected to the humiliation of a full body search. The guards said it was to keep prisoners from smuggling in drugs. We were allowed to dress, but they kept our shoes, socks, and scarves so we couldn't use our shoelaces or the other items to hang ourselves. We hadn't brought heavy coats with us, and late at night the room was uncomfortably cold. The concrete floor of the hallway was like ice under our bare feet.

We went through another metal door to a hallway with rooms opening off on either side. "Take a blanket from the stack and find yourselves a spot," the guard ordered as she clanged the door shut behind us. In the dim light, we could make out blanketed figures on the floor of the rooms. Though most of the women were asleep at this late hour, a few pairs of eyes followed us as we walked up and down the hall deciding which room to enter. We didn't need light to tell us the place was filthy beyond imagining; our noses told us well enough. The stench of sweat, vomit, and backed-up toilets was overpowering. It took all our self-control to keep from retching—in this moment, our empty stomachs were a blessing. The floor of the toilet area was awash in muck from two overflowing commodes; the trash bin was piled high with used sanitary pads.

After finding what looked like the least crowded room, we went back to a spot near the door to get blankets. They were loathesome—stiff with dirt and smelling strongly of urine, some of them still wet. They were all in about the same condition, but it was so cold we had to have something to cover ourselves with. We grabbed a couple that felt mostly dry and walked the few steps to our room, wrapped up as well as we could on the freezing floor, and huddled together, holding hands.

The onrush of emotions was like nothing I had ever experienced: bone-tired, confused, hungry, thirsty, repulsed by the foul air. How would our sisters and Christian friends find out what had happened? Would we be in here for a day? A year? Were our lives in danger? We were too tired to be afraid—it was all too new for us—though our future was completely unknown. It was more than we could absorb. All we could do was turn it over to the Lord.

We traded stories of our separate interrogations by Mr. Rasti, prayed to Jesus to protect us, and fell into exhausted and fitful sleep. It was to be our first of more than 250 nights behind bars.

CHAPTER 3

THE ROAD TO VOZARA

Marziyeh

"FOR GOD'S SAKE, WON'T SOMEBODY GIVE ME A DAMN CIGARETTE!"

The voice that jarred us awake was half scream, half animal cry, mixed with the grating, rattling noise of somebody shaking the bars of the cell-block door at the end of the hallway.

"Give me a cigarette! I know you've got them. Have mercy!" The words dissolved into a loud moan and what sounded like two women crying.

I woke up disoriented—stiff and sore from sleeping on the cold floor, confused at being in a strange place. It took a minute to remember that Maryam and I were under arrest and had spent the night in the detention center. It wasn't some crazy, terrible dream after all—it was reality. We buried our heads in our blankets for warmth, so that along with the sounds penetrating our consciousness there was the strong, sour aroma of stale urine mixed with the overpowering stench of the broken toilets.

"Give! Me! A! Cigarette!" The howling and begging continued, the bars shaking and clattering with each word. Maryam and I started talking quietly to each other, going over the events of the previous day and marveling that we had been able to sleep at all in these conditions.

Just then, we felt a kick at our blankets. We peeked out from underneath to see a wild-looking woman standing in front of us. She kicked at us again. "Can I have a cigarette?" It was the unmistakable voice that had screamed us awake. Now that she had found us, she made us the object of her insistent demands.

Although she was quite a young woman, she looked positively frightening—her filthy dress half unbuttoned, exposing one of her breasts, and her long, black hair matted in clumps and falling across her face. Her teeth were rotten, some broken and others missing entirely. She looked like a witch in a horror movie. When we said we didn't have any cigarettes, she turned abruptly and left.

The detention center was in a basement twenty steps down from street level, its walls lined with dark, damp, dirty stone blocks. Our cell was one of ten or so opening onto a narrow hallway. At the end of the hall, we saw the door in the wall of bars where we had come in. That door led to a small room with another wall of bars at the far end. In that far wall was another door, which opened to another long hallway. To the left in the hall was the entrance to the cell block with steps going up; to the right was an office or dayroom where the guards stayed. For now, the doors to individual cells were unlocked. We later learned that they were locked at night when the cells were crowded, and remained locked until morning. This solved the mystery of the terrible blankets. If a woman was forced to answer the call of nature during the night, she had no choice but to soil her bedclothes.

The door at the end of the hallway clattered open and two female guards, wearing masks to protect them from the nasty odors, came in and ordered us to fold our blankets and stack them in the corner. We could see now that there were fifteen or so women locked up in our area, ranging from teenagers to middle age. Some were well dressed, while others wore little more than rags. Over the next few days, we would see countless women come and go as they were either transferred to prison or acquitted and released.

The jail didn't serve breakfast, and of course we were unprepared. Fortunately, another prisoner kindly shared some biscuits with us. After we ate, we took our turn in the facilities. There were four toilets, two of which were broken and filled to overflowing with muck. There was no soap, tissue, towels, or running water in the sink. The floors were so filthy that the floor drains were clogged as well, leaving conditions we need not describe. And we were still barefoot.

With that memorable experience behind us, we set out to meet some of the other prisoners and learn more about the detention center. We saw the woman who had screamed at us and kicked us earlier, now sitting on the floor of the hallway smoking a cigarette a guard had given her. Next to her was a very beautiful young girl. Both of them were crying and shouting, occasionally calling out the names of Islamic prophets and asking them for help.

We sat down beside them without saying anything. This startled them. The Vozara Detention Center was not a place where strangers were friendly to each other, especially to crazy-sounding people who woke the cell block every morning screaming for a cigarette. We introduced ourselves and asked the two why they were there. The screaming woman told us her story, the first of many heartbreaking accounts of abuse and desperation we would hear behind bars in the days that followed.

Her name was Leila. She had been arrested two days before for buying drugs on the street. She was married and had a son. As a newlywed, she learned that her husband was addicted to opium. He pressured her into using it with him, and soon she became addicted too. Then he stopped taking drugs and threatened to divorce her unless she stopped as well. Instead, her addiction became worse and her habit grew to include cocaine and heroin. Desperate for money to buy drugs, she left her family and sold herself into prostitution, earning 4,000 tomans (about two US dollars) per time. She lived in a downtown park and slept in a cardboard box.

"I have prayed to Allah for help," she said, "but he has not answered my prayers." She started to cry again.

The young girl, Sephideh, was nineteen, with sparkling eyes and beautiful golden hair. After her parents divorced, her mother had disappeared and her father ignored her to spend time with his friends. She left home with her boyfriend, who introduced her to crack cocaine and opium. She had been arrested buying opium in a park; it was her second offense.

Leila and Sephideh asked us why we were in prison.

"For believing in Jesus Christ."

They had no idea Christianity was a crime and asked us to tell them more about Jesus. After we shared our testimonies, Sephideh asked if Christ could help her. With tears brimming in her beautiful eyes, she begged, "Please pray for my freedom. If I am released this time, I will give up drugs, go back to school, and get a good job."

Maryam and I spent the next half hour praying with Leila and Sephideh. They cried softly as we prayed for them and hugged us when we finished. "You are angels from the Lord," Leila said gratefully. They sincerely seemed to appreciate what we'd done, and after that they acted much calmer. We asked them to pray for us, too. This experience made us think that other women in the cell block might allow us to pray for them. We said good-bye to our new friends and took a walk down the hall.

We came to a cell that was still dark, with two figures wrapped in blankets on the floor. At the sound of our footsteps, they sat up—two girls in their late teens or early twenties, one with long, black, straight hair, and the other with a short, bleached style. We said hello and introduced ourselves. They were surprised by our gesture of friendship and asked why we were in prison. Again we shared our testimony, which put the girls at ease and led them to confide in us. They had been locked up for three days and were terrified of the other inmates, many of them rough and loud like Leila.

The girl with the bleached hair, Asieh, had gone to meet her new boyfriend for a date and took her friend, Sara, along because she didn't want to meet him alone. When the girls got to his apartment, he said he wasn't ready yet, but invited them to come in. While they were waiting, the *basiji* appeared and arrested them. The boyfriend had been using the apartment to meet a succession of young women, and the apartment manager had found out and sent the *basiji* to investigate. Everyone in the room was taken into custody for improper contact between unrelated Muslim men and women. The girls hadn't been allowed to call their families, so their parents didn't know where they were. They were terrified of what the authorities might do to them and of what their families would think when they found out.

We held their hands and prayed with them. Our suggestion that they put their trust in God seemed to calm them. Maybe they couldn't see a way out of their predicament, but He could. We told them about how Jesus loved them unconditionally and was always there for them. They asked if they could stay with us—and before we could answer, they picked up their blankets and took them to our cell.

We went to another cell, which was the biggest one on the hall. There were six or seven middle-aged women huddled together inside, well-dressed and obviously out of place. Maryam greeted them and asked why they'd been arrested. They seemed very fearful and hesitant to talk to us. They wanted to know why we were there. Once we explained, their silence was broken by a flood of questions.

"Is Christianity really a crime?"

"How long have you been Christians?"

"How did they find out about you?"

"What will happen to you now?"

They were intensely curious about this religion that was so harshly condemned by the authorities.

As we answered them, the ladies loosened up a little, and finally one of them told us their story. They were shopping at a bakery when a flash mob appeared to protest the high price of bread. The rally had been staged by a group called We Are, whose members don't know each other but are summoned by Internet messages to protest at a certain place. They would arrive at the location and at a predetermined time or signal, suddenly start chanting and clapping to make their point, then dissolve into the crowd. When the *basiji* came to break up the protest, they arrested anyone they could grab, including this woman and her friends. These innocent shoppers had spent the entire night locked in the back of a police car, all squeezed together, before being transported to Vozara. One of them had been beaten by a teenage *basiji* but hadn't had any medical attention during the three days she had been in jail. The women were all afraid of losing face with their families. We prayed with them that they would be released soon and that their families would understand they were innocent.

In the middle of the day, a guard unlocked the hallway door and slid a big saucepan down the grimy hall floor. This was lunch.

Many of the women, with Leila and Sephideh in the lead, dove for the pan, scooping the lentils and rice out with their hands or burying their faces in the dish like dogs. Maryam and I stood frozen in our tracks, gaping at the spectacle. Leila looked up at us, gobs of food caught in her hair and dripping from her face. "This is how they feed us," she explained between gulps. "No plates, no spoons." When we still held back, she added, "If you don't eat like this, you don't eat."

I looked at Maryam and said silently with my eyes, *Then we don't eat. At least not yet. We're not desperate enough to be fed like animals in a zoo.* The meal was symbolic of the way the detention center staff looked at everyone under their control: subhuman, unworthy of any respect, locked in filthy cages, and treated like mongrels.

A commotion at the end of the hallway caught my attention. Two young women, who had been arrested for attending a party where men were present, were banging on the bars of the cell-block door and calling for a guard. One of them badly needed a sanitary pad—her clothes were already ruined—and she was desperately calling for one. After a long time, a guard finally appeared. When the girl explained what she needed, the guard said, "Use one of the blankets."

"Please," the girl begged, "I'm bleeding."

"So go die," the guard replied. "It's not my problem."

"Please help me!"

"Shut up! Shut up! Shut up! Shut up!" the guard yelled, then turned away. An hour later, the guard came back with a single pad and threw it at the girl through the bars. "There. Now quit complaining."

Later that evening, another disturbance erupted as fifteen or so young women, all attractive and very fashionably dressed, were herded through the hallway door of our cell block. They had been arrested by the *basiji* at a weekend family party on charges of having unhealthy and un-Islamic relationships with men. Though they were Iranian, they spoke English to each other as a way to protect themselves. After a few minutes, several of the women came over to Maryam and me because they said we looked and acted differently from the rest of the prisoners. When we told them the charges against us, they asked us to pray for them, especially the one in their group who was pregnant. They couldn't all fit into our tiny cell, so they crowded in the doorway as we prayed that they would soon be released and that their families wouldn't suffer any harassment or embarrassment because of what had happened.

Prisoners came and went all day. By the end of the evening, there were considerably more women in custody than there had been in the morning. We moved to a slightly bigger cell so there would be room for us and our two new friends to stretch out on the floor. The day guards left and the night shift came on duty. Though these guards slept most of the night, they had to be there when new prisoners came in late or in case of a disturbance. The lights went out, and we were left alone with our thoughts and the night sounds of the detention center.

As I waited for sleep, I heard conversations, curses, coughing, and crying fade in and out of the darkness. For a moment, one voice rose above the rumble. I recognized it as Leila's, but this time she wasn't screaming, she was singing—beautifully. She had a mellow, haunting voice, so tender and sweet. I could scarcely imagine it coming from that frightful face and that mouth filled with rotten teeth. Maybe it represented a part of her, deep inside, that remained pure and untouched by all the sadness and tragedy in her life.

What a day! On the surface, our situation was a complete disaster; but in another way, it was an incredible blessing. In a sense, we had been preparing for this day for a long time. First separately, and then together, we had spent years working to share the truth about Jesus in a country where evangelizing Muslims was punishable by death.

| | |

MARYAM

The fact that we had even heard the truth about Christianity in Iran is a miracle. We grew up in a country that indoctrinates children in the state religion from the youngest ages, when they are most impressionable. Like all other children in Iran, we were told that Islam is the only complete religion. Teachers told us that Jesus was one of many prophets and that He was the prophet of love and peace, nothing more. Before school every morning we would line up to listen to one of the older children read the Koran in Arabic. Then we chanted, "Death to America! Death to Israel!"

though we had no idea what "America" and "Israel" were. All we knew was that they were unspeakably evil.

Every year on the anniversary of the Shah's downfall and the return of Ayatollah Khomeini, students still take part in huge demonstrations across the country. We did this too, because the authorities locked the schools and forced us to go. If we didn't pray the *namaz*, the Islamic daily prayers, they wouldn't give us our grades. Girls had to have their hair completely covered. If a teacher saw a strand or two sticking out from under our headscarves, she would pull our hair, hard.

Marziyeh and I were both born in Iran to Muslim families, yet as children both of us were thirsty for the truth and to know God. The Lord worked in amazing ways to call us to Him, and then to bring us together.

When I was growing up, I always had a lot of questions in my mind: What is the truth? Who is God, and how I can have a close relationship with Him? Why do I have to talk to God in a language I don't know, praying words I don't understand? I had many other questions about Islam and its rules, which frustrated and confused me.

I was eager to find the truth, so I tried to study and research other religions on my own. I read a Persian translation of the Koran and some other books—but not the Bible, because I couldn't find one. Sometimes I prayed *namaz*, and I also attended meetings of other religions from time to time. However, none of these efforts could quench my thirst.

At age seventeen, I was completely disappointed and thought it would be better not to follow any religion. I was tired of the meaningless rules and religious laws, and tired of a faraway God whose voice I never heard. I had always longed for two-way communication with Him but had never experienced it.

Eventually, I completely stopped doing research. But even then, sometimes when I was alone, especially at night, I looked up into the sky and asked God to reveal Himself to me and speak to me. At times, I would talk to Him in Farsi, like a conversation, for an hour or two, and enjoyed it very much.

One day my sister gave me a little booklet titled *His Name Is Wonderful*. It was part of the Gospel of Luke, from the Bible. Shirin said she had received it from a man at the church near her university. She knew I was searching to know God and that I would read any book on the subject. "Just don't read the last page," she warned, "because it is a confession prayer for anyone who wants to become a Christian."

I took the booklet from her and went to my room right away, closed the door, and started reading. From the first page, my heart was deeply moved. I started to cry because I could feel the presence of Christ in the room right in front of me. While I was reading, I felt as if I had already known and heard all of these words in the book and had just found what I had been seeking for many years: the love of Christ.

During those hours alone in my room, I realized why I had always felt a barrier between myself and God. As I read about the love of Christ and the work He did on the cross for my sins, I said to myself, *That is exactly what I have been looking for all these years: love without conditions.* None of those words sounded strange or unbelievable to me, even when I read that Jesus is the Son of God. I always tell people that Jesus Himself witnessed and delivered to me the Good News of salvation as a gift, even before I had spoken to anyone about Him or gone to church. He revealed His truth to me and prepared my heart for accepting it.

After two or three hours in my room, I knew I had discovered what I had been searching for; I felt like I had already known Jesus for many years. When I got to the last page of the booklet, I prayed the written prayer and gave my heart to Jesus without any doubt or second thought.

For two years, I attended a weekly Bible study in a woman's home in Tehran, taking the hour-long taxi ride each way from my home in Karaj. One day, she led a Bible study on the book of Acts and read about believers in the early church receiving the gift of the Holy Spirit and speaking in tongues. She spoke to me about her own experience. I was intrigued with the idea that God would give a gift to humans, a promise of a special spiritual experience. I wanted it for myself.

Later that day, in my room at home, I received this gift and spoke in tongues. I was surprised and overwhelmed with joy. Nothing like this had happened to me before. When I prayed, I knew what I was saying, and I knew that God understood.

I realize that not every Christian has this experience. The Bible describes many gifts, and this was one that I received. I believe that God, in His wisdom, uses whatever tools He has available to bring the gospel into people's hearts.

I wanted to be baptized in the official church in Tehran, where we attended, but the regime monitored the church closely and frowned on church baptisms. Instead, in 2002, I was baptized secretly at midnight in the basement of another small church. Though I was only nineteen, the pastors asked me to start serving in the church, speaking to new believers and working with a group of elderly ladies. The pastors said I had a great passion for evangelism, though when I boldly talked about Christ in the subway or riding in a taxi, the pastors said with a note of caution, "Save it for church!"

After I had served in that church for a year and a half, my pastor introduced me to Elam Ministries. It was while taking theology courses sponsored by Elam in Turkey in 2005 that I met Marziyeh.

| | |

Marziyeh

Ever since I was a young child, I loved God and wanted to find out more about His truth. I did everything I knew to get closer to Him. Because my family was Muslim, my only means of getting to know God were through Muslim religious teachings and things I learned at school. But I always had many questions about God that Islamic theology and Sharia law could not answer.

I used to think of God as a kind father who is closer to us than members of our own family, because I believed that the God who created my body was closer to my heart than my own flesh and blood. I had been taught the beliefs of Islam and debated them with friends and teachers in school; I could not accept the Koran's teachings, as they did not seem true to me. I did not accept the image of God that many Muslims have as one who harshly rules over the human race and punishes us for the slightest sins. That is a terrifying image of God.

I believed that the daily *namaz* prayers, bending several times a day in front of a God who was already in my heart, were a waste of time and unnecessary, and I could not accept them. I also had many questions about why I had to speak to God in Arabic instead of in Farsi, my native language. *Doesn't this God who taught me my own mother tongue know it Himself? Why should I pray to Him as if He's a great leader or ruler over me? Why can't I speak with Him in my own language?* These were the questions that had long occupied my mind. The answers I received at school were not convincing.

Despite my reservations, I did my best to fulfill my religious duties. I told myself that I might be wrong, and that the truth would show itself to me one day in the future. I prayed *namaz* for two years without fail. I used to read the Koran, and I would even wake up in the middle of the night and pray again. But these types of prayers and worship were not making me feel any closer to God. On the contrary, they created a greater distance from Him as they became a routine action that I was forced to do, not something that I wanted to do.

Even before I found Christ, I was certain that God spoke to me in dreams. In one dream, I was praying toward the sky when it opened up and a white horse came down and spoke to me: "Sit on my back," it said. When I obeyed, the horse took me to a city where worshipers coming out of a mosque were performing the Islamic Ashura and Tasua ceremonies, mournful chanting and self-beating. At first, they couldn't see me or the horse. But suddenly they appeared to change into wild animals with savage features, not like people at all. As soon as I saw them, they could also see me and tried to kill me. The horse ran like the wind to save me. As I held fast to its neck, I felt its love pouring into me with a power and purity I had never known. After we eluded our pursuers, the horse came to a fork in the road where one path turned up into the sky. As the tired horse started on the upward path, I awoke.

For a week after that, all I could think about was the deep love I had experienced in the dream. I have never since experienced love like that in this world. *God, why did You let me wake up? I wanted to be in this dream forever!* (That same horse has reappeared to me in a dream, with a message, every few years since then.)

After some thought and consideration, I came to the conclusion that the most important part of being a believer is my heart, and I decided to put aside my religion. I began to speak to God with my heart, in the manner of a relationship between a child and her father. One day, I heard from a friend of mine who had converted to Christianity that, in their religion, Jesus Christ is the Son of God and the Savior of humankind, who has come to the earth to free people from their sins. I became curious; I had not heard anything like that before about Jesus. I used to think He was just another prophet, as He had been introduced to us in our textbooks at school. I said to myself, *How do I know He is the truth?*

I decided to study different religions in search of the truth and began to read the Bible. After a while, I realized I could not possibly spend the many years necessary to study all the religions of the world, and that there might be some faith in the world that I would never be able to know in full. Therefore, I knelt and prayed, asking God to show me the right path to reach the truth. I said, "If Jesus is the truth, then You must guide me in the path that would take me to the truth and save me from being misguided."

The next thing that happened was a real miracle. During this time, I was invited to a church by a friend. On that same day, I had a medical appointment scheduled with a specialist. My visit to the church was an incredible experience. People were worshiping with joy and praying freely to God. Suddenly, in my heart, I heard a voice: *Marziyeh, you are healed.* I wanted to ignore this voice, but when I told my friend, she said it was Jesus and that He could heal me.

Later, at my medical appointment, the doctor picked up his pen to write me a prescription. Then he stopped. I waited, wondering why he was hesitating. Finally, he said, "I don't know why, but I cannot write a prescription for you. Come back another time." At that time, I sensed that God reminded me of His message in the church and told me to trust Him.

The symptoms were immediately cleared up. But even after Jesus healed me, I did not fully believe in Him. To me, the healing wasn't enough proof to convert to Christianity, so I asked God to show me more reasons. At the bottom of my heart, I had begun to believe in Jesus, but I still had my doubts. I had read about the Holy Spirit but could not fully understand.

I read in the Bible about the supernatural experience that the apostles had when they spoke in other languages, and also heard about it from my friend who had led me to Christ. At the time, I could not understand it. There were times when I prayed with friends and some of them prayed in tongues. At first, I thought they were a bit crazy, or that they were trying to mimic Armenian Christians whom they knew but who spoke their own language. Then I became curious, but thought it was impossible for me.

I had never prayed out loud in public. One day, some friends asked me to join them to pray together. The leader asked me if I wanted to pray, but I was shy. I was praying silently in my heart and said to God that I loved Him and wanted to talk to Him out loud. At that moment, the Holy Spirit came on me and I started to pray in tongues so all could hear. Even though I didn't know the meaning of my words, I could fully understand what I was saying to God. It was the first time I had ever been so close to God that I felt I could touch Him.

While I was praying, I could see Jesus in front of me for a few seconds. He was standing next to a large throne that was covered with shining gold. At that moment, I was not on the earth. The middle of my forehead was burning with heat, as if someone had branded it. Suddenly all my doubts disappeared, and I felt that God had removed a curtain from my eyes: I could now see the truth clearly. I could not control my tongue, but just kept worshiping Him.

When I got home, I wanted to thank God for His gift to me. I was surprised that the Holy Spirit came to me again and I prayed and sang songs of praise in tongues nonstop through the night until the early hours of the morning. My jaw was aching, but I did not want the experience to end. The sense of God's love was so powerful, and what had happened to me by then was just incredible, and I could not describe it.

No one had forced me into anything or hypnotized me. No one had cast a spell on me. The only explanation I could logically derive from that experience was that I had met with God through His Son, Jesus Christ. From that day forward, I dedicated my life to Jesus, I always felt God's presence with me, and I saw countless miracles and dreams from Him. Jesus is the only person who has been with me every single day of my life. Even when I've gone through very difficult times and was profoundly lonely, I have walked with Him next to me, and He has been my guide in life. I will never deny God's love or the life He has called me to; to do so would be to deny my very existence.

In time, I obtained certifications as a manager and trainer for hairdressers. Working with my salon trainees gave me opportunities every day to share the good news of Jesus Christ. Many women were eager to know more and gladly accepted a Bible from me. Friends suggested I start my own salon business, but I wasn't interested. My calling is with people's hearts, not their hair.

Though I was successful and secure in my profession, I was sure that the Lord wanted me to serve Him full time. During my years in Tehran, I had dreamed of financial independence and running my own business. Now that I had the opportunity, it meant nothing compared to telling the world about Jesus.

When a pastor friend suggested I study theology, I quit my job and traded a certain future for the unknown. I had started with nothing in Tehran and in five years had achieved worldly success. Now I was starting over again.

I planned to study theology in London, but was unable to get a visa. Instead, I traveled to Turkey for a study sponsored by Elam Ministries. That's where I met Maryam.

| | |

MARYAM

God made us a team and brought us back to Tehran, where we labored for three exhausting, exhilarating years, handing out accurate modern translations of the New Testament in Farsi to supplant the Islamic versions allowed in the public shops, which had been rewritten to support the Koran. We were always on the lookout for new opportunities to share the gospel.

God protected and guided us every day. Once a friend was helping us pick up some New Testaments and take them to our apartment. We had his van packed with three thousand Bibles and traveled at night because we thought it was safer. At the entrance to a bridge we had to cross, policemen were stopping and searching every car. By the time we saw what was happening, we were hemmed in by traffic and couldn't get out of line. All we could do was pray for the Lord to protect us. At that moment, a fight broke out between the police and a driver one or two cars ahead of us. While that was being settled, they stopped searching cars and let the rest of the line go on across the bridge. We gratefully thanked God for getting us through that danger safely.

Whenever Marziyeh and I walked around the city, we always carried ten or fifteen New Testaments in a backpack, in case we had the chance to give one away. One day, in a bookstore, I overheard a customer ask for a Bible. After the manager said he didn't have any, I followed the customer outside and gave him one. The man said he'd had a dream in which Jesus told him to get a Bible and go to a quiet place in the mountains where He could talk with him. The man had his hiking pack with him and was on his way to meet Jesus.

We often went to a place in Tehran where young people liked to go walking. One time, Marziyeh gave a Bible to a young man who said he was looking for the truth. Another time, in the same place, we met the man again. To thank Marziyeh for the Bible, he gave her a beautiful wooden cross he had treasured for years, decorated with pictures of Jesus and four apostles. We have it here beside us as we write.

There are two kinds of taxis in Tehran. The more expensive ones pick you up at a prearranged point and take you directly where you want to go. The other ones pick up and drop off customers like a bus, so that passengers don't have the taxi all to themselves. The driver tries to keep a full cab of four passengers as much as possible. These taxi drivers got to know us well because we would ride around and hand out New Testaments to other passengers. One day, I rode with a *sayed*, a man who claims to be descended from Mohammed, who was also *hadji*, meaning he had made a pilgrimage to the city of Mecca. These pilgrims consider Christians dirty, especially those who have converted. Usually they won't touch a Christian or even take anything from a Christian's hand. To my surprise, this man asked me many questions about Christianity and then invited me to visit an Islamic charity and go from room to room blessing it with Christian prayers.

Yet despite our commitment and dedication, for the last couple of months before our arrest, we had inexplicably been unable to evangelize. We didn't canvass the city like we had before, we had fewer meetings, and we didn't hand out a single New Testament. Something was holding us back. Now, surrounded by the dark, somber walls of the Vozara Detention Center, we could see it was the Lord protecting us and our friends. We had no idea that the *basiji* had been watching us, but their surveillance began right when our efforts began to wane. If we had continued as usual with the police on our tail, many others would have been arrested along with us for meeting with us and accepting a New Testament. God had saved all those people from the experience we were now enduring.

Most amazing of all, we were in the best place we'd ever been for witnessing to people hungry for the gospel of Jesus. We had spent ourselves and our resources traveling all over the country with the message of salvation, always mindful of the danger if the wrong person overheard us. Now we were stuck in jail, and God was bringing spiritual seekers to us in waves. The living conditions weren't very good, but we didn't have to deal with travel and traffic! And we could tell our fellow prisoners the story of Jesus openly because no one would come into this rat hole to spy on us.

We had prayed long and diligently for more chances to share our faith. Now the Lord was answering that prayer beyond our wildest expectations, though certainly not in the way we imagined. It was all so new and strange, unlike anything we'd ever experienced. We didn't know what to expect. What was the routine? What were the rules? What would keep us safe or get us in trouble? It was like being dropped into a completely foreign culture without warning and without a guidebook. Our only guide was Jesus. What blessings and opportunities would He bring us tomorrow?

CHAPTER 4

A SIGN OF HONOR

MARYAM

We had been imprisoned in Vozara too late on Thursday to go to court. Friday, the Muslim Sabbath, the courts are closed. So Saturday was the first day that our case could be heard. We awoke again to the sound of Leila screaming for a cigarette, visited the toilet facilities, and got a breakfast biscuit from the same generous woman who had given us one the day before. We hadn't eaten any dinner out of the community pan the previous night and were now extremely hungry.

The morning routine was for a guard to call out the names of the women going to court that day. Prisoners gathered at the cell-block door one group at a time as their names were called, depending on which court they were going to. Then a guard herded them upstairs to ground level. If it was a small group, the guard took them in a car or taxi to their court appearance. Larger groups traveled in a van. Because everyone in Vozara had come directly from being arrested, no one had any luggage or belongings beyond whatever they happened to have at the time. They took everything with them to court, in case they were set free.

In court, the judge would decide whether a woman would be released, returned to detention, or sent to prison to await trial. Inmates were not supposed to stay more than three days in detention. Because we had arrived late on Thursday, this was technically our third day in custody (though only our second morning at Vozara), and we expected to be called, have our case resolved, and be released. The chic young party girls who spoke English were all called, as were the women who had been arrested outside the bakery. As they left, many of them asked us to pray for them. We assured them that the Lord would never abandon them and that He could change their lives like He had changed ours.

After a while, the cell block was empty except for Leila, Sephideh, Marziyeh, and me. As we were walking up and down the hall to get a little exercise, two guards came to the hall doorway with some cleaning supplies. They handed us two brooms, a mop, and a bucket and ordered us to clean the cells. My immediate response was revulsion. How could we possibly tackle the filthy mess all around us? But then I thought, *What an opportunity! Not only will cleaning give us a way to pass the time, but we can also make this a more decent and humane place to live.* We asked the guards for some liquid soap, and they gave it to us, they were so surprised. Marziyeh and I swept and mopped the cell floors and the hallway, including the passage to the guard office, and last of all the toilets. Hours later, we had cleaned every surface, and though the smell was not entirely gone, it was far more bearable. The only disadvantage of all our work was that it made us even hungrier. Plus we were very thirsty; we hadn't had a drink of water during our two days in custody.

As we lay down for a nap, we heard Leila singing again, her beautiful voice echoing through the empty rooms. She started dancing, too, and the gracefulness of her movements was as surprising as the purity of her voice. But it wasn't long before she and Sephideh woke us up, shaking the cell-block door and screaming for cigarettes.

Late in the day, the other women began returning from court. The ladies from the bakery had been taken to Revolutionary Court, where political cases were decided, but the judge hadn't heard their case, so they were back in detention for another day. Several were crying in frustration, worried about their children and wanting some way to tell their families where they were. We heard that the big group of party girls had been released and the charges

against them dismissed. Also returning were two young girls with beautiful long hair, who had come in the day before charged with being improperly dressed. One of the girls had also admitted to having a boyfriend. Her parents had been in court when she was brought in. Her mother had known about her boyfriend but her father had not, and his look of shame and disapproval had devastated her. Now she was crying her heart out. I tried to comfort her, but for the moment I wasn't able to get through.

New prisoners also arrived, including an attractive girl of sixteen or seventeen with her hair cut short like a boy. Her name was Sahar, and she seemed happy, energetic, and full of life. All the older ladies wanted to mother her. She had run away from home and been arrested for shaving her head. Despite her fresh look and friendly ways, she made her living on the street as a prostitute. When she started talking about her sexual experience, she sounded like a woman of forty.

Another newcomer was a tall woman with a masculine build, extremely dirty and smelly. No one wanted to go near her because she looked so repulsive. Marziyeh and I went over and sat down beside her. Her name was Sayeh.

"What are you charged with?" she asked us.

"We believe in Jesus," I explained.

She laughed, a big laugh that showed her yellowed teeth and gave us a whiff of her terrible breath.

"What is your charge?" I asked.

"Being homeless and lonely, and having no one to go to. I was arrested for sleeping in the park. The police said I should have registered with social services."

Behzisty, the state welfare organization of Iran, is notorious for the abusive way it treats people who go there for help. I didn't blame her for staying away.

"I wish I had a comfortable place to sleep," Sayeh said, "or just someone who could help me. Anyone."

"You have a God who is with you wherever you are," I told her. "Have you ever asked Him to help you?"

"I've never had any help from the god of the Muslims. Perhaps your God can help me. Please pray for me."

As I prayed, Sayeh's eyes filled with tears. Then she listened carefully as I told her about Jesus and His plan for her salvation. She asked me about my own beliefs and then asked for the address of a church. After I gave it to her, she said, "If I ever get released and ever get away from Behzisty, I will go to church." In spite of her wild appearance, she had a tender and open heart. And in the Lord's providence, Marziyeh and I were there at that moment to share the love of Christ with her when she was most ready to receive it.

| | |

Marziyeh

The next morning, after the usual "alarm clock" of Leila screaming for cigarettes, Maryam and I visited the much-improved toilets, listened to name after name being announced by the guard, and watched as one woman after another left the cell block. After a while, she and I were the only two prisoners left. The place had been filled with chatter and commotion and people; now it was eerily silent. As we were about to return to our room to rest, we heard the guard call our names.

"Maryam Rostampour and Marziyeh Amirizadeh?"

"Yes?"

"It's time to prepare yourselves for court."

We were led to an inspection room where Sayeh was already waiting. The guard handcuffed the three of us together, with Sayeh in the middle, and took us up the stairs. The sunlight almost blinded us as we walked out the door toward the police car. We hadn't seen the sun since we'd been in Vozara. It was beautiful and felt so good on our faces. What a relief from the chill of the detention center! We couldn't take in the fresh air fast enough— what a blessing it was to be out in the world again, if only for a moment.

We heard our names and looked around. My sister, Elena, and Maryam's sister, Shirin, were running toward us. What an incredible joy it was to see them! The guards warned us to ignore them and keep moving; instead, we ignored the guards and threw ourselves into our sisters' arms, awkwardly hugging them despite our handcuffs, and weeping with joy and relief. They were shocked at how hungry, pale, and dirty we looked. "Are you being tortured? Are you being tortured?" they asked over and over. We assured them

we were not. We told them in a whisper about a supply of New Testaments the police hadn't found yet and asked them to hide them for us. They said they would, then handed us some chocolate and fruit juice. It looked and smelled so wonderful!

"You're not allowed to have that!" the guard barked at us. "That is not allowed."

We were so hungry we could almost taste the delicious treats in our hands.

"Into the car!" the guard ordered.

We handed the treats back to our sisters, gave them one last hug, and along with Sayeh, struggled into the backseat. The guard rode up front with the soldier who was driving. Both of them held their noses all the way to the courthouse.

After delivering Sayeh to the Family Court, Maryam and I went on to the Revolutionary Court, a huge brick building that is famous in Tehran. We came in through a back door, where prisoners enter so the public can't see them, then into a small room where guards searched us. We were led through a courtyard and through another door. Inside, the Revolutionary Court was a maze of rooms, long corridors, and elevators. Still handcuffed together, we walked upstairs to a waiting area outside Enghelab Court, Branch 2, of the Security Police. The ladies who had been arrested at the bakery with the We Are flash mob were there with their families and were happy to see us. They wanted to introduce us to their children and relatives. Our guard warned us to sit still.

"This place is covered with surveillance cameras," she said. "If you are caught talking, it will cause problems."

We exchanged brief greetings with the ladies and then sat down.

Next to us were two handsome young men in suits. They heard us talking to a couple of lawyers in the room about our charges and started asking questions.

"Why have you been arrested?"

"Because we are Christians," I said.

"Really!" one of the men exclaimed. "What a charge! They have no mercy on anybody. How did they know you were Christians? Were you involved in any church activities?"

At that moment, our guard told the man with all the questions to stand up. She then took his seat next to Maryam, leaned over to us, and said quietly, "These are plainclothes secret police, the *basiji*. They are trying to collect damaging information about you." This guard from Vozara had sympathy for us and was trying to protect us.

A group of men came in, some walking only with difficulty. They had been arrested with the women at the bakery and badly beaten by the *basiji*. The *basiji* who had hit them were the two handsome young men talking to us.

The ladies went into the courtroom, declared their innocence, and told the judge they wanted to file complaints against the *basiji*. The judge replied that if they would not file any complaints, he would release them on bail. If they insisted on pressing charges, they would stay locked up. The ladies were so relieved at the prospect of being released that they agreed to the deal. However, as so often happens in Iranian courts, the charges were not officially dropped. Once the bail was paid, the women were free to go, but the charges against them remained on the books indefinitely, in case the government wanted to pressure them in the future.

Every judge in the Revolutionary Court has a large, impressive office. We were called into the office of a fat, pompous man with a dark beard. He was Mr. Sobhani, the judge for the Revolutionary Court who had received our case from Mr. Rasti at police headquarters. He had a red mark on his forehead that devout Muslims get when they pray for long periods with a prayer stone pressed against their brow. However, I could tell that, like others we knew, he had heated the stone before using it. That made a red mark right away, displaying his devout status without all that time-consuming prayer. He wore a huge ring inscribed with verses from the Koran. On the wall were photos of Iranian soldiers fighting and dying, some of them covered with blood. There were photos of Ayatollah Khomeini, who had seized power from the Shah in 1979, and Ayatollah Khamenei, the current supreme leader of Iran. Some of the pictures looked to be of Sobhani himself. The courtroom was a monument to martyrs for Islam. The judge wrote out a list of questions for each of us and ordered us to write the answers without talking to each other. They were the same questions we had already answered many times, and our answers were practically identical:

Do you accept the charge of advertising activities against the regime and insulting religious authorities? *No.*

Do you accept the charge of promoting Christianity in Iran? *No.*

Do you accept the charge of distributing Bibles and evangelizing in a restaurant in Tehran? *No. We gave New Testaments only as gifts to people who asked for them. We did not initiate conversations about Jesus with anyone in a restaurant.*

What church do you go to? *We do not go to a church in Iran.*

Which church have you been baptized in? *Assemblies of God* (Maryam) and *Pentecostal* (me).

We continued on to the end, and then signed and fingerprinted our answers.

Back in the car, as the driver navigated the heavy noontime traffic, I assumed we were returning to the detention center. Instead, we were taken to the Gisha police station and soon found ourselves face-to-face again with our old friend Mr. Rasti.

"I hope you've been thinking carefully," he said, nibbling on a piece of bread. "Have you?"

I wondered if he knew how hungry we were, or if he always ate in front of prisoners.

"What should we have been thinking of?" Maryam asked.

"About telling us what we want to know about you and your activities, people you have worked with. We have other ways of getting prisoners to communicate. Tell us what we want or we will beat you. You might as well tell us now and save yourselves."

Mohammadi, the officer who had searched our apartment, came in with little signs and a camera. We had to hang the signs around our necks and have our pictures taken. The signs said, "Marziyeh Amirizadeh, accused of promoting Christianity in Iran," and "Maryam Rostampour, accused of pro-moting Christianity in Iran." We thought it was an honor to be identified that way, and we both smiled broadly for the photos, which made Mr. Rasti grumpy. We were supposed to be afraid, but his tactics weren't having the desired effect.

"I have checked your laptop and read all the evidence against you," he said sternly. "You must tell us everything about people you have contact with, which organizations you work with. Otherwise, we will lock your hands and feet together and beat you until you die. Think about that as you prepare for your interrogation."

Pushing back abruptly from the table, he walked out, leaving us with "Mr. Truth," the first policeman we'd met at Gisha the day of our arrest.

Mr. Haghighat took us to the basement of the police station to await our interrogation. It was a dark, damp, filthy room, reeking with the all-too-familiar smell of defective plumbing. As we eventually discovered, there actually wasn't any plumbing at all; the toilet was simply a hole in the floor. Roaches scampered around the opening and up the walls. It was cold, so we grabbed a couple of dirty blankets and wrapped ourselves up on the floor, huddling together for warmth. Who could have imagined that such a big, impressive-looking building contained such a squalid room? Of all the places we were imprisoned in the months ahead, this turned out to be the worst.

Despite our earlier bravado, we were afraid. For all we knew, this could be our last day on earth. We held hands and prayed to the Lord to calm our hearts. Our greatest fear was that we would break and say things outside of God's will. We prayed for strength. We wanted our captors to see that we were confident and brave. *If we are tortured, give us the power to stand fast.*

Praying made us feel better. Famished and exhausted, we fell asleep, even as we waited for the sound of death at the door.

The rattle of a key in the lock woke me with a start. Maryam and I held each other silently as footsteps approached. But instead of the rough-looking character we expected, a female guard came in with two young women, both of them crying. The women were sisters who had been arrested for using GoldQuest, an Internet business networking site that had been banned in Iran. After allowing us to pray for them, one of them said, "You are like angels in this place. How do you stay so calm and strong?"

"It isn't *our* strength," I explained. "Only the Lord is strong enough to get us through this." Within an hour or two, we were talking like lifelong friends. We held hands and prayed together. When we finished, the sisters kept right on praying.

We heard a key in the lock again and at the same time, the rant of a very familiar voice. *Leila!* The sight of her, screaming and struggling against the guard, petrified the sisters. I told them not to worry.

"We know her," I said. "She looks rough, but she has a tender heart. She told us she has a husband and a son."

Leila was overjoyed to see us. Somehow she had gotten down to the basement cells with a whole box of tangerines. She shared them with us and the sisters. Within a few minutes, we had gobbled them all down.

"We thought you were being released," I said. That's what she had told us when she left for court that morning. Her husband was coming to pay her bail and get her out.

"I thought so too," she answered. "But these bastards won't let me out unless my husband shows them a birth certificate or wedding certificate proving he's responsible for me. He said he couldn't find them and was going to bring them this afternoon. He's not here, so he can go die!"

"How about a cigarette?" she shouted toward the door. When there was no answer, she shouted again.

Finally, a guard appeared and said, "Shut up! Your husband should come and get you." As a married woman, Leila couldn't be released except to her husband, according to the law.

"Go to hell, coward!" Leila screamed. "Damn you and damn your Islamic religion! Death to you and to the regime!" The guard disappeared without a word.

As the day went on, Leila was told that if she could come up with bail money of 30,000 tomans (fifteen dollars), they would let her out. She had some of the money, and when I offered her the rest, she shouted for the guards to release her. But it was all a cruel joke, and they ignored her pleas. There had been no bail offer; the guards were only teasing. Later, they told her that her husband was on the way, and she cried with happiness at the news. But that, too, was a joke. Finally, they got him on the telephone for her. We could hear the two of them arguing before Leila hung up on him with a curse.

Completely spent by her raving, she fell asleep with her head in my lap.

Maryam and I both stroked her hair like she was a child. Goodness knows how long it had been since anyone had touched her with kindness and compassion. The sisters looked on amazed as she slept. It was such a contrast to her wild behavior to see this hard-looking, tough-talking, violent woman resting so peacefully.

When it was time for the guards to go home for the night, they couldn't leave as long as we were there, so they sent us back to Vozara. They handcuffed the five of us together, which meant that when one of us stumbled, we all fell. This prompted another string of curses from Leila. It was nearly midnight, so traffic was light, enabling the prison van to fly through the city streets, careening around corners, throwing us around in the back like a load of vegetables.

Despite the late hour, Elena and Shirin were waiting for us at Vozara with another supply of chocolate and juice. This time, we hid them under our clothing to eat later. This was when we first learned that others had heard about our arrest and were trying to help. In the days to come, our sisters would be our lifeline to the outside world. As our case became known, we hoped that news of Christians being threatened with torture or death by the Islamic regime would encourage the faithful to pray for us and work for our release. We hoped this meant our freedom was coming soon.

Inside Vozara, we were asked a now-familiar series of questions, this time by the warden of the detention center, before they allowed us back into our cell. Were we born Christians or did we convert? Why did we reject Islam? Why did we give out Bibles?

After some more questions, the warden demanded, "Who are you?!"

"I am a daughter of God," Maryam answered.

"Then I must be his son, right?" he replied sarcastically.

"Right!" Maryam said triumphantly.

The official jumped up, livid with rage. "Blasphemy! Stop with your blasphemy against Islam! Stop! Stop!"

His reaction frightened one of the guards, who advised Maryam to stop arguing. "These are dangerous people," she whispered. "You gain nothing by making them angry."

"The court will decide," the warden continued. "Then you'll see what's what!"

We went to the familiar detention cell block, chose a couple of stinky blankets, and wrapped ourselves up on the floor. We were both too exhausted to think. Images and experiences of the day swirled around inside my head like a crazy kaleidoscope. Yet we had survived so far! Without a bed, without a meal, without even a hint of justice, we had been spared by the mercy of God. I had no idea what the Lord had planned for us the next day. I only knew that whatever it was, His grace would be sufficient.

NEW FRIENDS, OLD QUESTIONS

Marziyeh

Monday, March 9, began with Leila's usual racket, though it was affecting us less every day because we were getting used to it and because we were waking up weaker from lack of food and exercise. The guard called out the names of women to be taken to court. The GoldQuest sisters were called, along with Sayeh, still disheveled and dirty. She asked us to pray to Jesus that she would go to social services and have a clean place to sleep. Leila was also called. The guards told her that since her husband had not come for her, she would be transferred to Evin Prison. The news threw her into a rage. Evin was notorious as a place where people who committed crimes against Islam—which were also crimes against the regime—were held indefinitely, often tortured, and sometimes killed. She was going there simply because her three days in detention were up. Now she would have a prison record for the rest of her life. As she left, she stopped screaming insults and obscenities long enough for us to say good-bye and wish her well.

Our three days of detention were more than up. If Leila was headed to Evin, we might be sent there too. But we had no news and didn't know what was next.

Only a handful of prisoners remained after roll call, including Sahar, the attractive young runaway with the close-cropped hair, and a new arrival we were anxious to meet, named Masomeh, a short, beautiful woman with friendly looking eyes. While the other women talked, Maryam and I started cleaning the cells and toilets. We had taken this on as our regular morning job. We asked the guards if we could clean around their office too. They were shocked that we would offer, and gladly accepted. If we did the work, it meant they didn't have to. The guards got their drinking water from the kitchen, which was off-limits to the prisoners. We asked permission to go to the kitchen for a drink. When they said yes, we were overjoyed, drinking our fill straight from the tap because we didn't have a glass. It was the first water we'd had in four days. We drank at least a pitcher each!

"You two are not like the other prisoners," one of the guards told us. "How did you end up here? What are the charges against you?" After we explained, she said, "You're too good to be here. It's a shame for innocent people like you to be locked up. I hope they release you soon."

Another guard, who had overheard part of our conversation, asked, "What are they here for?" When the first guard told her, she went berserk, flailing her hands at us and shouting, "They deserve to be in detention!" With surprising strength, she pushed us roughly down the hall into our cell and locked the door.

A little while later, we were taken outside the cell block to an office where two male inspectors and two female guards awaited us.

"What is your charge?" one of the men asked.

"Christianity," Maryam answered.

He looked at us with disbelief. "Christianity is not an offense."

"We were not born Christians. We converted eleven years ago."

"Oh, you converted! And are you advertising it too?"

"Yes, with friends and family who want to know more about Jesus."

The same familiar questions followed, as they had so many times before. The man said he wanted to know more about Jesus and the Bible because he might want to convert.

"Do you know Jesus?" Maryam asked.

"Yes," the man said. "He is one of the prophets."

"We believe that Jesus is the Son of God and the Savior of humankind, not just a prophet. He sacrificed Himself for our sins and rose from the dead."

"So you do not believe in Mohammed and the other prophets?"

"No, but I respect everyone's point of view."

To my astonishment, there were tears in the man's eyes. Looking down at the papers in front of him, he said quietly, "You don't need to tell anyone else what you have told me. It will cause problems for you." He then asked about our trip to the Revolutionary Court and what conditions were like in the cell block at Vozara. We told him how bad things were.

"But wherever the Lord puts us is the best place for us to be, even if it's here," I added.

"Be strong and hold on to your faith," he murmured. "I hope you will soon be free."

Back in our cell block, we introduced ourselves to some of the new prisoners. One was a short, chubby woman who had been arrested for check fraud. When we began sharing our story, she started to cry. "I believe in Jesus too," she said softly so no one else would hear. "A few years ago, in Sweden, I went to church and was baptized. I know about Jesus and His teaching, but I've never read the Bible." She asked us to pray for her, which we were glad to do.

Masomeh, the friendly looking woman we had hoped to meet earlier, turned out to be flinty and prideful. It's amazing how wrong first impressions can be. She reminded us that it's hard to know someone by their face alone. We had developed an idea of her character from her appearance and trusted her at first, but as we got to know her better, we saw a truer picture. Masomeh told us that her father was a martyr who had died fighting against Iraq. She didn't like her stepfather and had moved out to live on her own, supported by her father's inheritance. She had become involved in lesbian relationships with two women, who had accepted her money and favors but left her heartbroken. She later began a relationship with a man, lavishing gifts on him, including furniture and a car. Then one night the security police burst in on them in her bedroom. The rest of her story came out later: She had set the man up because he was wealthy. She told the police when they would be together and used her influence as the daughter of a martyr to convince the judge to order the man to marry her. When he appeared in court later that day, it was apparent he had already been lashed.

Emboldened by Masomeh's story, Sahar gave us more of her own history. She said she was sixteen and had a boyfriend who sent sex workers to Dubai. She wanted to go, too, but her brother found out and shaved her head and beat her. She ran away and was arrested. Her plans were to reconnect with her boyfriend as soon as she was released and get a job in Dubai. We tried to talk her out of it, but for her this was a ticket to freedom and financial independence.

Sex was a very popular topic in prison. It was impossible to know how much of what we heard was true and how much was bluster. Another new inmate, Tannaz, a sixteen-year-old girl from the city of Mashhad, wore skinny jeans and a revealing black top. She had been arrested while having sex in a park. She boasted that she had police files all over the country. When she heard our story, she declared that we must be executed as infidels. "My sins can be forgiven," she said harshly to us, "but you sinned against Allah, and that can never be forgiven!"

In the middle of the day, one of the guards, a woman in her mid-twenties, called us over to the hallway door and spoke to us through the bars. Instead of calling us by name, she called us "the Christian girls." She had started treating us with kindness and acted more gently toward us than did the other guards. She looked afraid, glancing from side to side as she talked.

"I have heard from some of the prisoners that you pray for them and your prayers are answered," she began. "Something bad has happened in my life. Could you please pray for me?" Maryam said we would be honored to pray for her. We held her hands through the bars and prayed aloud. She began crying softly, and when we finished, she joined us in saying, "Amen." We said a few words to her about Jesus, but she was afraid to stay any longer. "If your God answers me, I will go to church and I will read the Bible," she promised.

"I don't like this job, but I need the money," she added. "I'm in prison, too, just in a different way. The detainees come and go, but I'm stuck here day after day, month after month, in this horrible underground hole."

She went back to the office, but returned a little while later with a plate of pasta and two spoons. "I know you two haven't eaten the food," she said. "This is for you." We ate it gratefully. When we finished, she brought us a whole jug of water. What a miracle not to be hungry or thirsty for the first time in days.

As the afternoon wore on, prisoners began returning from court. We heard that the GoldQuest sisters had been released on bail and that Sayeh had been transferred to social services. Some of our acquaintances returned to the cell block while others we never saw or heard from again, and there were new arrivals constantly.

As incredible as our unexpected lunch had been, we got another big surprise at dinner. When the guard came in with the usual pan of lentils and rice, instead of sliding it across the floor to where the inmates waited to dig in with their hands, she shouted for the women to stand back.

"Nobody touches the food except Marziyeh," she barked, "because her hands are clean. Marziyeh will serve the rest of you."

I was stunned—the "unclean" Christian being chosen to handle everyone's meals—but I quickly stepped forward to do as the guard had said. Using one piece of bread as a utensil and another as a plate, I scooped up a helping and handed it to the woman nearest me, continuing in turn until everyone had been served. After dinner, Maryam washed the pan so that we knew it would be clean for tomorrow. It wasn't easy, but we found it was possible to establish a small island of decency, even in this hellhole.

| | |

MARYAM

The culinary surprises continued the next morning, when a guard brought all the prisoners breakfast: a small bag of bread and cheese, one bag for each two prisoners. We never knew why the meal routine suddenly changed, but I hoped it was because the guards were beginning to see us as human beings. We had refused to act like animals, so maybe they decided to treat us accordingly.

After breakfast, Marziyeh's name and mine were the first ones called. Instead of returning to the Revolutionary Court as we expected, we were again taken to the Gisha police station. There we were separated, and

Marziyeh waited while I went in for another interrogation with Mr. Rasti. A young female guard was also in the room.

Mr. Rasti invited me in with a smile and asked me to be seated. Could this be the same police officer who had been so rude and threatening before? Who'd had us hauled off to the Revolutionary Court in handcuffs?

"I hope you are well," he said in a friendly way. "Have you had any problems the last few days?"

"No," I answered. "Everything is fine. I have no complaints."

Mr. Rasti tried to hide his surprise and went on. "It's a shame for you to be locked up in a place like Vozara. We keep rough people there who have a lot of problems."

"I don't mind," I said. "They're all human beings, and they didn't always have these problems. We must look at their past and see what caused them to do what they did."

Mr. Rasti smiled. "Are you advertising Christianity in there, too?"

"Of course! We're speaking to every person you send us, especially the young girls. They are desperate for help, so we help them by praying for them."

"I guess it's not so bad for you in there after all," Mr. Rasti said. He shuffled through the contents of a file folder in front of him, selected a sheet of paper, and held it up. I could see it was in my handwriting. "Is this a list of people you're working with?" he demanded. "How do you know them?"

"Those are people we needed to pray for every day. I made a list so we wouldn't leave anybody out. We've never even met most of them."

"A notation here says, 'in hospital.' Did you visit this person in the hospital?"

I had, but I wasn't going to admit it.

The questions went on. "Did you visit this list of cities?"

"No, we made the list to pray for them."

"Did you prepare people to become Christians?"

"If they asked questions, we answered. As Christians, we want to share the Lord's truth with anyone who wants it."

As the same old questions dragged on and on, my mind began to wander, and I enjoyed the view through the big window behind Mr. Rasti's desk.

He held up a notebook. "This book is filled with names and addresses and phone numbers. Are these people Christians?"

They were, but I was not about to say so and risk their lives. "No. These are our friends, and most of them are Muslims. You can check if you like."

"Was your apartment used as a church? Did a group of Christians use it as a base?"

If you only knew, I said to myself. Marziyeh and I had spent hundreds of hours praying and reading the Bible with our friends. We hosted two home churches, one for young people and another especially for prostitutes. Often we met together twice a day to encourage and uplift each other. When we weren't feeding people spiritually, we were feeding them physically, filling the table night after night with good food to share as we talked about Jesus and His power in our lives. So many people had given their hearts to Jesus in that unassuming little place. If only the regime could realize how eager young Iranians are to experience Jesus. Many are desperate to escape but feel there is no way out. The rules of Islam are forced on them against their will. Several of these young people, when they first met Marziyeh and me, could scarcely imagine a Lord in human form who sacrificed Himself for them, a Savior who loved them unconditionally. That knowledge made them almost delirious with joy and thanksgiving. They loved Jesus because He first loved them. They readily chose Christianity over Islam. But they were not free to choose a new belief system. To leave Islam for Christianity was to risk torture and death.

"No," I answered confidently. "Our apartment has never been used as a church."

"Don't you think you're taking Islam away from our youth?"

"No. I don't want to change anyone's mind about their faith. I don't want to take Islam away from anyone. I only want to give young people a chance to choose their own religion. Is there a problem with that?"

Mr. Rasti ignored my question and plowed ahead with even more of his own.

| | |

Marziyeh

While Maryam was being interviewed, I waited in another room, handcuffed and praying. One of my two guards approached me hesitantly.

"I know why you're here," he said. "I want to know why you became a Christian."

I recognized him as the officer I'd seen on the day of our arrest, the one who had told me there must be a mistake and there was no problem with my car registration. Evidently, he knew nothing about the scheme to trick us into coming to the station. As I shared my testimony, the young man listened eagerly.

"I pray Islamic prayers every day," he whispered. "I believe in the Lord and in Christ, but not the way you do."

"This is something the Lord is trying to reveal to you," I said. "If you ask Him, He will help you to understand."

"Really?"

"Yes. Jesus says, 'Seek, and you will find; knock, and it will be opened to you.'[1] You need a heart that seeks truth, and the Lord will reveal the truth to you."

The other guard came over to where we were sitting. "I heard everything you were talking about. If you will answer some of my questions, I will believe in Jesus. How is it possible that a human being could be the Son of God? How could a person be the Lord?"

I explained the Christian idea of God in the flesh to him, but he was skeptical and kept challenging me.

"Do you believe the Lord can do whatever He wants?" I asked.

"Yes, I believe that."

"Then ask Him to explain it to you, since my words are inadequate. These are truths that only the Lord can reveal to people in their hearts. It isn't a matter of arguing or reading a book. If you really want answers, pray to the Lord in your own language—it is not necessary to pray only in Arabic—and ask Him to show you the truth."

The first guard was delighted with this advice, but his partner was still unconvinced. "If you sincerely want the truth and pray for it," I said, "the Lord will show it to you. But if you just want to argue, you're wasting my time and your own."

At that moment Mr. Haghighat came into the room and the conversation abruptly stopped.

After more than two hours, another guard came to take me for my interview. Maryam and I passed each other on the stairs.

"It's all right," Maryam said reassuringly. "We're not being tortured. Just tell the truth."

That's an odd thing to say, I thought. *One of my problems in life is that I can't lie even when I need to.*

In Mr. Rasti's office, he offered me a seat. "I'm so sorry to have to put you through this again," he said apologetically. "It's just that those are the rules."

I could not believe my ears. What happened to the curt, disrespectful Mr. Rasti I had met before?

"We found pictures on your laptop that were taken in Korea," Mr. Rasti began. "What is your relationship with the Korean church?"

"We were in Korea visiting a friend. While we were there, we went to a festival for women, organized by the church."

"Did you visit other churches there?"

"It is common for Christians to visit various churches when they travel."

"We know you operate a house church because we found these notes for a speech."

"Those are my notes for a Bible study," I replied. "You'll see I write about disappointments and difficulties, and the challenge of trusting the Lord during hard times, but that faith is the key to success. Is any of that incorrect?"

Mr. Rasti ignored my query and continued a long series of questions about photos, names, and other information he had learned from going through my private things.

Fortunately, no one had discovered any more information about the trip Maryam and I had taken to South Korea, where Christianity is thriving. Through a series of friendships, we had been invited to a leadership conference there, where the other participants were pastors' wives or other kinds of church leaders. We were just two Christian girls from Iran—it was a miracle we were there.

South Korea was clean and prosperous, and its Christians enthusiastic and compassionate. They showed their faith not only with words but with deeds as well. What a contrast it was to India, where we had gone to share the message of Christ with prostitutes and learn how to minister to them.

Fortunately, the Iranian authorities never found evidence of this work either. We were with a Christian ministry there that sometimes bought child prostitutes in order to rescue them. When we visited red-light districts where young prostitutes lived, we had to travel with bodyguards. It was a dangerous, filthy place. Many of the people had AIDS. Some prostitutes asked us to pray for them in church, which we were honored to do. We also spoke to a Christian congregation there and handed out Indian Bibles in the shops.

After my interrogation, I was reunited with Maryam and we compared notes on our sessions. We wondered why Mr. Rasti had behaved so differently toward us today than in the past. We were taken to a dirty, dark cell under the stairwell and left alone.

Later, a short, young, beautiful girl joined us. When we explained the charges against us, she asked us to pray for her. She had been married for six months. Whenever she refused to have sex with her husband, he tied her hands and feet and raped her. She escaped to her parents' house and filed for divorce. But under Islamic law, only the husband can seek a divorce. Legally, she could not get a divorce without her husband's consent. Still, she stayed with her parents and got a job.

One day, she accepted a ride to work with a male colleague. Her husband, who had been following her, alerted the *basiji* and had her arrested, claiming she was cheating on him with the man who gave her the ride. Even though the husband had no proof to support his charge, the word of a man officially carries twice the weight of a woman's testimony in Islamic court. She would remain in prison until she agreed to go back to her abusive husband (if he would take her) or until he agreed to a divorce.

Another prisoner came in, a slim girl with short hair, whose name was Sharareh. She had been arrested for drinking and dancing with some boys at an amusement park. There were wounds on her body where the *basiji* had hit her. One of the *basiji* had held her head down in the car so passersby couldn't see her through the window. Someone had also held her hands and feet. "Your body is so nice," her captor had said. "Why do you force us to beat you? Why don't you relax and let me sing you a little lullaby so you can fall asleep in my arms?" Though it was illegal for her to flirt with boys, it was evidently all right for the *basiji* who arrested her to flirt with her—even as they were beating her.

| | | |

MARYAM

It was nearly midnight by the time a guard named Mrs. Najimi came to take us back to Vozara. During the time when Marziyeh was being interrogated, I'd had a run-in with this guard. After my own interrogation, I had worried about Marziyeh and started praying for her out loud. Hearing the prayers, Mrs. Najimi had run into the room shouting, "Shut up! I don't want to hear your voice anymore! If I hear you once more, I'll come in here and strangle you!" Shocked and tired, with my resistance at a low ebb, I had dissolved in tears.

Now when Mrs. Najimi saw me, she said, "Maryam, are you all right?"

I assured her that I was fine.

"We're going back to Vozara," Mrs. Najimi continued, in a conciliatory tone, "but take your time, darling, and don't worry." Just as with Mr. Rasti, Mrs. Najimi's attitude and treatment of us was completely different than before. She went through the motions of following the rules but treated us with compassion and courtesy. She handcuffed me to Marziyeh and took us to the car. As we rode, she asked, "Why did they arrest you?"

"For being Christians."

"And what's wrong with that, my darling?"

"You'll have to ask Mr. Rasti."

"Something really bad happened to me this afternoon," she said haltingly. "I had an argument with my boss and he humiliated me. It left me crying the rest of the day." She was silent for a minute, and then turned to me again. "My darling, please forgive me for the way I treated you. I was nasty to you today, but I didn't mean it." She asked both of us about our faith, and we answered her questions all the way to the detention center.

Time and again, I was discovering that even the employees of the Iranian regime—guards, soldiers, police officers, court officials—yearned for the truth of Christ in their hearts, but feared to ask about Him because of the harsh punishment awaiting those who seek the truth.

When we arrived at Vozara, we couldn't be admitted because the guards had forgotten some papers. While the driver went back for them, Mrs. Najimi waited with us. She told us she lived in a poor area of the city and traveled hours each way to work every day. She didn't like her job, but her father had cancer and it was the only way she could make money to take care of him. She asked us to pray for her and her father. "I hope you will soon be free and that you have great success in your lives," she said, and gave me a big hug.

When the driver returned, we went down to our cell block, where everyone had waited up to learn what had happened to us: Masomeh, the martyr's daughter; Sahar, with the short hair; Tannaz, the flirtatious young girl from Mashhad; and others, along with several new prisoners, including a Korean woman whose visa had expired. She didn't speak Farsi, but she could speak a little English and a little Turkish, and so could we, so we were able to communicate. She was a Christian, and when she learned we were Christians, too, her face lit up with happiness. She asked to sleep in our cell, which was already crowded with other women, including Masomeh and Sahar, who all wanted to be near us like little frightened girls around their mothers. We made room for our new Korean friend and welcomed her in for the night.

CHAPTER 6

CELEBRATION OF FAITH

MARYAM

The next two days, Thursday and Friday, the court was closed, which meant Vozara was crowded and busy because new inmates kept arriving and nobody left. The first new prisoner we saw was a young woman who was very well dressed and seemed afraid of everyone around her. Her first experience behind bars had been watching Leila—who was back from Evin after only a short stay—go through her morning routine, screaming for a cigarette. It's little wonder the woman was frightened. When others approached her, she turned away and remained silent. Marziyeh and I introduced ourselves and answered the woman's questions about why we were there.

"This is such a relief!" she exclaimed. "I never thought people like you would be in a detention center."

She was a law student who earned her school expenses by giving skin and beauty treatments. After she leased space for a shop, her landlord made sexual advances toward her. When she refused him, he cashed her postdated deposit check ahead of the date they had agreed on. When the check was rejected by the bank, the landlord had her arrested. She was engaged to be married, and was grateful that her fiancé and her family were supporting her and working for her release. Even so, she was embarrassed and frightened at what might happen next. We began to pray for her. By now, our prayers were a familiar sound to our fellow prisoners, but somehow this time was different. As we continued, the other inmates stopped talking— one by one—and started listening, until our voices alone echoed off the walls of the cell block. When we finished and said "Amen," everybody else said "Amen" too.

The Vozara Detention Center had become a church.

Tannaz was the only prisoner who still shied away from us. She was the one who had told us that God would forgive promiscuous sex but would never forgive the worship of Jesus. I had seen her watching us as we prayed and talked with the others. Now, for the first time, she approached us. She was crying.

"What happened?" one of the prisoners demanded as the girl came closer. "Do you think their prayers aren't so worthless after all?" Without a word, Tannaz sat down in front of us.

"Would you like us to pray for you?" I asked.

"Yes, please," she said. "Pray that I would be freed soon and have a good life from now on." I took her outstretched hands and prayed for her until dinnertime, when a guard arrived with the big dish and everyone waited patiently while Marziyeh served up the meal on little plates of bread.

I noticed the Korean woman crying in a corner and asked if I could help her. Struggling with the language barrier, she explained that she had a newborn child and her breasts were full of milk. Because she couldn't nurse, they were very painful. The pain reminded her of how much she missed her child, and how hungry he must be by now. She also said she was still hungry. Marziyeh hadn't eaten yet, so she gave the young mother her portion.

It's hard to imagine a justice system worthy of the name that considers it essential to national security to separate a mother from her newborn baby over a visa problem. A regime that fears people like this is on very shaky ground.

Around midnight, I was awakened by the arrival of an attractive, athletic woman. The guards brought her to our cell so she wouldn't be as afraid. She had been skiing in the mountains with her boyfriend when the *basiji* stopped her and said her hair was not properly covered according to Islamic law. When the boyfriend confronted them for criticizing her, they were both arrested. She hit one of the *basiji*, who lodged a personal complaint against her on top of the other charge.

After daybreak, there were more comings and goings. Leila's husband arrived to pick her up, leading to whoops of joy. I thought she would literally fly out the door. As she headed for her freedom, Marziyeh and I reminded her of the promises she'd made to visit a church.

A group of half a dozen or so women came in together, very provocatively dressed and wearing heavy makeup. They were madams, arrested on the street for soliciting customers for their girls. One was a very aggressive lesbian who was immediately attracted to Marziyeh, eyeing her as she walked up and down the hallway to get a little exercise.

"Oh sister! What a piece of meat!" she exclaimed to her friends. "Honey, I'm sleeping with *you* tonight." When Marziyeh tried to ignore her, the woman made suggestive moves and did a little dance in front of her.

Fortunately for us, none of the madams ended up in our cell for the night, though I was awakened more than once by the sound of two of the women in the throes of lesbian passion. These were people who needed God desperately.

Sadly, most divorced or widowed women in Iran are destined for a horrible life. They have no legal rights, their families disown them, and the government gives them no encouragement or assistance. These women reminded me of our ministry to prostitutes in India, where the Hindu religion also enslaves women. One of our two home churches, a group we called Mary Magdalene, was for poor, divorced, or widowed women, who out of desperation had turned to prostitution to stay alive. Life was very difficult for them because many had young children and very few options for employment. Rather than offering assistance, the regime made the situation worse by forcing women to marry men they didn't love, forcing them to stay in abusive relationships, and making it almost impossible to get a divorce. The government used the façade of religion as an excuse to treat women like toys or commodities, such as with an officially sanctioned temporary marriage, or *sigheh*, which might last only an hour.

| | |

On Saturday, it was off to court for most of the prisoners, as usual. The skier was released on bail. Sharareh and Tannaz left the cell block and never came back. Two of the madams were summoned and the rest stayed with us. As we got to know them a little, we learned that some were in the sex business because they enjoyed it, some were saving money so they could stop doing it one day, and others had stories all their own. The aggressive lesbian was a transsexual who had been born a boy and sold himself for sex to make enough money for a sex-change operation. Now a woman, she seemed very satisfied with her new life. Another of the group had been raped as a young teenager in a house where she worked as a maid. When she found out she could get paid for sex, she loved the work for a while, but then came to hate herself for what she was doing.

"But how else can I survive in this country?" she cried. "I'm so tired!" All we could do was pray for her.

After Masomeh and the transsexual returned from court, the two of them got into a loud argument. We still weren't sure we had the whole story on Masomeh, the martyr's daughter who had set up her boyfriend to be arrested and lashed by the *basiji*. She started talking with the transsexual about her relationship with her boyfriend, claiming that she loved him so much. After listening for a minute, the transsexual asked if the apartment where they were caught was at a certain address. Masomeh said that it was.

"Six months ago, your boyfriend was one of my customers!" the transsexual crowed. "We went to that apartment, and he paid me 100,000 tomans to have sex with him!" Masomeh had said earlier that she'd bought the boyfriend a car and other expensive gifts. Now the truth was about to come out. She turned absolutely white. "He told me everything he had, including his car, was his to begin with, not presents from you!" the transsexual continued. "You weren't wealthy, and you weren't being generous. He was the wealthy one, and you had him arrested so you could take everything from him!"

Normally brash and outspoken, Masomeh was struck dumb by this exposé of her past. "I have to go to the toilet," she said, and left the room. Later, we learned she was having an affair with the judge in her case. He knew she was guilty of defrauding her lover; but in exchange for her sexual favors, the judge forced her boyfriend to marry her, and then sent him to prison so that Masomeh could keep his property and she and the judge could continue their relationship. This is not an uncommon situation. A different judge had offered to release one of the madams on bail if she would give him her phone number.

| | |

Marziyeh

Cleaning the floors and toilets had become an everyday routine for us. The change in hygiene and the improvement in the way our meals were served, small as they were, made a big difference in the comfort of our temporary home. One day, I even convinced one of the guards to take a little money from me to buy some cake and juice for everyone. It was the only relief we had from bread and cheese in the morning and lentils and rice the rest of the day.

Every morning, we also cleaned the hall in front of the guards' office. One day, a kind-looking middle-aged woman came to the cell block while we were cleaning and asked us why we were at Vozara.

"We're in jail for our faith in Christ," I explained.

She was the custodian, hired to clean the whole detention center. She admitted that, until that moment, she had never even been to our cell block. Perhaps tinged with guilt, she gave the floor a few halfhearted strokes with a broom and then said, "I hear you pray for everyone here. Could you pray for me?"

"Do you accept the way we pray?" Maryam asked.

"How do you pray?"

"We are Christians. We pray to Jesus Christ, our Lord and Savior."

"Okay, so you're Christians," she answered. "What difference does it make? I accept Jesus. Just pray for me."

We promised we would.

Late that night, a young girl, very thin and addicted to crack, came in. She was injured or sick, and crying in terrible pain. Though it was after midnight, I went to her cell.

"Why are you here?" the girl asked. "Why aren't you asleep?"

"Because I wanted to sit here with you," I said. I took the girl's head in my lap and stroked her hair. She was younger than my sister, Elena. I prayed silently until the girl fell asleep, and then sat with her a long time so as not to wake her.

Early the next morning, the girl sought me out and asked, "What kind of prayer did you pray for me last night?" I told her I had prayed for Jesus to heal her.

"I became so calm," she said, "and my pain is much less." Maryam and I told her that if she trusted Jesus and tried to change her ways, the Lord would always be willing to help her.

A woman in her forties arrived, whose husband was a pilot in the air force. They lived on a military base outside the city, and every aspect of their lives was monitored by the government: mobile phones, text messages, visitors—absolutely everything. The authorities knew more about them than they knew about themselves. Her elderly father had stomach trouble that he treated by drinking a little wine, even though alcohol is strictly forbidden by Islamic law. Because the family was under such close surveillance, it was impossible to buy wine without being seen, so they grew grapes and made their own. A neighbor saw the wine in a cabinet at their house and alerted the authorities. With the pilot and his family arrested by the *basiji*, the neighbor hoped to be promoted to the pilot's position. The woman was worried about her husband and also about their two young children. After she heard our story, she asked us to pray for all of them.

| | |

When a guard came for Maryam and me the next morning, we assumed we were going back to the police station or to the Revolutionary Court. We walked outside in handcuffs, but instead of the usual police car or van waiting for us, there was a taxi, and beside it stood a man who introduced himself as Mr. Yazdani. We didn't recognize him, but hoped that our sisters had sent him. Mr. Yazdani carried a dossier in his hand and seemed to know something about us and our case. "We're going to see what we can do to get you released in time for New Year's," he said. That certainly sounded encouraging!

On the way to the Revolutionary Court, he asked us why we couldn't accept Mohammed and Jesus both. "That's what I do," he explained matter-of-factly. "It's a shame that girls like you have been caught in this type of situation."

When we arrived at the courthouse, the driver told us the total fare. He insisted the police hadn't paid him. Mr. Yazdani hadn't planned to pay him, so I paid him.

Maryam and I waited in an outer room while Mr. Yazdani went in to talk to our judge, Mr. Sobhani. As we waited, we started talking, and eventually we were laughing. A young female guard came over to see what we were laughing about. We had simply gotten the giggles, and once we started, we couldn't stop. The young guard started giggling, too, and was soon red-faced and laughing as hard as we were. Just then, the office door flew open and a stern-faced Judge Sobhani came stalking out.

"Are these girls your prisoners or your friends?" he barked at the guard. She quickly stopped laughing and scurried to a chair across the room. After the judge disappeared back into his office, the guard resumed her conversation with us. She was a university student and very interested in Christianity. She wished us good luck and said she would find a Bible to read.

The door opened again, and Mr. Yazdani came out looking very dejected. "Mr. Sobhani doesn't want to see you today," he said. There was no one else waiting to see the judge, but he had been offended by our laughter. He tended to be far more lenient with prisoners who flattered him and begged for mercy. Every time we had seen him, we had seemed confident and courteous. This aggravated him, and therefore he declined to see us.

It was nearly midnight by the time we returned to Vozara. A new prisoner lay on the floor in front of our cell, a teenager addicted to crystal meth and going through withdrawal. She was nearly comatose, unable to stand and seemingly unaware of what was happening. One of the guards was kicking her.

"Get up! Get up!" she yelled. "Get in your cell, you stupid trash!" The girl was completely helpless. The guard kicked her into our cell like a pile of old rags.

| | |

The next morning, I woke up with a terrible pain in my abdomen. Some kidney problems I'd had in the past were flaring up again, thanks to the stress, bad food, and cold floors. I called for the guard to unlock our door so I could go to the toilet, but my cries went unanswered. By the time the guards came to open the cells for the morning, I had wet myself. I feared I might be losing control altogether and hoped the problem would not be with me from now on. When the door was unlocked at last, I washed my clothes in the sink and wore my coat while they dried.

With the New Year's holiday approaching, most of the prisoners were called and set free that morning, leaving only a few of the madams, the young addict from the night before, and Maryam and me. Though the girl still seemed dazed and uncomfortable, she was better than when she'd come in. When we asked how we could help her, she said only a few words before starting to cry. Her voice made a strange, weak, raspy sound. As we comforted her, she told us her story.

She was so addicted to meth that she ate some of it, which had damaged her windpipe and vocal cords. Her family had tried to help her, and she was able to give it up for a while, but recently relapsed. She walked through Tehran looking for a treatment center until a kind man picked her up, gave her some money, and dropped her off at a hospital. The hospital staff told her they weren't a detoxification center and sent her away. Walking the streets again, she had asked some policemen for help. Instead, they beat her and drove her to Vozara.

"There's no one on earth who can help me," she said through her tears.

"The Lord will help you," I assured her. "He will not answer your cry for help with kicks and punches." Maryam and I told her a little about our lives and our Christian walk. "Trust God. Go to a church when you get out, and they will help you."

The girl's expression changed from despair to bright hope. "I will go to church, and I will never touch drugs again," she said with confidence. I held her while she cried, gave her a little money, and wished the Lord's blessing on her.

By the end of the day, every prisoner except the two of us had been called to court, and all but one had been released on bail. The pilot's wife was the last one to go, and she was sent to prison. We were left in the cell block completely alone.

We walked down the hall together, going into each cell and remembering the women we'd met there. By law, prisoners were to spend no more than three days at the Vozara Detention Center, yet we had now been there for two weeks. During that time, we had witnessed to dozens of women we never would have met if the authorities had followed the usual three-day rule. What a miracle it was that we'd been able to meet and encourage so many women. What man meant for evil, God used for His good and His glory. The people who arrested us thought we were suffering in misery. In fact, we had shared the gospel more openly behind bars than we had ever been able to do on the outside. Even two guards who had been especially rude to us apologized during that last day for the way they had acted, and they asked us to pray for them.

Now, as we entered each cell, we prayed for all the people who had been locked up there. We hoped they now had their freedom, that we had been faithful witnesses to them, and that they would continue to listen for the spirit of Christ moving in their hearts. Then we started thinking about the women who would be locked up there after we were gone. How could we reach out to them? There were damp places on the walls where little chunks of plaster had fallen off. Using these pieces of plaster as chalk, we wrote Bible verses and Christian messages all over the walls, and on the ceilings where prisoners could read them as they fell asleep. We prayed aloud and sang songs until late in the night. All alone in an underground prison cell, we shared a joyous celebration of faith.

| | |

The next day—March 18, 2009, in the West—was known as Esfand 28 in the Muslim world, one of the last days of the year 1387. Maryam and I went back to the Revolutionary Court and waited outside the magistrate's office while Mr. Yazdani went in to talk to Mr. Sobhani again. This time, the magistrate gave us an option for gaining our freedom, knowing it was impossible for us to carry it out. If we could come up with two hundred million tomans ($100,000) per person by five o'clock that afternoon, he would release us on bail until our case went to trial. Otherwise we were to be transferred immediately to Evin Prison. Prisoners have to be offered bail before they can be transferred to Evin, so the court had to go through the motions, even though we couldn't possibly arrange for that large of a payment on such short notice.

Our families owned property that they could pledge in order to get the money, but on the afternoon before one of the biggest holidays of the year, all the banks would be closed and our sisters could not collect the necessary documents. We knew we'd never get it back, even if we were acquitted. Christians typically forfeit all of their property in cases like ours.

Our two faithful sisters, Elena and Shirin, came to the detention center every day, in case we were taken somewhere. They followed us to court or to the police station to exchange a few words and slip us something to eat or drink while we walked from the car into the building. Today they were behind the police vehicle when our driver had a minor accident. While we waited in the van for the police to sort everything out, we had a solid hour to talk to them—by far the longest conversation we'd had since our arrest. One small luxury we enjoyed was trimming our fingernails for the first time in two weeks!

After being taken to the police station to get some forms, we were shocked to discover we were headed to Evin Prison. It was hard to believe that we were about to enter one of the world's most notorious prisons, imprisoned only for our faith in God.

Elena and Shirin waited at the prison entrance to say good-bye and wish us well. We hugged and cried and promised to pray for each other. Then we walked through the tall, imposing entrance gate with "Evin Prison" written across the top, out of the spring sunshine and into another world.

CHAPTER 7

EVIN, OUR CHURCH

MARYAM

The entrance to Evin Prison was on a hill. A few guards standing around kept people from stopping or gathering there. In contrast to the huge front gate, the door we passed through next was small. The first little room inside led to two reception areas, one for men and one for women. We went through the women's entrance into a tiny office with broken-down furniture and a box of dirty, smelly *chadors*.

A chubby woman with glasses sat behind a small metal desk. "What's your charge?" she asked.

"Christianity," we answered.

Her brow furrowed in disbelief. "I've never heard of someone being brought to Evin for Christianity," she said suspiciously. "You probably did something else. You were probably advertising and promoting your faith."

"That's correct," I said. "We spoke to people about it."

"I told you!" she said with a note of triumph. "Your charge is participating in political activities against the government."

We said nothing. It seemed like every time someone mentioned our offense, they described it differently. We had not seen a written copy of the allegations against us, nor had we been allowed to speak to an attorney. We later learned that the official charges were "acting against state security" and "taking part in illegal gatherings." They couldn't legally arrest us just for being Christians, according to Article 23 of the Iranian constitution: "The investigation of individuals' beliefs is forbidden, and no one may be molested or taken to task simply for holding a certain belief." News of this constitutional guarantee would have come as quite a shock to many of the country's policemen and law enforcement organizations, not to mention its citizens.

We handed over all our possessions to the woman behind the desk. She searched us and ordered us each to put on one of the filthy *chadors*. Fortunately, we had gotten used to such horrible smells at Vozara that we could at least tolerate these. The woman led us past a beautiful green court-yard with flowers and trees that was evidently used by the staff as a break area; it looked more like a park than a prison. No doubt visitors were impressed by it. After waiting a few minutes in another office, we were fingerprinted by a man wearing black cotton gloves. It would be *haraam*—sinful—according to Islamic law, for him to touch the bare skin of a woman he didn't know. (The long list of *haraam* offenses includes everything from murder and premarital sex to eating pork or getting a tattoo.) With our hands blackened by the ink, we had our photos taken again. Someone entered our names and information about our "crimes" into a computer, which spit out white identification cards for each of us. We were now officially prisoners of the Islamic Republic of Iran.

A guard led us out a back door into the main prison yard, which was huge and covered with so many red brick buildings it looked like a town. After a ten-minute walk, we arrived at the women's prison block. Our guard rang a bell, gave our cards to the young woman who opened the door, and left. We were called one at a time into a small room, where we had to strip naked and submit to the indignity of a full body search. They ordered us to squat and stand three times. When Marziyeh challenged this instruction, they made her squat and stand six times. Though the women who searched us looked and acted like guards, they were actually prisoners. As we soon learned, the inmates did most of the work inside Evin, which made life easier for the guards and staff and gave certain prisoners the chance to earn special favors.

After we dressed, we were led up a long flight of stairs to an office outside the cell block, where women prisoners were coming and going. Some were leaving with their luggage for a New Year's holiday parole with their families. Others were being released, hugging each other and saying goodbye. A clerk called our names and held up our two cards.

"What did you do?" she demanded.

"We are Christians and we promoted our faith, so we were arrested for activities against the regime."

"Why did you do such things to yourselves?" she asked in a gruff voice.

Another guard led us to Ward 2. She opened a door and gestured through it to the hallway beyond.

"Ask for Mrs. Mahjoob," the guard instructed as she locked the door behind us. "She'll tell you what to do."

Mrs. Mahjoob was well dressed, with small eyes and simple makeup. She was the prisoner in charge of Ward 2, keeping order among the inmates and acting as a point of contact between prisoners and prison staff. Ward 1 was for drug offenders. Ward 3 was for prisoners with mental problems—and as the newest and cleanest part of the women's prison, was usually the only part shown to visiting inspectors or other outsiders. Ward 2 was for everyone else and was divided into two parts: women accused of murder or prostitution were downstairs; women charged with fraud or crimes against the state were upstairs.

"What have you been charged with?" Mrs. Mahjoob asked.

"Believing in Jesus," I said.

"Come over to this room until I decide where to put you."

There were six cells upstairs in Ward 2. Mrs. Mahjoob led us to a room that was already so crowded there was scarcely room to sit. It was about fifteen-by-twenty feet and jam-packed with eight triple-bunk beds. Women who didn't have a bed slept on the floor. Under the lowest bunk in each set were three or four wicker baskets, one for each person in the room, the only personal storage space the prisoners had.

There was a loud rumble of conversation among so many women in such a tight space. Some were knitting. Others were talking or sleeping. One or two were climbing in or out of the upper bunks, which took some effort because there were no ladders. Still others were coming and going to "the shop," a tiny window down the hall where prisoners bought supplies, snacks, and little luxuries from the prison commissary. The commissary would be closed for the New Year's holidays in a few hours, and women were rushing to stock up.

As newcomers, we were showered with questions about our lives and the charges against us. "You have become apostates," one woman said harshly after we told her our charges. "This is very dangerous."

Someone in the room yelled, "Look at them! They're not crying. Newcomers always cry for an hour before they settle down."

Another woman shouted back, "Political prisoners don't cry, because we haven't done anything wrong!"

"Don't worry," the woman who had mentioned crying said, "we're all political prisoners in this room." She introduced herself as Tahereh. She and eighteen others had been arrested on their way to visit their children in Iraq. The children (and likely their mothers, too) were members of the *mujahideen*, loosely organized opposition groups that had repelled the Soviet army in Afghanistan with help from the American CIA and were now fighting for ethnic autonomy in Iran. Their children lived in Ashraf City, a *mujahideen* refugee camp near Baghdad that had been under US control but had recently been handed over to the Iraqi government. The women had not seen their children for years and decided to travel to Iraq as a group. They were arrested at the airport and brought to prison.

While Tahereh was talking to us, one of her friends offered us cups of tea. It tasted wonderful! It was the first we'd had since our arrest. The *mujahideen* women were the most welcoming and generous of all the inmates we met that day.

"Perhaps you would like to have a shower," Tahereh suggested diplomatically. "Come, I'll show you."

Perhaps we would! We hadn't bathed or even brushed our teeth in fourteen days. Other women gave us shampoo, towels, and combs, and a woman named Sepideh led us to the bathroom, where several women were washing dishes in the sink. There were six showers, very dirty and matted with hair that stuck to our feet. The water was like ice. But for the first time in two weeks we felt relatively clean.

Mrs. Mahjoob was in our room when we got back. "You can stay here," she informed us. "All the other rooms are too full."

We found space to sit on the floor in front of a plastic shoe rack along one wall. Some of the women with lower bunks allowed their friends to sit on their beds; otherwise people found a spot wherever they could. The door at the entrance to Ward 2 was locked, but women could move freely among the six cells, the bathroom, and a small room with four telephones and the little window for commissary purchases. We would have liked to buy a few things, but we had no way to pay for them. When the guards took our money at check-in, they were supposed to give us commissary vouchers. We hadn't received them yet, so we'd have to make do with whatever the prison gave us until the holidays were over, along with any help our fellow inmates might offer.

A loudspeaker crackled with the names of several prisoners, who jumped up to report to the office. Would they be released? Paroled? Taken to court? Executed? Every inmate both loved and dreaded hearing her name called— loved it because of the hope that she would be released from Evin Prison, dreaded it because the news could also be devastating. In this case, all the women called learned they were to be set free. They screamed and jumped with joy, accepting the congratulations of all the others. Then they gathered their few possessions and disappeared through the door.

A woman who sat next to me, knitting, stared at me for a moment. "Why have you converted to Christianity?" she demanded. "My mother is a Christian and my father is a Muslim. I follow both religions equally and am a member of a church. You've made a great mistake by leaving Islam." When I started to tell my story, she looked down at her knitting, refusing to make eye contact. "You made a mistake," was all she would say.

I overheard two women talking about Marziyeh and me.

"What is their crime?"

"Converting to Christianity."

"That isn't a crime! They must have done something else. Everybody who comes into this prison says, 'I've done nothing wrong.' If they'd done nothing wrong, they wouldn't be here."

This woman seemed extremely upset and angry, and I soon found out why. She was a widow who taught kindergarten to support her two children.

She had been behind bars for two years because her brother had written a bad check on her account to settle a debt. When the check bounced, she was arrested. He promised every day he would work to get her out, but instead he did nothing. She missed her two children and had thought she would be granted New Year's parole to see them, but her request was denied. She hated her brother for destroying her life.

She started to cry. "I don't even say Muslim prayers now! I'm angry with this God who does not command any justice. I do not believe in this God!" Her sobs grew louder as she spoke.

I asked if Marziyeh and I could pray for her. Her grim and angry expression softened into a broad smile. "Yes, of course," she said gratefully. We prayed for her peace as the tears continued to flow. After we finished, she thanked us profusely.

I heard a clattering sound and someone shouting, "Dinnertime! Dinnertime!" A pot of food appeared as the women prepared to eat. In addition to Mrs. Mahjoob, who was in charge of all of Ward 2, each room had an inmate leader who assigned sleeping space, settled arguments, reported problems to the guards, and collected and served food for that room. Our room leader was Mrs. Pari, a plump, middle-aged woman with extremely heavy makeup, black hair, and an unusual accent. Her most noticeable feature was her heavy, black, painted eyebrows in the style of the Reza Shah era or Hollywood movies of the 1940s and '50s.

"Finally, we have succeeded," Mrs. Pari announced as she brought in the food. "We kept asking Mr. Sedaghat for eggs and potatoes, and here they are!" A cheer resounded off the concrete walls. Mr. Sedaghat was the prison warden. Perhaps in honor of the holidays, he had granted their request. Mrs. Pari looked at Marziyeh and me. "You brought luck to the ward," she said. "We've waited months for this."

The women had their own dishes, stored in the wicker hampers under the beds. By now, they all had plates in their hands and had lined up for this special treat. As Marziyeh and I tried to fold sheets of newspaper into makeshift plates, an elderly woman who had been watching us quietly ever since we arrived spoke up. "I have some extra plates in my basket. You're welcome to them, and you can sit here in front of my bed to eat."

Each woman received one egg and one potato. We received the smallest potatoes in the pan. "You are newcomers and haven't been deprived of good food as long as we have," Mrs. Pari explained. *If only she knew!* But we took our portions without complaint.

The woman who gave us plates later told us that when she and her two sons sold a piece of land, there was a problem with the title. When another man claimed the property was legally his, this woman was charged with trying to sell something she didn't own and sent to prison. She called us her daughters and asked us to call her "Mommy." After dinner, she gave us the rundown on all the long-term residents of our room. She was part historian and part town gossip.

Marziyeh and I went for a walk along the corridor to get more familiar with our new surroundings, weaving our way through the crowd waiting for the telephones and on to a quieter part of the hall. "Hello," a voice said. We turned around to see a woman in her early thirties with long hair that was prematurely gray. "My name is Silva Harotonian. Some friends told me there were two new Christians here. I'd like to get to know you. I'm a Christian too."

Her honest, open approach made us suspicious. Was she a plant to extract information from us? Had the authorities sent her to get the names of our Christian friends? Ward 2 had surveillance cameras in the ceiling of every room, including the toilets. We were constantly monitored and thus wary of anyone who seemed unusually friendly. We said we were in prison for believing in Jesus Christ.

"I can't believe that," she replied. "How can they put somebody in prison because of their faith?"

Without going into too much detail, I said we were accused of activities against the regime. Sensing my hesitancy, Silva shared her story with us.

"I am Iranian, but my family heritage is Armenian," she said. "I went to Armenia about a year ago to work for International Research and Exchange, an American charity. I helped offer Iranian experts in mother-and-child health care the opportunity to travel to the United States and consult with their counterparts there. I often traveled back to Iran to meet with Iranian applicants for the program. I was introduced to Drs. Arash and Kamiar Alaei, widely known for their work on AIDS and international health.

"My last visit ran far longer than I expected. In June 2008, the security police came to my apartment in Tehran and took me to a hotel for questioning. They told me they had been following me for months, recording every move with a security camera. I didn't think they had any problem with my work. In fact, the Iranian government had invited IREX employees to Iran a few years earlier, though this was during the era of the reformist president, Khatami.

"After spending the rest of the day answering questions, I asked the police if I could attend a friend's wedding later in the evening. 'You're not going anywhere for some time,' they replied. So that night, instead of celebrating with my friend, I was brought here to Evin Prison."

She went through intense interrogation the first few days and was kept in solitary confinement. "They demanded I confess things that weren't true. For example, they wanted me to say that the Alaei brothers were leading the programs I was handling at IREX. But it wasn't true and I refused to say it."

Three weeks ago, she had been transferred to Ward 2 and was now very happy to meet two Christian girls. Her story won us over; we believed her.

Throughout the evening, the loudspeaker announced the names of people who were being set free. By 10:30, the bed above Mommy's was vacant. Knowing that Marziyeh's back had been bothering her for some time, I took a spot on the floor so she would have a better chance to get some sleep in the bunk. Around that time, the lights were turned off, except for a small spotlight in each cell, though the individual rooms were not locked.

After midnight, a group of *mujahideen* women were released, which freed up some additional bunks in our room.

"You're lucky," one of the women told me as I climbed into a newly vacated bed. "Most people have to sleep on the floor for the first week or so." After sleeping on the floor at Vozara for the past fourteen days, even a thin and dirty mattress in Evin Prison felt like a cloud.

| | |

I woke up to the sound of yelling. For an instant, I had a flashback to our first days at Vozara, when Leila welcomed the morning by screaming for a cigarette. But now it was Mrs. Imani—a young, thin, jumpy woman who read the Koran and fingered her worry beads for hours at a time—screaming over use of the telephone. Each inmate was allowed to use the phone once a day. Established prisoners received more minutes than new arrivals, and those with longer sentences got more time than the rest. Prisoners could sell their time to other inmates, usually for snacks from the commissary. Mrs. Imani spent every moment possible on the phone every day, trading for some of the time, badgering inmates out of more, and simply taking it whenever she saw a chance. Whenever a phone was available, she wanted to put it to good use.

Marziyeh and I had breakfast with Mommy. We noticed that others in the room steered clear of her and that she kept to herself. We felt sorry for her. Because she had a hard time walking, we washed her dishes for her and helped her to the toilet. With six toilets and sinks for more than one hundred women, the wait to use the facilities was often long, especially for an elderly woman who could barely stand.

Later that morning, we had a long talk with Sanaz, the woman imprisoned for her brother's bad check. Being separated from her children during the holidays was very hard for her. "I don't know why God doesn't solve my problem," she said dejectedly.

"Maybe God is using this to prepare you for something better," Marziyeh suggested. "Instead of complaining, ask for wisdom to understand what He is trying to teach you. Leave your problems to God. Perhaps God wants to give you a great gift and has put you here because it was the only way to get your attention."

Sanaz thought for a moment. "Maybe you're right. I always pray only for God to solve my problems, never for the sake of honoring Him. From now on, I will ask God to show me the truth. Thank you." From that moment, our friendship with Sanaz grew closer every day.

As time for the New Year's celebration approached, we went back to our room, where a crowd was gathered around a small TV set waiting for the festivities to begin. The spring equinox, March 20 or 21 depending on the year, is the first day of Nowruz, the Persian New Year. The actual moment comes when the sun crosses the equator. When the announcer said the new year had arrived, we all cheered and congratulated each other. For many, it was a bittersweet moment as they clutched photos of their children and families on the outside. It's hard to celebrate when a prison wall separates you from the people you love.

Many inmates tried to observe the Nowruz tradition of Haft Seen, setting the New Year's banquet table with seven items beginning with the Farsi letter *s*, symbolizing the various parts of creation: a mirror, representing the sky; an apple, representing the earth; candles, representing fire; rose water, representing water; grain, representing plants; goldfish, representing animals; painted eggs, representing humankind and fertility. Of course, no one had most of these things, so they substituted, say, a hairpin bent into the shape of a stalk of grain, or a picture of a goldfish cut out of the newspaper. Inmates displayed their Haft Seen, one per room, in little piles on the floor or on the beds. It was a way to connect with the outside world and memories of happier days.

As the commotion marking the moment of Nowruz died away, I noticed Mrs. Mahjoob crying quietly on her bed. Not knowing what troubled her, I asked, "Could we pray for you to find peace in your heart?"

"Yes, please."

As Mrs. Mahjoob cried, we prayed—not loudly, but not hiding what we were doing. Gradually, the women around us stopped their conversations to listen. By the time we finished, nearly the entire room was silent. Someone called out, "Your heart is pure and God will listen to your voice. Will you pray for me, too?"

Evin Prison, the dreaded hellhole of Tehran and symbol of radical Islamic oppression, had become our church.

And so we prayed on.

CHAPTER 8

CHILDREN OF GOD

Marziyeh

Of the six rooms on our floor, Room 3 was the only private room. Mommy's description of the distasteful character who lived there only reinforced our impression that Mommy was quite the gossip. She was eager to share personal tidbits about everyone, but the resident in Room 3 triggered a reaction like no other inmate. We had seen this woman during the Nowruz celebration, when everyone was going from room to room wishing each other Happy New Year. She was immense, weighing at least four hundred pounds, and was so fat she could scarcely walk.

Mommy told us the woman's name was Soraya and that she had been in prison for eight years on fraud charges.

"She thinks she owns the place," Mommy sniffed.

Everybody was afraid of Soraya. Because of her size, she could not get on and off the toilet, so instead she used one of the showers to relieve herself. One shower of the six was for her exclusive use, and she put a sign up to make sure no one invaded her private territory. She had a long list of medical problems and took a big handful of pills every day. She was allowed to take extra food from the kitchen, which she gobbled loudly as everyone else made do with their scarce rations.

Just before dinnertime on New Year's Day, Mrs. Mahjoob came into our room holding a beautiful little boy in her arms. I couldn't believe the sight of this child in a dirty, overcrowded prison. At first, I assumed he belonged to one of the guards or someone in the warden's office. Mrs. Mahjoob explained that Room 4 of Ward 2 was for prisoners who were mothers of young children. The children lived in the cell with them. This boy, whose name was Armin, was two years old and had beautiful fair skin. Maryam and I went with Mrs. Mahjoob to Room 4 to meet the boy's mother, a very tall, slender Afghan woman, imprisoned on drug charges. I could tell she tried to be a good mother behind bars, because her son and his clothes were so clean. Staying clean was almost impossible, and her success was proof of how hard she worked to make his life better. She said she had six other children living on their own in Tehran. The oldest, a girl of sixteen, was taking care of the others.

While in Room 4, we met some of the other mothers and their children. One boy, Aboubakr, had the biggest, most beautiful brown eyes imaginable and lots of blond hair. His mother was another tall Afghan, locked away on drug charges. She was depressed because soon her son would be taken from her. Children could live in the prison only until they were three years old; after that, they were separated from their mothers by the authorities and sent to an orphanage if no other family members were available.

Hamid was the child of his mother and her lover. When the woman's husband learned she was pregnant, he attacked her. She stabbed him to death in self-defense and was sentenced to life in prison for murder.

Hapal was a beautiful but pale and frail-looking little girl who was always dirty. Her hair was a matted mess and her face and clothes were covered with grime. She had been born in prison. Though she was at least two years old, her mother still breast-fed her, smoking cigarettes as she did so. The mother was as dirty as Hapal was and had only a few yellow or blackened teeth remaining. She was a drug addict who, like several other inmates, earned pocket money and extra food by cleaning the toilets in Ward 2.

Though Armin was the favorite child of all the women because he was so beautiful, Maryam and I were drawn to Hapal and even made up a pet name for her. She was delighted to get attention from us, and soon would come running into our arms whenever she saw us. Her mother seemed grateful for the attention we gave her daughter.

Like every other rule at Evin, the rule about mothers with children living in Room 4 was not strictly observed. A curly-headed girl named Kasra was the daughter of a woman who lived downstairs, where the cells were darker, dirtier, and thick with cigarette smoke. Kasra was the pet of the women's prison warden, Mrs. Rezaei, and was the only child she showed any affection.

Kasra's mother was a beautiful, aggressive lesbian, whose young lover, Vida, was known as "the jail child" because she had been born in prison and had lived most of her life there. Vida had no family on the outside, so every time she was released, she committed a crime in order to return to the only real home she'd ever known. She had black hair and a dark complexion. Her face, chest, and arms were covered with scars from knife fights.

These two were known as bullies in Ward 2. They spoke openly about their relationship and had regular sexual encounters in their room, despite the security cameras. Before the cameras were installed, lesbian assaults and rapes had been commonplace, so most of the women welcomed their presence, even at the cost of constant surveillance.

| | |

Though outright violence was under control at Evin, homosexuality remained a powerful and ever-present force. Since we had first come into the Vozara Detention Center, we'd seen lesbian behavior in some form every day and felt the tension it brought to a roomful of women locked up together. The situation at Evin Prison was as bad or worse—taunting words, suggestive movements, and open expressions of physical love were so common that they were taken for granted.

Another well-known couple were Reza and Arash, boyish-looking girls with short haircuts to match their male names. They had been in prison for two years on drug charges and lived downstairs. During the holidays, Maryam and I went downstairs to exercise in the little courtyard, where we mixed with the Ward 2 prisoners from the lower floor. The outdoor space was paved with rough stones and had high walls so that all we could see was a square of the sky. There were a few pieces of broken-down exercise equipment in one corner, just for show. One lone tree added a touch of life and greenery to the scene, but during our stay in Evin the guards made one of the prisoners cut it down.

One of the long-term inmates was able to borrow a CD player so we could have music for dancing. Some of the women were excellent dancers, especially Reza and Arash, who danced like professionals and took it as seriously as if they were in a competition. They were both rough-looking characters, with knife marks and broken bones in their faces. Their hands were sliced with so many scars that they looked like zebra skin.

At first, we hesitated to talk with strangers during our breaks outside because we didn't know who might be spying for the regime or who might try to hurt us. And since we didn't see the women from downstairs at any other time, it took us longer to feel comfortable around them. After a few days, we gradually started mingling with them and began looking for a chance to start a conversation with Reza or Arash.

One day, we saw Arash trying to wash her clothes in a bucket, holding the hose in one hand and a cigarette in the other.

"Do you need some help?" Maryam asked.

"Yes, pretty woman," Arash answered in an unusual accent. At close range, we could see that she had only a few blackened teeth left and that her face and neck were completely covered with scars. Maryam held the hose so she could wash. We asked her name.

"My real name is Maryam," Arash said.

"That's my name too," Maryam said with surprise. "My friend and I are in prison for our belief in Jesus. I have been a Christian for eleven years."

Arash looked up from her laundry. "That means you are an apostate and you will be executed. Why did you do this?"

Maryam explained how she had come to know Jesus and read the Bible, and how she had learned that Jesus is the Savior of the world and was crucified for our sins.

Arash looked surprised. "What do you mean He died for our sins? Does that mean we're no longer sinners?"

"If you believe that Jesus died on the cross for your salvation, then for the sake of His blood you are forgiven in the eyes of the Lord," I said.

Arash's eyes widened. "What a wonderful thing He has done, then!"

she exclaimed. "I always liked the Christians. I've never seen any benefit in Islam. I was married at twenty to a drug addict who beat me. He made me an addict and our daughter, too. She's eleven. I miss her so much!"

Women who saw us talking to Arash warned us to stay away from her because anyone who had a conversation with her was suspected of being a lesbian. Clearly, this was a topic about which we still had a lot to learn.

Samaneh and Sima, both in prison on murder charges, were the most notorious couple at Evin. I saw Sima for the first time during a break when she came into the courtyard to dance to the music. She looked nothing like anyone else I had seen behind bars. She had creamy white skin and straight blonde hair that fell to her waist. She wore expensive, stylish clothes, including very tall high heels. Her dancing was incredible, with her long hair flying and her beautiful legs visible beneath her skirt.

Her case had been a big story on TV and in the newspapers when she was arrested eight years before. I remembered it well. Who would have ever thought I would be standing beside her in prison? She was a glamorous young woman who fell in love with a national sports celebrity. They began an affair, even though the man was married with children. He and Sima established a *sigheh*, a temporary marriage contract under Islamic law, which allowed them to have sex, because Islam permits men to have up to four wives. A *sigheh* can be as short as one hour, and is very convenient for turning a session with a prostitute into a legal Islamic marriage, or an affair into a legitimate relationship. Of course, the man's wife has no say in the matter.

According to the rumors flying around her case, Sima killed her lover's wife when the lover was out of town. Sima, it was said, sneaked into their house with a key he had given her, waited in the basement for the children to leave for school, and stabbed the wife to death. Sima denied the charges and was still fighting them after eight years in prison. During that time, her celebrity and personality had made her the most powerful inmate—the boss of bosses—in the women's prison at Evin. The years had also turned her into someone who would do anything to satisfy herself and stay on favorable terms with the prison officials. She had become an open, aggressive lesbian. Other prisoners hated her because she treated them so scornfully and because she turned them in for rules violations in order to enhance her position with the staff. They could hardly wait for her to be executed.

When she was in charge of frisking prisoners for drugs, some inmates said she took the job to extremes, putting her finger inside their bodies or making them relieve themselves in front of her to ensure there were no drugs hidden in the most private of places. If she found drugs, she always turned the person in. At least two women had been executed after she set them up. This made her a favorite with the warden, and Sima hoped it would extend her stay of execution. It was very sad to see how life in prison had made her willing to do anything to survive, even sending other women to their death. Maryam and I were trying to bring these same women to life.

I used to think of murderers as evil, heartless monsters with the faces of demons. Sima had a beautiful face, even after eight years behind bars. She had been a poor, beautiful girl swept up into the life of a wealthy, successful, famous man who already had a wife and children. Under Islamic law, he could legally satisfy his lust with her. If she did murder the man's wife, it was a terrible crime. But what made the crime possible? A law that allows men unlimited freedom to play out their sexual fantasies with women who are nothing but toys to them.

For every hard-hearted prisoner like Sima, there were many who were kind and friendly to us. Arezoo was a widow with two children, who claimed she was falsely accused of stealing jewelry. She was offered bail, but the only way she could get the money was if her mother mortgaged her apartment, which she refused to do. Arezoo had been locked up for two years. Her best friend was Rozita, who looked very young, although she already had three children. Rozita had been in prison for three months. She told us she had signed checks for the steel company where she worked, not knowing the checks were worthless. After creditors accused her of being an accomplice in an embezzlement scheme, she was sent to Evin.

| | |

MARYAM

Sepideh, one of the *mujahideen* women who had been so nice to us when we first arrived, soon became one of our close confidantes. She was an educated woman, a publisher and political commentator whose family was known to the regime as activists. Her husband was living at the Ashraf *mujahideen* camp in Iraq. Her brother was a prisoner at Evin and had survived intensive interrogations in Ward 209. Sepideh had been in 209, too, and shared a cell there with Silva, the kind Christian woman who had introduced herself to us on New Year's Day. Another prisoner in Ward 209 with them was Shirin Alam Hooli, a member of the Kurdish opposition group known as PJAK.

"Shirin is the strongest girl I have ever met," Sepideh said. The more she talked about Shirin, the more we wanted to meet her. Silva and Shirin lived in Room 2, next door to us.

At first, Marziyeh and I had beds in different parts of Room 1, so we couldn't talk after lights out. However, my bed was next to Sepideh's, allowing us to talk far into the night during the holidays, when the guards relaxed the rules about silence at bedtime. Sepideh was very interested in Christianity and why I believed in Jesus. I told her about Christ coming into my heart, changing me from the inside out, and about His love and sacrifice for humankind. Tears welled up in Sepideh's eyes as she whispered, "I never thought I could be so moved by the story of Christianity. I look at your life and the path you've chosen with more respect than ever. I would like to have the same thing happen to me. I would like to meet Jesus Christ. Could that be possible?"

"Yes, indeed," I assured her. She and I talked late every night until an empty bed opened up next to Marziyeh and I moved over there.

After about a week at Evin, I saw Shirin Alam Hooli, a slim young woman with shoulder-length hair, alone in the courtyard. We both wanted to speak to each other, but neither wanted to go first. After a moment, when she and I happened to look at each other at the same time, we both smiled and introduced ourselves. Shirin had heard about "the Christian girls" in Room 1 and had many questions about faith, which I answered as best I could.

"I don't believe in any faith," Shirin declared, "but I respect those who do. Each person must be free to choose her own faith. Nobody has the right to tell us what to believe."

When Shirin asked me if I promoted Christianity, there was something about her openness and self-assurance that prompted me to trust her. "Yes," I said, "I did promote and advocate Christianity, especially among young people."

As we walked in the courtyard, Shirin told me the story of how she had become involved with the Kurdish nationalist group known as PJAK

(Partiya Jiyana Azad a Kurdistanê), or Free Life Party of Kurdistan, which seeks to establish political rights for Kurds in Iran and create an autonomous Kurdish state.

She was from Deym Gheshlagh, a village near Maku in the West Azerbaijan province of Iran. She was introduced to PJAK through a friend and went to their training camps in Turkey and Iraq. In 2008, she was arrested by the Sepah Corps in the Shahrak-e Gharb district of western Tehran on charges of carrying explosives and being a member of PJAK. The Sepah Corps are the most ruthless soldiers in the Revolutionary Guard, cruel murderers assigned to protect the Islamic system of Iran from internal enemies. (And if there were any doubt about their intent or tactics, their symbol is an upraised arm holding a machine gun.)

They took Shirin to Ward 240, where political prisoners arrested by the Guard go for special interrogation. They interrogated her for a month, though she didn't understand their questions very well because they spoke Farsi and she only knew Kurdish at the time. She had since learned Farsi in prison. The language problem was actually a help, because it was an excuse for her not to answer their questions.

For twenty days, she wouldn't tell them anything, not even her name. It made them furious. They kicked her in the stomach until she vomited blood, slapped her, and hit her in the face. They whipped the soles of her feet with leather belts. They suspended her upside down from the ceiling. They banged her head against the wall over and over. They screamed in her ears so loudly that she thought her eardrums had burst. They held a gun to her head and threatened to shoot her.

One of the guards who tortured her washed his hands as ablution before prayers and said that what he was about to do to her was a holy act for the sake of God. He would look up to heaven and say, "My God, please accept this sacrifice from me." Then he would beat Shirin for hours until it was time for the next Muslim prayer. At the prescribed time, he stopped beating her and knelt in prayer. When he was finished, he resumed the beating.

One time, after an especially severe beating, Shirin was unconscious for three days. During that time, she was transferred to Ward 209. When she woke up, the interrogations continued, but they weren't as severe.

I took Shirin's hand and we continued to talk as we walked in slow circles around the courtyard. She spoke of the terrible poverty and restrictions imposed on Kurdish girls and said that her greatest wish was to be able to help them somehow. Though she was only twenty-eight, I could see a lifetime of pain and sadness in her face and sense the heroic struggle in her eyes. Her hair was thinning, her face and skin were dry, and her eyes were failing because of malnutrition.

Later, I introduced Shirin to Marziyeh and we all became close, trusting friends. After hearing Shirin's story, Marziyeh said to me, "We must learn from Shirin how to struggle for justice. If she is prepared to suffer so much to defend her nationalist and political beliefs, shouldn't we be able to do the same when our beliefs come from our faith in God?"

Shirin's story was an inspiration. Though she had suffered terrible brutality, she was never mean to others and never talked behind their backs. She was a tower of courage and resolve. She bravely kept her thoughts to herself, though there were times when I heard her crying quietly under her blanket at night. She especially loved the children from Room 4. Whenever one of us picked up a little one, Shirin would playfully shout, "Give me that baby before you kill it! I know everything about bringing up children. I raised all my brothers and sisters." It was almost impossible to watch her play with such tenderness and compassion and know she had been tortured for days on end for the crime of *moharebeh*, fighting against God.

| | |

Some days, during break, Marziyeh, Shirin, and I would go together to the courtyard and talk to the girls who lived downstairs. Shirin listened closely to what we said. One day, when she was alone with me, she asked, "Do you think what you say to these people will have any effect on them? Do you think they will ever change?"

"Possibly," I said. "We have to do our part. The rest is up to God."

Shirin laughed. "Sure enough, they had a reason to arrest you! You really were proselytizing!" She gave me a good-natured poke. I poked her back. We giggled and poked at each other until we dissolved into laughter.

As Marziyeh and I befriended more women, Mommy grew extremely jealous of our time and attention. If she saw us speaking to someone else, especially if we were comforting or hugging someone, Mommy pouted and called us to come sit beside her.

We had started helping her go to the toilet, doing little chores for her, and helping her go into the hall when the clinic worker came to give her an insulin shot—even though the guard yelled at us for being there when we didn't need treatment. We had started serving her food out of compassion and courtesy; now she expected it. These tasks changed from favors into assistance that she thought she deserved. We were becoming her servants. Though we didn't want to insult her or make her cross, especially since we had to live in the same crowded room with her, we were going to have to change our relationship. We started finding ways to be busy elsewhere at mealtimes.

The food in Evin Prison was awful. One regular meal was a stew consisting mostly of water and fat with a few unpeeled carrots and potatoes. The vegetables hadn't been washed, so the water was always full of dirt. It was more like eating mud than stew. Another dish on the weekly menu was dried, tasteless rice with no cooking oil or spices, plus a few potatoes and some tomato puree that often tasted spoiled. We also had *gheimeh*, a pea soup with a little fat and potatoes. Once a week we had sausage, which was horrible and gave many of the prisoners diarrhea every time they ate it. Marziyeh and I ate only the bread and cheese at breakfast, except for the one day each week when they served potatoes and boiled eggs. For me, that was the only meal worth eating. The food was also laced with formaldehyde, which was supposed to suppress the inmates' sex drive. This made the food smell and taste even worse, ran the risk of poisoning us, and is a hazard to a woman's reproductive system.

Twice a week, the prison cooks baked what looked like whole wheat bread. At first, we were excited to see a fresh alternative to the bland white bread stuffed with fillers that we usually got. That was before we discovered that the prison bread routinely contained flies, hair, pieces of plastic, and an occasional tooth.

Though we were hungry from eating only one meal six days a week, we avoided most of the sickness that the prison food caused so frequently. Unfortunately, that wasn't enough to keep us healthy. And we soon learned that the medical care in Evin Prison was every bit as bad as the cooking.

CHAPTER 9

FEEDING THE HUNGRY

MARYAM

By the time we transferred to Evin, we had already spent two weeks in detention at Vozara without a decent meal or a bath. Within a few days of our arrival at the prison, Marziyeh got sick after showering in the icy cold water. What started as a sore throat quickly became a serious infection. She had chills, a high fever, and aches all over her body, and she couldn't keep her balance. When I told Mrs. Mahjoob, the prisoner in charge of Ward 2, that Marziyeh needed to see a doctor, she said he was on vacation for Nowruz and wouldn't be back until after the holidays. Mrs. Mahjoob brought Marziyeh some antibiotics that were past their expiration date and said it was the best she could do. Marziyeh stayed in bed for nearly a week, miserable, shivering, and exhausted, relieved only by the tea or fruit juice other prisoners brought her once in a while and a few bootleg painkillers. All I could do was pray.

Marziyeh's sickness aggravated her back pain. The springs on all the beds were completely shot, so most prisoners used two of their three blankets as a mattress pad and the third to sleep under. Marziyeh thought it might help her back to sleep on her blankets on the floor. But if she gave up her bed, another prisoner would immediately claim it and it could be weeks before she had a bed again. Because the bed was the only private space she had in the room, she didn't want to lose it. I pressed the prison office for medical care, as did some other prisoners who were sick, but the answer was always the same: "The doctor is gone for the holidays. There's nothing we can do."

| | |

Between the crowded conditions, lesbian drama, constant petty squabbling, and Mrs. Imani screaming about the telephone, Ward 2 was a noisy place, making it even harder for sick patients to rest. The political prisoners were always the quietest, calmest, most polite members of the ward. Many spent the day knitting—the one productive pastime inmates were allowed. Some of the ladies had become very good at it and made beautiful shawls and other clothing to sell for spending money. Our new friend Shirin Alam Hooli was an expert, and she taught me how to knit while Marziyeh was in bed with her fever. As the weeks crept slowly by, she and I passed many hours knitting and talking together.

The courts were still closed for New Year's, which meant that few prisoners entered or left Evin. We'd had no new arrivals for a week, when a group of about ten women came who were members of the One Million Signatures Campaign, an organization formed to promote human rights— and especially women's rights—in Iran. One of the leaders was Mrs. Mahdieh, a very slim woman with dark curly hair. She had been in prison several times and considered it helpful to her research into the treatment of women by the regime and also as a way to meet other activists. A friend of ours, a kind woman in her sixties named Mrs. Azam, connected quickly with Mrs. Mahdieh and her associates. Mrs. Azam had been in prison for nearly three years on charges of acting against national security by joining a rally in support of women's rights.

Mrs. Mahdieh was very interested in how women were treated at Evin. She struck up a conversation with me to learn about our experience. I explained about our arrest, detention at Vozara, and transfer to Evin. When

Mrs. Mahdieh found out we were Christians, she asked me why I had chosen Jesus. After a short conversation, it was clear that Mrs. Mahdieh had a badly distorted view of Christianity that came from falsehoods she'd been told and from reading the Barnabas Bible, the corrupted version sold in Iran that falsified the life of Jesus to suit Islamic ideas. Even educated people in Iran have no idea what the Bible really says, because they've never read it.

"Then where is the true Bible?" Mrs. Mahdieh wondered. "Where can I find one?"

I wrote down the address of a church. "When you get out, go here," I said. "They will give you a true Bible and answer your questions about it." Mrs. Mahdieh said she wanted to know more about Christianity and would study it.

After she told her mother during a phone call that she had met some Christians, her mother asked Marziyeh and me to pray for her because she had been sick in the hospital. It was interesting that this woman thought our prayers had power, even though we'd never spoken to her.

Since our arrival at Evin, Marziyeh and I had not been allowed to use the telephone. Now, after two weeks, we would have a chance to talk to our sisters, Shirin and Elena. A prisoner named Emma was in charge of scheduling telephone slots. When we asked for telephone time, we learned that other prisoners had been using our time and didn't want to turn it over to us. The call time allotment was something the prisoners worked out on their own; the prison didn't officially hand out telephone minutes. The long-term inmates had come up with this system to give them control of the phones and ensure themselves the time they wanted.

Though we were now wary of Mommy's behavior and her motives, we still considered her an expert source of information on rules and relationships. We asked her about the telephone rules. We had scarcely finished our question when she brushed past us, walked into Room 2, and whispered something to a heavyset woman who was knitting a scarf. The woman jumped up and started screaming hysterically, swearing at Marziyeh and me.

"You stupid political prisoners!" she hollered. "Idiots! Greedy animals! One day you say you don't need any telephone time, and now you complain that you don't have enough! Who are you to accuse me of deceiving you and abusing your rights?"

We tried to interrupt her to find out what Mommy had said, but it was no use. She was too enraged to listen. We gave up and went back to our room while her ranting continued. When Mommy came back, we told her not to get involved in every little problem we had, but to let us handle things. We had worked hard to get along with the other prisoners, even when it meant giving up little privileges such as a good place in line at the shop window or a bigger serving of potatoes and eggs, the one meal a week we would eat. We were afraid Mommy's lack of tact had compromised our reputation for getting along.

Our friend Silva told us that the angry woman's name was Shamsi. She had been in prison for eight years on fraud charges and would not be released until she repaid her creditors. Her debt was so large that she could never repay it from prison, which meant she would likely be locked up for the rest of her life. She was notorious for her prickly attitude, especially toward newcomers, in order to show them she was in charge. Later, Shamsi apologized for her outburst, explaining she thought we were accusing her of stealing our belongings. This conversation marked the beginning of another wonderful friendship.

| | | |

Marziyeh

Since our good friends Silva and Shirin lived in Room 2, we spent a lot of time there getting to know others who lived with them. Marjan was a cheerful girl who was always cracking jokes and trying to make everyone around her happy. When she met us, the first thing she said, with mock seriousness, was, "Oh my God, more Christians in this ward? First Silva and now you! I can't stand this!" Marjan said she'd been in prison for two years because a former friend stole a pre-signed check from her office, made it out to herself for a large amount, and cashed it. When the check bounced, the friend sued Marjan and had her sent to prison.

"I'm not sure I like you as much as you like me," Marjan insisted. "Please don't try to make me like you, because it won't work!" From that moment on, she was one of our best friends.

Naseem, also in Room 2, was the person who had frisked me so rudely when we transferred to Evin. Though she was accused of murdering her mother-in-law, as we got to know her we found she was a kind and gentle woman.

"My dear Naseem," I asked, "why did you frisk me so roughly when I arrived? Why did you make me squat and stand six times? Did you think I could lay eggs like a chicken?" That question drew a laugh from everyone who heard it.

"It was nothing personal," Naseem said, apologetically. "I had to obey orders."

One of the best times to meet newcomers or women from downstairs was during break periods when we were all allowed to walk in the court-yard. One day, a beautiful, young, pregnant girl named Pouneh introduced herself to Maryam. She had been in prison for eight months on murder charges, even though her husband had committed the crime. After he had broken into a rich old woman's house to steal her money, the woman walked in on him, they struggled, and he killed her. In a panic, he had called his wife to the scene. A few minutes later, the police arrived and arrested them both. If Pouneh's husband were convicted alone, he would be executed. If they were convicted together, they would get life in prison. She shared the blame in order to save his life.

"I learned I was pregnant in prison," she said. "My husband doesn't know. My baby is due in a few weeks." Her chin trembled, the tears welled up in her eyes, and she started to cry. "Please, for God's sake, in the name of Jesus Christ and Holy Mary, pray for me! I have no one to care for me. I am completely alone. I can't even hire a lawyer to defend my rights. How on earth can I spend the rest of my life in prison with my child?" She left in tears, headed back inside with the rest of the "murderers." When the baby was born, Pouneh would be transferred upstairs with the other mothers. Then we would get to see more of each other.

Another prisoner, Mana, was only twenty-three, but it was hard to tell because she wore so much makeup that she looked like a clown. Though wearing makeup was against prison rules, Mana and some other prisoners wore it at night after dinner when the guards seldom came around. Despite being a naive girl, she thought deeply about many things. We teased her good-naturedly about her heavy makeup, saying we could understand how the old women would want to paint themselves, but she didn't need to do that. She listened to us patiently and wore her silly makeup just the same.

Mana was one of the inmates who scheduled telephone time for Ward 2. Unfortunately, the other inmates took advantage of her naiveté and cheated on their calls. When she figured out she had been deceived, she would throw the phone logbook on the floor and say she wouldn't do the job anymore and the office would have to get someone else. Then, after a while, she would calm down and resume her work.

One day at break, Mana said she wanted to know more about Christianity. She had wanted to ask for a while, but her telephone duties kept her too busy.

"I'm not a spiritual person," she began, "but I'm very interested in Jesus and Christianity and want to know more about it.

"For many years, I've had no faith in God. Years ago, I actually tore up a copy of the Koran and set it on fire." (This is a terrible sin under Islamic law. The faithful are not to deface the Koran in any way. They're supposed to wash their hands before even touching it.) "I think God doesn't love me anymore because of what I did. I'm being punished for my lack of faith.

"I was born into a rich family. My father was a self-made man who was also involved in politics without the rest of his family knowing about it. He was killed under very suspicious circumstances. The authorities gave us his body without explaining how he died. I was young at the time, and his death was a terrible blow. We lost our fortune and our standing in the community. That's when I lost my faith and burned the Koran."

"I'm very sorry to hear about your father," I said. "But you must know that God has not abandoned you. He still loves you as much as ever. You may have lost your earthly father, but the real Father of us all is our Lord, and He would never leave you. You assume God has abandoned you for burning the Koran, when in fact it is you who are cursing yourself and abandoning Him."

Mana explained that she and her husband had been in prison for three years for stealing money from the government. Their plan was to get out on parole, retrieve the money from its hiding place, and flee the country for a life of leisure abroad. She saw it as a way to avenge her father's death.

"How can you and your husband build a happy future together based on this logic?" I asked. "I don't believe this is a path to prosperity. I don't mean to meddle in your personal life, but I beg you to start repairing your damaged relationship with the Lord by talking to Him tonight. Pray for yourself and your husband to survive these hard times by seeking the truth. He will certainly answer your prayers."

"Do you think God will ever forgive me and welcome me back?"

"Absolutely! He has already paid the price for you. Besides, I don't think you and your husband will ever prosper with this money. It won't buy you happiness. Money that belongs to others will not bring you a better life. Without God's love, all the money in the world will not make you happy."

Mana asked for prayers for herself, her husband, and their family. As I prayed, Mana hugged me tightly and started to cry. "I feel so relaxed and peaceful," she said. "Maybe this will help with my nightmares. I have a hard time sleeping, and when I do fall asleep, I have terrible nightmares." That night, I prayed for hours that God would grant Mana solace and peace of mind and guide her in His path.

Late the next morning, Mana burst into our room so happy and excited. "Look!" she said, opening her hand to reveal a beautiful wooden cross. "I can't believe this! Last night, I spoke to God for the first time and asked Him to show me the truth about Jesus Christ. Then, as I was lying in my bed this morning, a friend who knew nothing about my prayers handed me this cross and said, 'Mana, I made this at the craft center and wanted to give it to you today.'

"I can't believe God would answer my prayers so quickly with this wonderful gift! I know it's a sign and that all your words about His love are true."

Mana started coming in almost every day with exciting news about some other sign that God was listening to her. She started talking about how much she would like to have a Bible to read. She told me, "I believe what you said about seeking and finding a new path for my life. I want to see the Bible for myself and know God's message firsthand."

Though I had no way to give her a Bible, her request was another reminder of how easy it was to witness behind bars compared to the work we had done on the outside. Maryam and I didn't have to look for prospects or sneak New Testaments into their mailboxes. We could talk to them openly, rather than hiding behind closed doors or in basements. Our fellow prisoners were hungry for the truth. Desperate for it. The guilty ones felt the weight of sin for their crimes and believed Islam condemned them to punishment or death. They had lost all hope until they heard news of the true God. On the surface, the prison environment seemed to be a dead end. At the same time, the truth of Jesus, His love for sinners, and His atonement for their sins, was a miracle to these inmates, a balm for even the oldest and most painful wounds in their souls. Most of these women had lost all hope of salvation because of Islam's depiction of God as a god of retribution and revenge, a god who demanded impossible standards and had no mercy on those who failed to achieve them. The realization that God is their Father and loves them unconditionally just as they are was a life-changing revelation. And because we were already in prison for promoting Christianity, we figured we might as well shout the good news of Jesus Christ from the rafters.

| | |

Not long afterward, as I was cleaning the floor under Mommy's bed, I discovered a long-forgotten box of what looked like trash. I asked Mrs. Mahjoob if she knew whose it was. Mrs. Mahjoob said that some prisoner who was gone must have forgotten about it and left it, and I should just throw it away. As I carried the box to the trash, I looked through it, just in case. Even trash might have some value in prison. To my surprise, I found a pocket-size Gospel of Luke mixed in with the scraps and castoffs.

I quickly slipped it under the blanket on my bed. I could hardly wait to get to bed that night and start reading. When it was time for lights out, I retrieved the little book and opened the cover. On the flyleaf was an inscription and the signature of Archbishop Ramsey, the former archbishop of Canterbury and leader of the Anglican Church worldwide, who had evidently given it as a gift. What a treasure and miracle it was to find it!

It's hard to describe the feeling of being able to read Scripture after being away from it for a month. Every page, every word, every letter was a blessing. A banquet for the starving soul. Maryam and I decided to share it with people who might be interested. First we loaned it to Mrs. Mahjoob. After she finished with it, we gave it to Mana. When she saw it, her eyes widened in shock and amazement.

"God has answered your prayers," I said, handing it over. "Now you can read a portion of the authentic Bible you've always wanted." As word got around, many, many prisoners wanted to read it. Before long, dozens of women had their first look at the true Christian Scriptures, reading the little volume signed by one of the most powerful men in the church, who had died more than twenty years before and whose little pocket Gospel had miraculously turned up under a bed in a women's prison in the middle of Islamic Iran.

The holidays were coming to an end. The courts would soon reopen, and the little freedoms we had enjoyed would likely be curtailed. Often in the afternoons Maryam and I took walks in the courtyard or up and down the hallway with Shirin and Silva. On one of the last days of Nowruz, at sunset, we were looking up at the sky. To look at the sky from behind the high walls of a prison is like a stone weight on the heart. Sometimes, feeling the wind on our faces, we imagined we were the birds we saw flying so gracefully above, floating and free. We looked through the only window in the hallway at the one hill we could see in the distance and wondered what it would feel like to run barefoot along the ridge.

Shirin asked, "Do you think God is looking at us? Do you think He can see us at all?"

"Yes," Maryam said, "I think He can see us."

"Then why doesn't He do something? Why is He silent in the face of so much injustice? Does He like the oppressors better than us?"

"I don't know why He doesn't do something," Maryam said. "Maybe He does, but we can't see it. I don't know why He is silent. But I don't believe His silence is forever. Sometimes God is silent, and sometimes He speaks."

"I don't understand this God of yours," Shirin said. "What kind of God would see all these years of misery and hardship and do nothing to help us? Is He waiting until all the young people in Iran are killed, and then maybe He'll do something?"

"I have many similar questions," Maryam admitted, "but God hasn't answered all of them yet. Even so, I am sure God loves His children more than you and I do."

Sometimes the four of us sat in front of the hallway window, looking at our hill, the sky, and the birds, singing hymns. We envied the birds their freedom, their ability to see the whole sky instead of the little square visible to us. As we watched, we took turns singing. Shirin's Kurdish songs were beautiful and sad. She always asked us to sing the hymn with the words, "My heart is in Your hand. My life is filled with Your love. I am held by the world. You are my Savior." When we sang, people who passed by the corridor would stop and listen. Now, as the holidays were coming to an end, we enjoyed our little ritual again.

After the songs were over, we talked some more as we looked out at the bright spring sky of a new year, the carefree birds, the distant mountains, and the billowing clouds above. And we thought of the presence of the one true and all-knowing Lord Jesus Christ listening, watching, and loving us.

CHAPTER 10

A NASTY REPUTATION

MARYAM

On the thirteenth and final day of Nowruz, known as Sizdah Bedar, the prisoners were allowed to spend the whole day outside, visiting, dancing, drinking tea, and savoring the final hours before the normal prison routine resumed. Somebody borrowed a CD player from the office again, so that music filled the courtyard all day. Some couples danced like two women, some danced like two men, and others like a man and a woman. There were prisoners who danced beautifully with graceful, artistic moves, while others pulsed and gyrated to the pounding beat of hip-hop music. The lesbian girls kept eagle eyes on their partners. They flirted and teased, told dirty jokes, and kissed each other passionately without any concern for privacy.

The first day after the holidays, we were jolted awake at 5:00 a.m. by the scratchy sound of *azan*, the Muslim call to prayer, over a speaker that was so loud it rattled the windows. Everyone who wanted to be counted a good Muslim, which meant nearly everyone but Marziyeh and me, had to get up and bow in prayer toward Mecca. We stayed under our blankets, but our reprieve didn't last long. At 6:30, a guard's voice, badly distorted and incredibly loud, boomed over the loudspeaker, ordering everyone into the courtyard. "Register time! Register time!" This was the mandatory headcount of all prisoners taken every morning and again at 7:00 p.m. every night. Though roll call had been neglected during Nowruz, it would now be part of our daily routine. Some prejudiced guards forced prisoners to pray *omalyajib* Islamic prayers. "Swear to God that Mohammed is the prophet of God," they ordered. "Say your prayer ten times and God will answer." We stood in the freezing cold for an hour waiting to be counted. At last, one of the guards and Mrs. Alipour, a prisoner who worked downstairs, came out to do the job.

The end of Nowruz also meant that the prison shop would reopen. Our sisters had set up an account for us so we could buy snacks and a few other small luxuries. We stood quietly in the queue. The moment the window opened, there was a mad dash as dozens of women scrambled to be first in line after two weeks without shopping. Others jumped in front of us, shoving and yelling. Soon they were pulling each other's hair, screaming, and swearing. We backed farther away, saying, "Please go ahead." It wasn't worth it to fight for a spot. We could wait until tomorrow. We turned and started back toward the ward.

The only quiet place was at the very front of the line, where Soraya's gigantic bulk nearly blocked the view of the window for everyone else. She was first, and for all the other squabbling and pushing, no one dared lay a hand on her. Seeing us retreating, she headed toward us, calling out, "You silly girls, why do you let others cut in line ahead of you?"

Before we could answer, she grabbed us, one with each hand, and led the way back, barreling through the swarm like a ship parting the sea, straight to the head of the line. "Here you go. Now do your shopping, my dear girls." No one dared dispute her decision—including us.

The shopkeeper was a young woman who also worked in the office. She took one look through her little window at us—the Christian girls!—gave a sudden scowl, and said curtly, "The shop is closed!" sliding the panel shut in our faces. We waited for an hour until the window reopened, and then placed our order. But instead of handing us our items, the girl threw them through the window so that they either hit us or fell on the floor. Our natural impulse was to shout back at her or complain. Yet, we thought to ourselves, our little inconvenience and embarrassment was nothing compared with what Jesus endured for our sakes. We had no need to complain, though we surely had the right to. We knew we were there as part of God's perfect plan to do His work. The incident tested us and reminded us of how hard it is to remain silent and Christlike in the face of even the smallest challenge. We prayed that God would always give us the power to forgive and a sense of compassion for everyone, even those who mistreated us.

| | |

For all the time and trouble it took to get it, the food from the shop was a terrible disappointment. We learned by trial and error which items were worth buying. The canned tuna and chicken were awful, supplied at inflated prices by one of the Mafia-like gangs that control much of the prison system. Most of the other snacks were no better. There were no dairy products or anything fresh, so there was little relief from the nasty prison food. The potato chips were good, and also the chocolate. We bought a sup-ply of chocolate and the best snacks to give away to the poorest prisoners who couldn't buy anything. We also gave a lot of items to the children, who, if they weren't nursing, had nothing to eat but the disgusting prison food. Some of the mothers could never afford to buy their children anything. The kids loved the chocolate, cookies, and other treats, so we always tried to have some handy for them.

The cultural center, which had closed for the holidays, reopened. Many of the prisoners in our ward went back to bed for a couple of hours after roll call, then had their breakfast and went to the cultural center. Some took a snack lunch and stayed there all day. At first, we didn't go, but passed the hours knitting, talking, walking in the courtyard, and doing exercises. When one of our friends suggested we go to the center, too, we decided to try it.

The cultural center was the cleanest, roomiest place we had seen since our arrest. There was a small sports hall with table tennis in one corner; a little library with a handful of brittle and worn-out books; a handcraft area for making pottery, dolls, and textiles; and a computer center with a few computers that were all turned off. There was also a class about the Koran. Other classes were scheduled, but some were listed just for show and never actually held. The prison authorities portrayed the cultural center to the outside world as one of their strong points: a place where inmates got healthy exercise, expressed themselves artistically, and were instructed in the Muslim faith.

We took a look around to see which activities we'd like to register for. Marziyeh, who is a good table tennis player, started a game with another prisoner. When the woman in charge saw how well Marziyeh could play, she invited her to compete in an upcoming tournament. Meanwhile, I went to a woodworking class in the craft room and started a project. The teacher there asked me what I was making.

"It's a cross," I said, holding it up.

"Are you really here on charges of believing in Jesus Christ?" the teacher asked.

"Yes. My friend and I converted to Christianity and have been charged with acting against the state."

"What's wrong with Islam?"

After I shared my conversion story, I asked the teacher if she'd ever read the Bible.

"No," she said. "I can't find a copy anywhere. Is it in the bookshops?"

"No," I answered. "You have to get it from a church." I wrote down the name of a church and handed it to her.

"I hope you'll register for this class," the teacher said. "I'd like to talk with you some more."

| | |

Marziyeh

The next day, I went to register Maryam and myself for classes. One of the women in the office asked me what the charges were against us.

"We are charged with following Jesus and promoting Christianity," I said.

The head of the cultural center, Mrs. Ghanbari, overheard the exchange. "What?" she said with a note of surprise. "Since when is believing in Jesus Christ an offense?" She thought for a moment. "Maybe you should say you're an apostate." Believing in Christ was one thing; telling anyone else about it was another matter entirely. Her tone turned suddenly angry. "Who let you into the center anyway?"

Her attitude shocked me. "Aren't all prisoners allowed to use the cultural center, regardless of their charges?" I asked.

"Yes, but not those who have renounced their religion. In fact, hell-bound infidels like you must be executed!"

"I've done nothing wrong," I declared. "I have no reason to be ashamed of my charges. In fact, I'm proud of them." As I turned to go, I saw a quotation written on the wall: "Blessed are those who are rejected by their fellow human beings, but not by their God." The Lord was speaking to me even then, reminding me of His love.

There are no secrets in prison. Soon everyone knew that Maryam and I had been denied access to the cultural center, and many were angry that we would be treated so unfairly. Our friend Silva wanted to help us, but she was waiting for parole, so we encouraged her not to stir up trouble with the authorities. When Mrs. Pari, the woman in charge of our room, went to the cultural center manager to speak for us, Mrs. Ghanbari angrily told her, "Those girls are apostates. They must be executed because their presence corrupts the others. At least they should be in solitary confinement."

Hearing the word *executed* was startling. Could we really be executed? We hadn't even seen the formal, written charges against us. After six weeks in custody, we had not yet been allowed to speak with a lawyer. From that time on, we heard that the Koran teacher talked about us often in class, criticizing and condemning us and our beliefs. On the other hand, our many friends in the ward became bolder about their friendships with us. "Come sit by us to eat your meal," they would say. "We feel like being corrupted and unclean today," or, "May God forgive us for sharing our food with these nasty Christians."

Later, Mrs. Pari shared a secret with us: Her daughter was a Christian and attended a home church. The daughter had told her that our presence in prison was God's message to her that she should convert. Mrs. Pari was more worried, though, about what would happen if her daughter were arrested.

"Should my daughter use the *taqiyya*?" Mrs. Pari asked. "Why don't you use it and get out of here?" The *taqiyya* is an Islamic tradition that allows a lie of convenience in times of life-threatening danger.

Though we had sometimes shaded the truth since our arrest to protect our Christian friends, we would never deny our faith to save ourselves. "There's no such thing in Christianity," I said. "We don't care if they kill us, because our faith is the most important thing in our lives. It's more important than life itself."

Mrs. Pari walked away with a troubled look.

| | |

When we were first arrested, all we could think about was getting out. Now, we were comfortable in the place where God had sent us. In the mornings, we knitted, exercised, and talked. In the afternoons, we invited everyone in Room 2 and our other friends in for tea and snacks and spent the whole afternoon in conversation. The most important topics were always prison conditions and the status of various inmates. Whoever had the latest news would share what she knew. With the courts back in session, new inmates arrived every day. We always invited them to our gathering and tried to make them feel welcome.

No visitors had been allowed at Evin Prison during the holidays. Now at last we would have the chance to see our sisters for the first time since we'd transferred from Vozara. Tuesday was visitors' day. By law, each prisoner was allowed a noncontact visit every week, and one contact visit per month, when we could hug and touch our visitors. In practice, the head of the women's prison, Mrs. Rezaei, and the prison staff reserved contact visits for their friends, and in exchange for bribes from other inmates. Contact visits were very important because they were an inmate's only physical contact with the outside world, and it was when friends could smuggle in food, fresh clothing, and other contraband.

After roll call and breakfast, a guard called the names of everyone who had visitors. We waited an hour for the small, dirty minibus that took us across the prison complex to the visitors' building. Because we were outside, we had to wear *chador*s and dirty prison slippers that were far too big. The bus was so small that I had to stand with my head bent over. We were packed in like cattle. The road to the visitors' center was lined with trees and lush flower gardens. *Visitors must think Evin is a beautiful place.*

We went inside and down a long staircase into the basement. After another wait, we were called into little booths separated by glass from the visitors on the other side. Family members were already seated, so prisoners rushed in like a herd of buffalo to find their visitors as quickly as possible because we only had ten minutes.

Our sisters, Elena and Shirin, were waiting for us. What a blessing it was to see them! We did our best to act happy, avoiding stories of what life in prison was really like. For the first time, we heard that our sisters had asked Mr. Soltani to be our lawyer. He was well known for his fierce opposition to human rights abuses and was a very effective attorney. In order to represent us, he had to have our written consent. He had been to Evin Prison twice already to have us sign the form, but was not allowed to see us. Hoping to get around the officials, he sent a female assistant. She got as far as the office of Mr. Sobhani, the prosecutor. When the prosecutor denied her permission to see us, she demanded that he put his denial in writing. Mr. Sobhani refused, saying it was against the law for him to deny our lawyer permission to see us so of course he couldn't write it down.

There was still the matter of the bail he had set for each of us: two hundred million tomans (about $100,000). Miraculously, our sisters had been able to secure mortgages on family property and were seeking to have us released until our trial. When Mr. Sobhani learned they had come up with the bail, he insisted he had never authorized bail in our case and refused to accept it.

After our visit, we talked with two friends who worked in the prison advisory services office about getting permission to see our lawyer. A woman there named Mrs. Soroosh seemed very interested in us and in Christianity. We thought if anyone could help us, she could. But after reading our file, she told us sadly, "I'm very sorry, but I can't help you at all. In most political cases, and in a few rare unusual cases like yours, our office isn't allowed to help the prisoner." It was a fresh reminder that what happened to us was in God's hands alone. Whatever crazy rules existed in this place didn't seem to apply to us.

| | |

MARYAM

Easter was coming on April 12, and in honor of our Lord and His goodness, Marziyeh and I decided to fast from Good Friday through Easter

Sunday. Silva joined us in this. The three of us formed what we called "our community." Each day, we spent the morning together praying for the inmates, for ourselves, and for a renewed vision of how to serve God better while we were in prison. Our fasting created a sensation in the ward. One woman in particular, a fanatically religious Muslim from the holy city of Qom, had never said a word to us. When she learned of our fast, she said, "Good for you, girls, you are really pure. Pray for us." Everyone was talking about our fasting and praying. Many women asked us to pray for them. On Easter Day, the whole ward congratulated us. Some people gave us presents they had knitted or made at the craft center.

The most miraculous gift of all came from Silva's mother. During a contact visit after she had taken Easter Communion at church, she brought Silva bread dipped in wine at the Communion rail to share with us. It is impossible to put into words the feeling of taking Communion secretly together inside an Iranian prison. What sweet fellowship our community shared with Christ Jesus that day! It's unlikely we'll ever experience another Easter as precious and full of meaning.

Our fasting was an outward expression of our faith that the other women could understand more easily than Scripture or theology or principles. It encouraged prisoners who had been hesitant to reach out to us before to make contact.

One day during break, a tall woman named Shahin approached me in the courtyard. "I have wanted to talk to you, but was afraid," she said. "When I saw you alone in the courtyard, I told myself I had to speak to you today." She was trembling with fear, constantly looking around to see if anyone was listening. "What I have to tell you is completely private. No one else must know about it."

When I promised to keep her secret, Shahin said, "I am a Christian too. I'm a member of a house church. At first, I was so excited about Jesus that I told my family. After they turned against me, I kept going to church in secret. I'm in prison because my husband and I owe my brother money. He could forgive me, or at least pay my bail so I could be with my daughter, but he wants to keep the pressure on my husband to pay the entire debt. A friend of mine in prison told me about you and said I should ask you to pray for me."

Her friend was Ziba, a woman we knew who lived downstairs because she'd been arrested on prostitution charges, but who worked upstairs on our floor during the day. Ziba had separated from her drug-addicted husband, but couldn't get a divorce without his permission. After going to live with a female acquaintance, she had noticed various men coming to the apartment who said they were relatives. One day, the police raided the apartment. That's when Ziba learned that her host was running a prostitution ring from her apartment and had planned to bring her into the business. She had now been in prison for three months and had no way to raise bail. Her only hope was from an elderly neighbor of her sister's. He offered to pay her bail in exchange for sexual favors in a *sigheh*, the Islamic temporary marriage. So far she had refused, but she was getting desperate to see her young daughter.

"Please pray for me," she asked. "I feel completely hopeless."

"If you repent and have faith, God will help you out of this situation," Marziyeh assured her. "This is a test of your faith. If you choose the *sigheh*, it means you have not relied on God."

"But I've been in here for three months," she said, dejected. "What could possibly change that would help me?"

"God's works are amazing," Marziyeh answered. "He may help you in ways you never imagined. But first He is testing you. I think you should pray for help, and also pray for that neighbor of your sister's who made the offer to you."

"Do you think he would ever change his mind?"

"For God, nothing is impossible. I feel that you will be released in two weeks' time."

Skeptical though she was, Ziba prayed faithfully for the ability to forgive her sister's neighbor and for his heart to change. We prayed for her too. In the end, Marziyeh's timeline was just about right. One morning, Ziba came running to us beaming with joy.

"I just phoned my sister," she said. "You won't believe this! Her neighbor came to her to say he was sorry for suggesting the *sigheh* and asked for forgiveness. To get God's pardon, he has offered to put down a deed to property as bail so I can get out and see my child. He said he regretted his earlier demand, but he couldn't explain why he had changed his mind."

"I think this has happened because of your faithful prayers," Marziyeh said. "Don't forget your promises to God. Don't forget to put your faith in Him."

"I will never forget!" Ziba said, lightheartedly. "And I will never forget your kindness and the hope that one day you also will be free."

"Don't worry about us," Marziyeh assured her. "Our time will come."

Within days, Ziba was released. She wished us good-bye with hugs and tears. We never saw her again.

| | |

Soon after Easter, Mrs. Imani, the woman who seemed so crazy and was always desperate to use the telephone, gave us new evidence of what many prisoners really thought about Islam. She was one of the extremely pious inmates who seemed to despise us for being Christians. She fingered her prayer beads and read the Koran for hours at a time. Now, Mrs. Imani was beginning to suspect that what she'd heard about Christianity was not true, and she asked us for some real answers.

"Is it true, as I've been told, that Jesus Christ believed in Islam? Is it true that Jesus was a prophet who promised the coming of a more complete religion after him? Is it true that a person can believe in Islamic principles and say the Islamic prayers five times a day and still believe in Christ?"

"No," I said, "none of that is true." She had also been given completely false information about baptism, Communion, and other things. We had seen this so many times in our ministry, how some Iranian leaders, desperate to hold back the tide of Christian belief, had systematically spread lies to keep people from learning the truth.

"I thought this might be the case," she admitted. Lowering her voice, she went on. "I have two children in school in the Ukraine. They have become Christians and receive so much joy from Christian worship and Christian prayers. What they described didn't sound like what I had heard about Christianity."

For several nights in a row after that, Mrs. Imani asked a lot of questions about Jesus and His church. "I love the church," she said at last. "I think

Christians are much better than Muslims. As soon as I get out of prison, I'm going to the Ukraine and going to church."

For all her newfound passion for Christ, she didn't change her outward habits. It was clear that inmates who seemed to be fanatical believers—praying, reading the Koran, and fingering their beads for hours on end—did so not necessarily because they believed any of it, but to gain favor with the prison officials. Acting like a faithful Muslim gave them the best chance of getting contact visits, leave, pardons, and other advantages. There were many inmates like Mrs. Imani who found Islam to be empty and false, but pretended to follow it in order to make their lives a little easier and to reduce pressure on their family, contacts, and social position on the outside. That kind of religious charade doesn't happen only inside Evin Prison. It is a part of life in Iran.

Many of the prisoners went through the motions of Islam because they felt they had no choice. Yet every day we saw the power of Christ at work, drawing these broken, frightened, sinful people to Himself with a message of hope, strength, and forgiveness. More important, the prisoners felt His power too.

WILLING SPIRIT, WEARY FLESH

Marziyeh

There was a prisoner downstairs named Mercedeh, a rough-looking character whose arms were covered with knife scars. Ever since I'd first seen her during the Sizdah Bedar celebration in the courtyard, I had felt God calling me to pray for this girl. One day during a break, I noticed Mercedeh looking out at the courtyard through the window of her room. I introduced myself and told her I had been praying for her.

"Why do you do that?" Mercedeh demanded sharply.

"I don't know. Sometimes God doesn't tell me why, just that I should pray. I've been locked up for six weeks on a charge of believing in Jesus. Can you tell me something about yourself?"

As Mercedeh was telling me that she had been in prison a year and a half for armed robbery, another woman walked up behind her and interrupted, shouting, "Who are you talking to?" She leaned toward the window and said sharply to me, "Who has allowed you to talk to this girl?" Then she pulled Mercedeh away from the window and slammed the shutters closed.

A few days later in the courtyard, I asked Setare, another friend of Mercedeh, what was going on. Setare was in her early twenties and had hair down to her waist, and her once attractive face had been ravaged by years of drug abuse. "The other girl is Nazanin," Setare explained. "She is madly in love with Mercedeh and won't let anyone else talk to her because she's afraid they will try to steal her. Mercedeh never comes outside, because she takes ten sleeping pills a day and spends all day asleep.

"Mercedeh and I were best friends when we were teenagers," Setare continued. "I hadn't seen her in years until I ran into her in prison. Nazanin forces her to obey her and completely runs her life now. Mercedeh puts up with it because she says Nazanin takes care of her. Leave it to me. I'll make sure you have a chance to talk to her."

"What about you?" I asked. "What are you in for?"

"My husband and I are drug addicts. We got caught stripping cars for money to feed our habit."

"Why don't you quit doing that and get a regular job?"

"Who's going to hire a drug-addicted criminal like me? Besides, I could never earn enough to pay for the drugs. I've tried to quit a thousand times, but nothing works. I can't wait to get out of here and get my next hit of *shishe* [crystal meth]. For a few hours, it takes you out of this filthy world and all its filthy problems."

"There is another way out, Setare, and that is relying on God's help."

"God? What God!" she said angrily, her voice rising. "When was the last time He heard our cries—the cries of His miserable people? We are in deep dung [but she didn't say 'dung'] and covered with sins! Where is God in all this?"

"My dear Setare, God hears you right now in the depth of your misery. He hasn't abandoned you; you've abandoned Him. God loves you and has never left you alone."

Setare stopped, a puzzled expression on her face. "Are you saying God can hear my cries and help me right now?"

"Of course He can." I told her the story of my own faith journey and the circumstances that had brought Maryam and me to Evin. Then I prayed that Setare would have a bright future. She again promised to make sure I got a chance to speak to Mercedeh.

Because Mercedeh, Setare, and Nazanin had no friends on the outside to send them money, I bought some treats the next day and handed them to

Setare through the bars of her window. She was startled by the gift and kept repeating, "You shouldn't have done this! You shouldn't have done this!"

| | |

By the time I finally met Mercedeh, I had learned the basics of her story. She was charged with armed robbery, and her victim had demanded eight million tomans (about $4,000) compensation, which she could never pay. The victim had offered to withdraw his complaint if Mercedeh would become his sex partner. She had said no and would stay in prison as long as she refused.

The first time Mercedeh came out to the courtyard, Nazanin swooped in and took her away as soon as she started talking with me. When Maryam went to Nazanin and assured her that I had no sexual interest in her friend but only wanted to get to know her better, Nazanin agreed to meet with us in the courtyard, along with Mercedeh and Setare, and allow Mercedeh and me to talk privately for a few minutes.

Though Mercedeh was only twenty, all the freshness of youth was gone from her features. Her face was slashed with scars. Most of her teeth were missing or broken, and the few that were left were yellow or black. She said her teeth had been knocked out by her interrogators when she first came to prison. She had been tortured and her mouth smashed. She raised her pant legs to show the deep scars left from being whipped with steel cables. There were scars on her hands from guards putting out cigarettes on her skin.

Her arrival had made headlines: "Girl Behind Multi-Million Tomans Robbery Arrested." To pay for their *shishe* habit, she and a friend had dressed in provocative clothes and stood at a busy intersection asking for rides in luxurious cars. When someone picked them up, they offered to go to the driver's house for sex. There they drugged their victim with a drink. As soon as the man fell unconscious, the girls left with all the cash, jewelry, and other valuables they could find in the house. When occasionally the drugged drink wasn't strong enough, the girls would slash their wrists to force the men into paying them to leave. After Mercedeh was captured, the prison guards had tortured her to reveal the names of her robbery victims.

Gradually, Mercedeh and Setare became friendly with us, though

Nazanin continued to resist. She planned to go into business making *shishe* pills after she got out and was expecting Mercedeh to help her. Our suggestions and prayers were a threat to those plans. Nazanin advised Mercedeh to go into business with her; we encouraged her not to accept, but with the Lord's help to take her life in a new direction.

Maryam and I wanted to give Mercedeh a gift as a token of our affection and a reminder that the Lord was always with her. Because we weren't allowed contact visits, we arranged for one of our sisters to buy a gold cross necklace and smuggle it in through another visitor. A couple of days after we'd made these arrangements, but before we had received the cross, Mercedeh met us in the courtyard and said she'd had a dream the night before that someone had given her a beautiful gold cross necklace. When the real necklace was given to her, she was speechless with joy and surprise. She said it was exactly the one she had seen in her dream.

The shimmering beauty of the cross around Mercedeh's neck was a stark contrast to her sad, grim, disfigured face. It was a reminder of the beauty and purity of Jesus Christ and how He descended from heaven to earth, suffering terrible pain and humiliation, to save the sinners of the world. Yet despite our sins, He doesn't leave us to perish, but leads us out of the darkness into His shining light of salvation.

| | | |

While spiritually we were strong and fulfilled, physically we suffered along with the rest of our fellow inmates. The filth, bad food, poor medical care, and lack of exercise and fresh air in prison made it practically impossible to stay healthy. Prisoners saw their hair become thin and brittle from malnutrition, like Shirin Alam Hooli's had done; their skin, eyesight, strength, and ability to sleep were all degraded by the conditions. And woe to anyone who had the misfortune to actually get sick—the inept medical treatment was likely to do more harm than good.

Maryam and I both felt ill during much of our time at Evin. I struggled with a chronic sore throat, splitting headaches, backaches, and kidney problems almost from the beginning. Several times, I visited the clinic, in another building across the prison yard from the women's prison. It was three or four stories tall, with the second floor reserved for female patients. There I saw addicts from Ward 1 for the first time. These women were in frightful condition, little more than toothless, ragged skeletons because of their drug habits. They could get their fix more easily inside the prison, because the prison officials readily sold drugs supplied by the same organized crime group that controlled sales at the prison shop.

The women's doctor, Dr. Avesta, was prejudiced against Christians the same way many of the guards were. She prescribed antibiotics for me every time I went to the clinic, though she never examined me and seemed to have very few medical instruments in the room. I picked up my medicine from the pharmacy downstairs, but the drugs did nothing to relieve my symptoms. I would suddenly get a severe headache and have to go to bed. I spent part of every day doing exercises to try to relieve my back pain. At times, my back hurt so badly that I would cry involuntarily until my face turned blue.

For years, I'd had powerful, vivid dreams that I believe the Lord used as a way to communicate with me. One night, in my misery, I dreamed that nails were being driven into my hands the way nails had been put into Christ's. In the dream, my right hand had a hole in it from the nail, and I heard Jesus say to me, "I have let you taste a little of My suffering." When I awoke, I thanked God for the strength to survive in prison, even though I saw myself as weak and disabled. My suffering there was nothing compared to what Jesus had endured for my sake.

By the time I felt better—a testament to the natural healing powers of the human body, not to the medical services supplied by the Iranian government—Maryam had fallen dangerously ill. It all started when a serious virus spread throughout Ward 2. When Mommy caught it, she developed a high temperature, chills, and an eye infection. Because she was so unpopular, none of the other inmates wanted to risk catching the disease by taking care of her. I was too sick to help, but Maryam nursed Mommy, even though we had decided to keep our distance from her because of all her gossip and backbiting.

Mommy had a strong constitution, and because she had clout with the guards, she got plenty of fresh fruit and nourishing hot soups. She recovered within a week. By then, Maryam had come down with the virus and was beginning to suffer. It started as a cold and progressed to a sore throat and an ear infection that got steadily worse. Within a few days, the agony of her earache drove Maryam to bed, where she wrapped the covers around her head to try to reduce the pain. She couldn't sleep, and along with the pain came dizziness. The next morning, when I awoke, Maryam was lying so still beneath her blanket, and her face was so pale, that I became alarmed. I shook her by her shoulder until she opened her eyes, but when I spoke to her, she couldn't hear a word I was saying. She had become completely deaf.

I quickly reported this serious problem to the guards and tried to get Maryam a clinic appointment. But one of the guards looked at Maryam and said, "She looks all right to me. There's nothing wrong with her." I pleaded with the guards for hours until they finally relented—which they did mostly to silence me and the other prisoners who were arguing on Maryam's behalf.

When another guard came to escort Maryam to the clinic, he said harshly, "You could have waited a few days. You wouldn't have died." He turned her over to a female prisoner who worked in the office, with orders to take her to the clinic. The woman was angry because it was lunchtime, and she forced Maryam to stand in the corridor for half an hour while she left to eat.

Once again, the clinic was full of drug addicts from Ward 1. They looked like African famine victims, ravaged by the effects of drugs and without money to buy any food to supplement their prison meals. After waiting a while on a bench, Maryam went into Dr. Avesta's office. The doctor took her blood pressure, and before asking any medical questions, asked, "What are you charged with?" Maryam could sometimes hear a little and was able to figure out what the doctor was saying.

"I'm here because I believe in Jesus Christ."

"Is that a crime? Were you involved in any activity?"

"I converted to Christianity. Converting is a crime."

"Yes, and a very dangerous one." Dr. Avesta shook her head. "If you are an apostate, your sentence will be heavy."

After Maryam described her symptoms, Dr. Avesta gave her some erythromycin, an antibiotic useless for treating a virus and which no sensible doctor would prescribe. Maryam started taking it, and also took some pain pills that other inmates gave her. Her condition only got worse as the infection spread to her eyes, causing a painful discharge that restricted her vision to nothing more than shadowy images. Two days later, she developed a sharp pain in her stomach and a terrible headache. Waves of nausea washed over her. I helped her to the toilet, where she knelt on the floor and vomited for hours. Others in the ward called for the guards, who looked at Maryam through the bars without opening the door.

"She's very sick," I insisted. "She has a bad eye infection and can't see."

One of the guards looked at Maryam's red, pus-filled eyes. "She's been crying too much. That's why her eyes are red. Calm down. She'll be all right." With that, the guards left.

Exhausted from all the vomiting, Maryam was too weak to climb into her bed. Shirin Alam Hooli and I, and a few others, wrapped Maryam in blankets on the floor and held her. Shirin massaged her head, hoping to relieve some of the pain. A few days later, when Maryam started feeling better on her own, some of our friends and I convinced the guards to take Maryam once more to see Dr. Avesta. After Maryam explained what had happened to her, the doctor said, "It doesn't matter. The medicine I gave you probably poisoned you. But don't worry. Your eardrum will heal itself." With that, Maryam was brought back to the ward. In time, her body did indeed heal itself. By then we had been in prison for almost forty days.

As soon as we felt well enough, we resumed praying for other prisoners. New prisoners, strangers to us, approached us regularly now. "We've heard you are Christians and that God answers your prayers. Please pray for us," they said.

"Of course, we'll be happy to pray for you," we always replied, "but we can't promise you will be released. If God wants you to be free, you will be free. And you can pray for yourself, too. God will hear you."

| | |

MARYAM

Two newcomers were very young girls terrified of being in prison. They asked Marziyeh and me to pray for them and were disappointed when they didn't get out the next day. They asked us to pray again. Instead, we started walking with them and talking about how they could call on Jesus themselves to save them. They thought being a Christian had to do with going to church and observing certain rituals.

"No," I explained, "Christianity isn't church rituals. It's a matter of believing in Jesus Christ in your heart. Then your sins are forgiven." They both promised they would talk to Jesus when they were alone and pray for Him to reveal Himself to them.

Two days later, they excitedly told us they would be released that day. "We really believe in Jesus Christ," they declared. "He heard us!" They wanted the location of a church. We had no paper, so I wrote the address on the backs of their hands. As I was writing, the girls' names were called from the loudspeaker, and they were set free.

Friends warned me that the prison staff knew we were praying for people, and that we should be careful. "Praying is not a crime," I said. "We don't force anyone to have us pray for them. Many Muslims in here pray as much or more than we do, but people prefer to ask us to pray for them in the name of Jesus. That's their choice."

Marziyeh and I had both prayed often for Shahin, the secret Christian who'd been imprisoned for owing her brother money. We had told her she should forgive her brother for bringing charges against her, just as Christ had forgiven her for her sins. She prayed faithfully for Jesus to help her, but it was a struggle. Finally, she decided to call her brother and say she had forgiven him for keeping her in prison. When she called her husband a few hours later, he had incredible news. "Your brother has forgiven you!" he shouted. If her husband promised to pay the debt, her brother would pay Shahin's bail immediately. Not only that, but her brother also apologized for what he had done, admitting that his wife had pressured him into doing it. What had seemed a hopeless situation was miraculously transformed in a single day.

Usually, prisoners were excited to hear their names on the loudspeaker, because it meant they were being released, or that at least their case was moving forward. At the same time, it could be a sign of something bad, such as a trip to court for sentencing. Six weeks after our arrest, we heard our names on the loudspeaker at Evin Prison. It made us apprehensive and our friends even more so. Our dear friends Silva and Shirin came into our room at once to ask if we knew why we were being ordered to report to the prison office. We had no idea.

We put on the required *chador*s and went to the office. A woman behind the desk said, "You are being transferred to Ward 209. You will go downstairs and wait for a guard to escort you."

Just like that—no warning, no explanation. Without ever seeing the charges against us in writing or speaking to a lawyer, we were being sent to the dreaded 209, the section set aside for political prisoners, where Silva had been kept in solitary confinement for eight months and where Shirin had been beaten unconscious and had her teeth knocked out.

We went back to the ward to say a quick good-bye to Silva, Shirin, and the others we had come to love so much. The news of our transfer stirred up memories of their own awful experiences in Ward 209, and they were terrified for us. After giving our sisters' phone numbers to Silva and Shirin, with instructions to get in touch with them if we didn't return, we hugged everyone and went downstairs. After half an hour, a rotund, bearded, middle-aged guard appeared and barked, "Wear your *hijab* properly and follow me." The *hijab* is the Islamic head scarf that must hide every strand of a woman's hair in public. There was nothing wrong with the way we were wearing ours; he only wanted to show off his authority.

We walked behind him for a hundred yards or so until we came to a small white door in a red brick building. He told us to wait and not to talk to each other; then he disappeared inside.

After a minute, he returned with a blindfold in each hand. "Put these on," he ordered. We covered our eyes and tied the cloths behind our heads. "Now follow me," he said gruffly. "Look under the bottom of your blindfold and watch my feet."

We stumbled inside and heard the door lock behind us.

CHAPTER 12

FAIRNESS AND INTEGRITY

Marziyeh

We followed the guard down a narrow hallway until he told us to stop and face the wall. "Don't talk to each other," he ordered. We waited for more than half an hour. Standing still aggravated my backache, so I began transferring my weight from one foot to the other, trying to get some relief. Finally I whispered to Maryam, "I can't stand up anymore."

"Who has permitted you to talk?" the guard demanded. Neither of us said another word. Compared to the noise of Ward 2, this place was eerily quiet. Nobody spoke. Even the footsteps seemed silent; we wondered if the guards wore special shoes.

A different voice said, "Follow me. Look down and watch my shoes. Be careful not to fall." This man's voice was not as harsh as the other one's. We followed him up a long staircase and down another narrow hallway. There wasn't a sound anywhere. All we could see around us was pairs of shoes. The guard took us into separate little rooms, about six feet square. There was a door open between the rooms, so we could hear each other.

The new voice belonged to Mr. Mosavat—another pseudonym; *mosavat* is the Farsi word for "fairness." These officials had quite a sense of humor when picking their professional names. A second man in the room with him was Mr. Sedaghat (Farsi for "Mr. Integrity"), an interrogator in Ward 209 who had the same last name as the warden of the public part of Evin Prison. Mr. Mosavat did most of the talking in a calm, friendly tone. He gave us both a list of questions to answer in writing and went back and forth between our two rooms asking more questions.

He started with me. "Well, Miss Amirizadeh, how are you today?"

"You should know that, the way you seem to know everything else," I answered. "We're fine."

Mr. Mosavat maintained his cool demeanor. "You were in the Vozara Detention Center for fourteen days, and now a month and a half in Evin. Surely this has taken a toll on you." I remained silent. "In fact, that's why you're here today. Whether by our error or sheer bad luck, you were arrested by a rather extremist group. I am with the Ministry of Intelligence and usually handle the cases of Christian prisoners. Unfortunately, this extremist group has had your case file. We have been struggling and reasoning with them to turn your case over to us. We're here to make sure you will be released and back home as soon as possible.

"By the way, how are you getting along with the conditions at Evin? I hope you haven't had any problems."

What a hypocritical weasel! "I think you know about the conditions and problems at Evin," I said. "There's no need for me to remind you."

"Of course you're right," Mr. Mosavat said. "I'm just concerned for a lady like you being in such an unsuitable place. That's why I'm trying to have you sent here to Ward 209, to conclude your case and have you released."

"What do you mean 'unsuitable'?" I asked.

"There are many criminals over in the public side of the prison, and it isn't appropriate for people like you to mingle with them."

"Those criminals are also human beings," I said. "We have no problem mingling with them. In fact, we like being with them."

"I suppose you've been speaking to them about Jesus," Mr. Mosavat ventured.

"Of course we have. And we don't even have to approach them. Because the charges against us are so unusual here, their curiosity gets the best of them. They want to know what we believe in that's worth going to prison for. We tell them about Christianity and Jesus. So actually, you're to blame for spreading Christianity, because by keeping us here you make people notice us and become attracted to who we are and what we believe."

Mr. Mosavat's cool suddenly evaporated. "No!" he said angrily. "What you're doing is not right at all! You're making our young people lose their identity and turn away from Islam!"

"Is this the identity Islam gives the youth of your country?" I fired back. "An identity that leaves women no hope? No choices in life? That makes them property of their husbands no matter how abusive they are? That promotes one-hour marriages? That ruins young girls' lives, driving them to prostitution and drug addiction? That gives them no legal representation once they're here?"

"I think you have learned a lot during your stay," Mr. Mosavat observed.

"I certainly have! Don't think I'm unhappy about being here. Yes, the conditions are hard. But I've learned more about Iran and Islam at Evin Prison than I could have learned in any university. It has transformed my life. I am a different person than I was."

Mr. Mosavat tried a new angle. "Of course, our argument is not only about your faith. I believe every religion must be respected." I couldn't suppress a smile at such a blatant lie. "Our problem is that you are promoting your faith. You do not have the right to speak to our people about Jesus. I have worked on Christian cases for many years and have read the Bible in full. Your Bible says you must follow the laws of the country where you live."

"I don't think you've read the Bible correctly," I said. "Jesus tells His followers to spread His gospel message. When the law of men and the law of Christ differ, I follow Christ."

"But Miss Amirizadeh, you don't have the right to convert your fellow citizens to another faith. In an Islamic state this is a criminal offense."

"The government tricked us with lies into coming to the police station. The *basiji* ransacked our apartment and took our belongings without a warrant. These are the illegal acts of a dictatorship."

"Miss Amirizadeh," Mr. Mosavat said with an icy tone, "you must understand: I am the law. And no one should dare oppose this."

"If God showed His face to you today and said you must tell your people the truth, would you follow His order, or the law of Iran?" I asked.

"This is impossible!" Mr. Mosavat declared. "God would never issue an order that would cause strife or chaos among His people. In any case, if you continue your activities here, it will be very hard for you."

"Do what you wish," I said. "Unless you cut out my tongue, I will keep feeding the people's hunger for the truth about Jesus. And if you do cut out my tongue, I will share His gospel with sign language!"

Mr. Mosavat was livid, his voice strained, his fury scarcely under control. "So I suppose you are not looking forward to your release."

"No one would want to stay in this place," I replied. "But I respect God's will above my own, and I think His will has been for me to come into this prison to witness the suffering and injustice here. You are not fighting me. You are fighting the will of God. In the end, His truth will prevail."

"I have to go away for a week," Mr. Mosavat said. "I advise you to carefully rethink your position until I return. This is in your own interest."

"I will think about it," I said, "and you'd better think about it too. If you're such an expert in Christianity and know all about the Bible, have you ever read the story of Paul?"

"Who's Paul?"

"If you don't know who Paul is, there's no way you could have read the Bible. Paul arrested and tortured Christians on behalf of his government. One day, the Lord appeared to him as a blinding light on the road to Damascus and challenged his brutal acts of repression. After that, he became Jesus' most important supporter. Eventually, he sacrificed his life for the gospel. Think about the years you've been persecuting Christians the way Paul did, and how you might one day see the light as Paul saw it."

"I'll think about it," Mr. Mosavat said. "And you think about why most Christians get out of prison in a week or two but you're still here."

| | |

MARYAM

While Marziyeh was being questioned by Mr. Mosavat, I sat alone in my tiny room, listening to their conversation. Blindfolded and facing the wall,

I thought of all the women who had sat in this chair. Had Shirin and Silva been in this spot? It was probably where Shirin had sat blindfolded when she was slapped until she was dizzy.

While I waited, I answered the long list of written questions, beginning with how I had been arrested and who had arrested me. I peeked under the bottom of my blindfold so I could see the pages to write.

Behind me, I heard two people enter the room. One of them took the questions and answers from me.

"Miss Rostampour," the voice of Mr. Mosavat said reassuringly, "I am here to help you. Unfortunately, the people who arrested you are a fanatical group, and it has taken us this long to get your case and fight them on your behalf. This is an intelligence case, not a security case. We only ask you to cooperate so we can close your file and release you and your friend as soon as possible.

"Miss Rostampour, I have seen these questions already and studied your answers from before. You previously confessed that you owned a large number of Bibles and were active in spreading Christian propaganda."

"We had only a few New Testaments among our personal belongings," I answered. "And anyway, are you sure those answers are mine?"

"What do you mean? Didn't you answer the questions? Christians don't lie!"

"Mr. Rasti at the police station asked me the questions aloud and wrote down my answers himself," I explained. "I had to sign the statement without being allowed to read it. Therefore, I refute everything put down in writing, because I don't know what he wrote."

Mr. Mosavat and the man who was with him were stunned into momentary silence. Then they spoke angrily to each other about how stupid Mr. Rasti was. Mr. Mosavat's cool façade slipped for a moment, before he brought it back under control. "If that is true," he said calmly, "we'll have to ask the questions all over again, and you must answer in your own handwriting so you cannot deny it this time."

"I don't mind."

There were some new questions this time around. "Why did your sister give an interview to Voice of America? Did she tell the truth? Were you really sick?"

I tried to hide my surprise and excitement. This was the first time Marziyeh or I had any idea that someone on the outside, other than our sisters and friends, knew about our situation. Voice of America is a worldwide news and information network, uncensored by the Iranian government and heard and seen in secret by people all over Iran.

"Yes," I said. "I still have symptoms of my infection, and my hearing is still damaged. If my sister were in here and I were in her place, a TV interview is the least of what I would do."

"Do you know that talking to foreign TV reporters is a crime?" Mr. Mosavat demanded sternly. "We could put her in prison for this. But we understand she did it only out of concern for you. We know she is a member of a church and has been baptized. Be sure we would have arrested her already if we intended to do so."

Suddenly he sounded concerned. "If you still feel ill, you can go to the doctor here in 209."

"No, thank you. I had all the prison doctoring I want in Ward 2."

"You sound upset. What did they do to you there? Tell us and we will investigate."

"You are totally aware of the situation there and at Vozara—the malnutrition and mistreatment. Why pretend to be ignorant? The health and lives of prisoners are worthless to you—"

"They are convicts," Mr. Mosavat snapped, interrupting me, "and they should be treated as such! You two, on the other hand, are distinguished ladies and shouldn't be kept with prisoners. If we had known about your detention at Vozara, we would have brought you here sooner.

"I don't want to know about other prisoners," he continued. "Have you yourself been mistreated in any way? Is there anything you want to report?"

"First of all," I said, "those 'other prisoners' are human beings. And they're not all guilty. You seem to have convicted them already in your mind, but most of those people shouldn't be here at all. This oppressive culture has branded them as criminals for claiming the right to think as they please—the most basic human right. The head of the cultural center shouted at us, saying we weren't allowed to use the center, that we were apostates and should be executed. My friend and I have been sick repeatedly and have been refused medical attention. Even when I was poisoned by bad medication, no one would help me."

"This is impossible!" Mr. Mosavat exclaimed. "How can someone who is poisoned not be taken to the clinic?"

"Eighty prisoners will say they witnessed it."

"We will definitely look into this." Mr. Mosavat paused briefly. "However, Jesus Christ teaches you to forgive, so let's forget the matter."

"I don't know why your case has taken so long. Far more important people than you—priests and bishops—have been here, but none stayed more than a week. We will transfer you both to Ward 209 next week, though if you're unhappy in Ward 2, we can have you transferred tonight."

"Thank you, but I'd rather stay with the 'criminals' over there. They are my friends, and I'm more comfortable with them."

"All right. I'll be studying your case file. I just received it from the police this morning. We've been so busy with your situation that I can't fall asleep at night for thinking about it."

I suppressed a laugh and only smiled beneath my blindfold.

"I know you don't believe it," Mr. Mosavat went on. "You've been so mistreated that you've lost confidence in us. But we'll do everything in our power to set you free as soon as possible.

"During this next week," he added, "take some time to rethink your position."

| | |

Marziyeh

Our separate interrogations lasted three or four hours. By the time we got back outside and took off our blindfolds, it was dark. We followed a guard across the yard to the women's prison and Ward 2. He told the guard there that we were to be sent to separate rooms and were not allowed to talk to each other, even during breaks. This was Mr. Mosavat's way of punishing us for standing our ground during his questioning. One of us had to go to one of the dirty, smoke-filled cells downstairs. We were completely drained from the interrogation, both still suffering from our sicknesses. Each of us wanted to let the other stay upstairs with our friends. In the end, I insisted the most forcefully and went downstairs to live with the prostitutes. Of course, this was an opportunity to witness to them. Mr. Mosavat's intended punishment opened the door to bring the gospel of Christ to a whole new audience.

While Maryam was welcomed back to the ward by Silva, Shirin, and other friends, I had to get used to my new surroundings on the first floor. All our shared dishes and snacks were upstairs, so our friend Arezoo brought food, blankets, and a few other things downstairs to me. While she was there, she spoke to the leader of the first floor, Mrs. Niromand.

"Marziyeh is one of our friends upstairs. We will need to come and see her from time to time. She has to stay here for a while, but if anything happens to her, we'll know you are to blame." After two years in prison, Arezoo was not shy about speaking up, especially to people in authority who were prisoners themselves.

"Don't worry, my dear," Mrs. Niromand said. "I'll take good care of her."

While I was still getting settled, Mercedeh and Setare came into the room. When they saw me, they screamed with joy and ran to give me a hug. Setare offered me some fruit, partly in thanks for all the little treats I had given her over time.

It was soon clear that the women here treated each other differently than the women upstairs did. Prisoners on the second floor were generally better off financially, but were very selfish with their belongings. Downstairs, most of the inmates were very poor, yet they freely shared what they had. The cells were darker and grimier than upstairs, and the women spoke only in whispers; yet it was a much warmer atmosphere of friendship and trust: no gossip, no betrayal to the authorities, only mutual help and support.

Even so, the harshness of prison life was never far away. During dinner the first night I was there, two prisoners got into a fight. Mercedeh went to intervene, but I pulled her back. Mrs. Niromand rushed in, separated the girls who were fighting, and slapped them both hard. They settled down immediately.

After the meal, several of the women turned their dishes upside down and started banging on them like drums. Other women started to dance; even Mrs. Niromand came and joined the festivities. The sight of these women dancing and having some fun together was a welcome surprise that lifted my spirits. They found joy in living, even when life seemed so depressing and hopeless.

The next day, I saw Maryam at break time, but we didn't speak directly because we'd been warned not to. Instead, our friends carried messages back and forth for us. The day after, however, we decided to talk despite the ban. No one tried to stop us. We even ate together, sitting on newspapers outside on the ground. Silva, Shirin, and some other women joined us. After lunch was over, we moved into the corridor and spread our newspapers there. Each day, more women joined us, so that soon there were fifteen or more gathered around us every afternoon, some with food and tea like it was a picnic. We had long, meaningful conversations with them and answered countless questions about our charges and our own personal faith journeys. It became more than a picnic: it developed into a worship experience. That crowded hallway was now our church.

Living downstairs gave me lots of time with Mercedeh, Setare, and Nazanin. I finally convinced Nazanin to talk about her relationship with Mercedeh to Maryam.

| | |

MARYAM

A day or two later at break, while Marziyeh talked with Mercedeh, I had an opportunity to talk with Nazanin.

"Why do you seem so possessive of Mercedeh?" I asked.

"I can't stand to see her talking with anyone but me," Nazanin said.

"Do you have a homosexual relationship?"

"No. We used to, but Mercedeh doesn't want to anymore. Not since she was tortured. But I love her so much!"

"Do you think God would approve of two people of the same sex having a romantic relationship?"

"I don't know. But aren't you and Marziyeh lovers? Wouldn't she be jealous if I held your hand?"

"Marziyeh and I share an apartment and love each other very much. But it isn't romantic love. We feel no sense of possession toward each other.

We're very different in some ways, and we allow each other to do what we want. We speak to young people like Mercedeh all the time to tell them about Jesus, but not to have a sexual relationship."

While we spoke, Nazanin watched Mercedeh across the courtyard like a hawk.

"Are you still angry at Mercedeh for talking to Marziyeh?" I asked.

Nazanin lit a cigarette. She started shivering and began to cry. I took her hand.

"God understands your feelings—"

"No He doesn't!" she shouted. "He doesn't love me! He has never helped me! I hate men, and all I have left is Mercedeh. If I lose her, I lose the only hope I have left in life."

"Why do you hate men?"

"I was not always homosexual. I had a boyfriend I loved very much. Then my father raped me. After that, I couldn't have any relationship with my boyfriend again. I hate myself. I hate my father. I hate everybody but Mercedeh, and I want to save her."

We stood holding hands for several minutes without speaking, as Nazanin cried and looked over at Mercedeh. My heart was filled with thoughts of my own father, who loved me so much and whom I loved in return. How I wished Nazanin could have known such peace and security in her past. I prayed for her that she would feel a father's pure love from her heavenly Father and that she would be surrounded by the kindness of Christ. Whether the message penetrated or not, I couldn't tell.

| | |

A girl we hadn't seen before was assigned to the first floor, and Marziyeh had a chance to meet her the first night she was there. We both saw her the next day at break. She was in her twenties and very thin, a quiet, polite girl who was unusually neat and careful about her dress and manners. She seemed isolated and lonesome. We learned her heartbreaking story from Arezoo.

The girl's name was Zeynab Nazarzadeh, and she was from a provincial city. She had been in prison for three years on a murder charge. As a young girl, she had been forced into an arranged marriage with her cousin. From the beginning, he had beaten and humiliated her. No one would help her, and a divorce—difficult to get under the best of circumstances in the provinces—was impossible without her husband's permission. One day when he attacked her, hitting her and swearing, she threw a mallet for crushing ice, hit him in the head, and killed him. Her aunt filed charges against her, demanding retribution by execution for her son's death.

In Iran, the law is in the hands of the aggrieved parties. They can choose to press charges, agree to some kind of compensation, or forgive the offender. This means there is no consistency or accountability in the law. The legal system in Iran is based on revenge, not justice. The aunt demanded Zeynab's life in return for the son's.

We prayed with all our might that the aunt would change her mind or that someone would come to Zeynab's defense. She had never seen a lawyer during her three years of imprisonment because she couldn't afford one. In three years, she had never had a single visitor. That night, we noticed other women paying special attention to her and trying to make her happy.

At ten o'clock the next evening, the loudspeaker called Zeynab's name and she reported to the office. Her friends were frightened. Once an execution is ordered, the prisoner is taken into solitary confinement for her last night. This is typically the first and only indication that an execution is about to be carried out.

Hours later, we heard that Zeynab's aunt had accepted her apology and forgiven her. Our celebration of joy lasted late into the night. But it was a false hope. The next morning, we awoke to the sound of *azan*, the call to Islamic morning prayer. That was when we learned that Zeynab had been executed by hanging shortly after midnight; her aunt had claimed the "honor" of pulling the chair out from under her, dropping her to her death. The execution had to be carried out after midnight but before *azan*. The false news that she was alive had been spread because the prison officials feared an uprising once word got out of what had really happened.

Mrs. Niromand said she had told Zeynab before she was hanged that the reason her mother had never come to see her was that she had died of a heart attack on the day Zeynab was jailed. She said that Zeynab welcomed death because it would reunite her with her mother. She had never complained about anything during her three years in prison and didn't complain at the last—never begged for her life, never asked for mercy. Mrs. Niromand said that even the prison guards were crying.

It was the first execution of someone we knew. There are no words to describe the pain and sorrow we felt. This was an act of injustice and evil beyond the power of expression. She had been a prisoner for years in a marriage that was a nightmare of abuse, forced to remain there by a law that holds a man's sexual pleasure above the most basic rights of human decency and dignity for women. This is the law of the land. She killed her husband because he attacked her and she feared for her life. There was no investigation, no attempt to collect the facts, no consideration of the horrific circumstances that caused her to commit a crime accidentally and in self-defense.

Her husband wasn't murdered; she was.

Two days later, the prisoners held an Islamic memorial service for Zeynab, standing around her empty bed praying, the tears flowing freely. Her friends handed out food to the poorest inmates as an act of charity in her memory. Marziyeh and I were there, along with Silva, and the other ladies thanked us time and again for joining them even though we were Christians. Of course we wanted to be a part of the ceremony. Our hearts were broken for the tragic injustice of Zeynab's death. This sweet girl's sad and lonely life should never have ended this way.

Zeynab's barbaric execution brought the whole horror of the radical Islamic regime into focus for us as never before. Her story, so poignant and sobering, is a symbol of the lives that millions of women experience under the oppressive government in Iran. Anyone who says Islam is a religion of peace and equality should spend a week with the prisoners of Evin. Poor, defenseless Zeynab! Married against her will while scarcely in her teens— in the Islamic tradition. Beaten and abused from the beginning by her husband, who acted with impunity—in the Islamic tradition. Denied any fair chance of escaping her abuse by legal means—in the Islamic tradition. Denied a lawyer, her life dependent on the whim of her husband's angry relatives, who likely helped arrange the marriage in the first place—in the Islamic tradition.

How savage the culture whose survival depends on abusing and killing helpless girls! Cruel, heartless, indefensible—and all in the name of Allah.

The leaders of Iran are right to fear Jesus, because He is infinitely more powerful than they are—and they know it! Still, for now, they rule by force and terror, holding back the truth at all costs, imposing on their people a religion that the leaders can control.

God bless the precious memory of Zeynab Nazarzadeh. And may God deliver the people of Iran.

CHAPTER 13

BLINDFOLDED AND BLESSED IN WARD 209

Marziyeh

After living on separate floors in Ward 2 for a week, we were taken again to Ward 209. Our first trip over there had lasted only half a day, and all they did was interrogate us. We didn't know whether to expect more of the same treatment as full-time inmates, or if this was when our torture would begin. We said a tearful good-bye to our friends—especially those who had been to 209 and knew what could happen—and placed our few personal possessions into bags. Again we were led across the prison yard to a brick building with a small door. We put on blindfolds and went inside.

After shuffling down a hallway, peering out as best we could through the bottom of the blindfolds, we were ordered into a tiny cell about six feet square—the size of a closet. A guard told us to take off our blindfolds and all our clothes, and then gave us men's prison uniforms that hung on us like sacks. We couldn't keep from laughing at each other.

"Silence!" the guard ordered. She was a hefty woman of about forty who wore glasses. "Keep quiet. That's the rule here. If you talk, talk softly. Don't yell for us and don't knock on the door. When you have to go to the toilet, press this button on the wall and someone will come for you."

She left us to look around our new home, but there wasn't much to see. Grimy carpet covered the floor. A few dirty blankets were tossed in a corner. The only furniture was a small metal sink. There were no windows in the tall steel walls, which were painted white. The only natural light and ventilation came from a skylight covered with a heavy metal screen that blocked most of the light and air. A bare lightbulb in the ceiling, we soon would learn, burned day and night. We sat talking quietly for several hours. There wasn't another sound anywhere—quite a change from the constant noise and commotion of Ward 2. We had no knitting, nothing to read. Shirin and Silva had told us to pound on the walls to see if any other prisoners heard and answered back. At first there was no reply, but then we heard an answering knock.

In response to our pounding, the cell door opened and a young, heavyset guard stood glaring at us without a word. We stared back for a moment before collapsing on the floor in laughter. We were not going to allow prison to rob us of our sense of humor. We needed it to survive.

"So this is what you do!" the guard said. "Don't do it again!" She slammed the door and disappeared.

Sometime later, a tall, young guard, scarcely more than a girl, came in with plastic plates of food. There were decent meatballs in the dish, and it was hot! It was the first time since our arrest we'd had a good, hot meal served to us on plates. Silva had told us that the guards in Ward 209 feed the inmates better because they are political prisoners and news of their treatment is more likely to get out. This made about as much sense as anything else in the Iranian justice system. If we were going to be tortured, at least we'd be well nourished.

The combination of a hot meal and the quiet surroundings made us very drowsy, and we soon drifted off into a deep sleep. When we awoke, we needed to use the toilet. Though we pressed repeatedly on the buzzer, no one came. Finally we banged on the door. After a minute the older guard with glasses threw open our door.

"Do you know what time it is?" she huffed angrily.

"No, we have no idea," I said. "How could we possibly know what time it is?"

"It's three in the morning."

"I'm sorry. I didn't know. But the buzzer doesn't work."

"It's not a buzzer," said the guard, exasperated. "It blinks a light to let us know you want to go. Here, put on these blindfolds." We covered our eyes and followed her down the hall.

Except for breakfast at 7:00 a.m., our other meals, and trips to the toilet or the shower, our only activities were talking or sleeping. We slept a lot just to pass the time. Every two or three days, we had the chance to go on a break to a larger room with a clear skylight, but we turned it down in protest over our tiny, windowless cell and lack of books or other diversions. We made up nicknames for the guards based on our impressions of them: Mommy, a kind, older woman who was the head guard and usually brought us our food; Auntie, a short, fat, comical-looking woman; Cousin, another chubby guard; Iron Woman, who had braces on her teeth; Grumpy, who was always in a bad mood; and the Ghost, who never spoke or made an unnecessary move.

| | |

After a few days, we were transferred to another small cell, the same size as our old one, where we scarcely had room to lie down, but which we would now share with a third woman, Munis, who had been in Ward 209 for three months. She and her former cellmate, Roxana Saberi, were the ones who had answered our knocks the day we arrived. Roxana was an Iranian-American journalist falsely accused of espionage and sentenced to eight years in prison. Our friend Silva had met her in 209 and had told us to look for her. Because of pressure from the international community, including the American president, Barack Obama, Roxana had recently been released. (She later wrote a book about her experience, *Between Two Worlds: My Life and Captivity in Iran*.)

Munis was a publisher and a leader of Al-e Yassin, an ideological group based on Islam, but which respects all religions. Later that day, a fourth prisoner was added to our cell, a girl of about sixteen with long black hair. When she and Munis saw each other, they embraced with shouts of joy. They had met earlier, but then had both been placed in solitary confinement. The new girl's name was Mahtab, and she had been imprisoned for belonging to the *mujahideen* organization. She was arrested while walking in a park with her fiancé. She believed it was a way for the regime to harass her father, who had already spent a year at Evin, leaving her mother and ten-year-old brother to fend for themselves. Her father was in the public ward of the prison, and Mahtab had been allowed to see him only once.

Munis and Mahtab had both endured intense interrogation during their time in solitary, living in cells half the size of the one we were in, which had scarcely left them room to sit. Mahtab's interrogator had sat close in front of her, opening his legs and moving his body in suggestive ways. She'd had the good sense to tell him to stay away. She might be young, but she knew how to stand up for herself.

"We've heard about the dangerous, high-profile political prisoners in 209," I said. "Who would have believed this teenage girl has put the national security of our country in jeopardy!" When we laughed this time, no guard came to shut us up.

"Before I transferred to this cell," Mahtab said, "the interrogators told me I would be with two girls who had run away from home and converted to Christianity. They said I might be able to convince you to recant and return to Islam."

We couldn't help laughing. "We're not runaways, and we didn't leave our families," Maryam explained. "Your interrogators have tried to shape your perception of us with lies before you even met us." For a minute, we suspected that she had been sent to spy on us; but we soon realized she was a brave and very honest and naive young girl. Her interrogators had sent her in to change us. What eventually happened was that our testimony changed her. In time, she would become a Christian.

With four women in the cell, there was scarcely room to lie down. The air became thick and stifling as we did our best to get comfortable. We arranged our pallets on the floor, wedged ourselves next to each other, and fell into an exhausted sleep.

| | |

MARYAM

The next day, I was blindfolded and taken away to another cell, separating Marziyeh and me once again. My new cellmate was Fereshteh, a middle-aged woman with short, scruffy hair, who looked like a walking skeleton.

She had large, sunken eyes that contrasted sharply with her starkly white skin, and her dark, bleeding gums were a testament to long periods of malnutrition in prison. Her whole body shuddered and wheezed with every breath, and she was so weak that her voice was almost inaudible.

"Don't sit here," Fereshteh said in a worried tone when I took a step toward her in the tiny cell. "Sit on your blanket in your corner. They're watching us on the security camera, and they can also hear us."

"Don't worry," I said, trying to calm her. "I don't think it's that important to them."

"You don't know these scumbags! You're so naive."

To avoid upsetting Fereshteh, I sat in my own corner and we began to talk quietly. As I related my story of being arrested for being a Christian, Fereshteh constantly warned me to be quiet and to be careful what I said, or else the guards would take me away and she would be alone again. By the time I finished my story, Fereshteh had calmed down enough to tell me her own.

"I have been here in solitary confinement for about three months," she began in a thin, soft voice. "Until yesterday, I was interrogated every day. I've been on a hunger strike for a month, taking only dates and tea, to protest against my treatment. I've been charged with belonging to the *mujahideen*, but I'm not a member of that or any other movement or political party. My real crime is being a mother who loves her children and wants to stay in touch with them.

"My two daughters live at the Ashraf camp for *mujahideen* in Iraq. After I visited them last year, I stayed in contact by telephone and e-mail. One day, coming home from an Internet café, I saw several men lounging outside our apartment. I could tell they were from the ministry of intelligence. I called my husband and told him what was happening. We hid in the street, watching the men around our door, and knew we had to decide right then whether to leave our entire lives behind and escape from the country that day, or face the agents and try to sort everything out. We decided to face them. They ransacked our apartment, arrested us, and separated my husband and me.

"I have been interrogated seven or eight hours every day until yesterday. I haven't been tortured, only hit in the head and slapped, but I still have terrible headaches. I have multiple sclerosis. I'm too weak to be a political activist, too weak to endure torture beyond what they're already doing. That's why I shake all the time. If my MS isn't treated, my doctor has told them I will soon be paralyzed and blind. But these vile, inhumane people have no conscience whatsoever.

"There have been times when I thought I couldn't endure another day. I've tried to kill myself, but have been too weak even to do that. The guards have promised me I will either die of MS in prison or commit suicide. They say I'll never walk out of 209 alive."

"Dear Fereshteh," I said, "why are the authorities punishing you so harshly for sending e-mails to your children?"

"As a student, I was politically active and wrote political articles," Fereshteh said. "I wanted to do something good for my culture and my people. When I was twenty-two, three weeks after my wedding, I was arrested and sentenced to five years in prison. I went to Ghezel Hesar Prison, in Karaj, with some other women from various groups, including the Daftar Tahkim Vahdat student association. For a month, my husband didn't know where I was, and he thought I'd been killed.

"In Karaj, we were stripped naked, blindfolded, and put in a cold, empty hall. One by one, we were taken for interrogation and torture. Some women, especially the young, pretty ones, were raped; others whipped with cables; others, including me, beaten in the head until we had concussions and blood streaming from our noses. My MS dates back to this time. I was whipped on the soles of my feet so that I couldn't walk or stand for days at a time. I had buckets of scalding water poured over my head. Some of us were led blindfolded into the execution chamber, where corpses still hung in their nooses. They made us walk around inside the room for hours. When we bumped into a body, a guard would announce that person's name.

"My husband finally found out where I was and came to see me. 'Forget about me,' I told him. 'Go find a new life for yourself.' After a year, I was transferred to Evin and spent four more years here. By then, most of my friends had been tortured to death or executed. When I was released, I went back to my husband.

"You must excuse me for talking so much," she said. "I haven't had anyone to talk to in so long and I have all these feelings inside me. I feel like I'm going to explode! From the first moment I saw you, I prayed to God that you would come in here with me because I could see you smiling below your blindfold."

"Dear Fereshteh, could I pray for you?" I asked.

Fereshteh laughed, a strange sound coming from such a cadaverous form. "Of course. Why not? I love Christians."

I sat beside my new friend and prayed for her and her family. When I finished, Fereshteh put her head on my chest, and we sat together silently for a while.

"I guess you're unlucky to have been sent in here with me," Fereshteh said. "But I am very lucky that God sent you to me."

"Please don't say that," I replied. "If I had been through what you have, I'd be in much worse shape than you are."

With some gentle urging, Fereshteh ate a little of her lunch and, later, all of her dinner. After dinner, a guard brought her a handful of sleeping pills.

"I have to take these for my condition," she explained. "I must apologize, but once I take them I can't stay awake very long." True to her word, she fell asleep within half an hour.

Too keyed up to sleep and now with a pounding headache, I tried to relax by walking around the cell. But it was only two steps across, and walking soon made me dizzy. I sat staring at the white walls for hours, thinking of all the heartache, injustice, and agony those walls had seen visited upon the lives of women like Fereshteh, the ocean of innocent blood spilled, tender lives like Zeynab's snuffed out by evil forces. At last, exhaustion mercifully overcame me and I settled into a fitful sleep.

| | |

After breakfast the next morning, I pressed the button to summon the guard to escort me to the toilet. She came to the door, blindfolded me, and led me down the hall. Once inside the washroom, I was allowed to remove the blindfold. A reflection behind the sink caught my eye. Between the basin and the wall, balanced on a water pipe, was a cross made from the foil top of a yogurt container.

Marziyeh is trying to communicate!

I knew if she was using the same facilities, it meant she was on the same floor. My heart was filled with joy as I hid the token in my pocket and put my blindfold back on. I could hardly wait to tell Fereshteh.

Later that afternoon, I made a similar cross and left it in the same spot in the washroom. When I heard someone in the next cell leave for the toilet, coughing and dragging her slippers in a distinctive way, I knew it had to be Marziyeh, letting me know she'd received the message. I tried a few exploratory knocks on the wall, and the rapid response confirmed that Marziyeh was just next door.

On my next trip to the toilet, I couldn't wait to check the hiding place behind the sink for another message. This time, I found a note made from torn-out letters from a newspaper stuck to a piece of tissue with toothpaste. It said, "how are you who are you with."

Elated, I now had to figure out a way to answer. The only paper in my cell was Fereshteh's copy of the Koran, which I didn't dare damage. As I scanned the spare, small room, my eyes were drawn to a tube of toothpaste, still in its carton, resting on the edge of the sink in the corner. I removed the tube, tore open the carton and flattened it out, and then smeared a light coating of toothpaste on the blank inside surface of the cardboard. Once it was dry, I used my fingernail to scratch my response: "Fine. With Fereshteh." On my next visit to the toilet, I left the note behind the sink.

Our "underground spy" communication system survived for as long as we were separated. We wrote notes in toothpaste and sent each other crosses, stars, and flowers made from yogurt lids or orange peels. Once, when the guards discovered one of our notes, they were angry and threatened us, but we kept up our correspondence without a pause. God was protecting us every minute.

| | |

Marziyeh

After Maryam and I were separated, I thought hard about how I could find out whether she was still close by. I had no paper and nothing to write with, so a note was out of the question. I talked with Munis and Mahtab about it, and they suggested some kind of symbol that Maryam would recognize. Munis warned me that if the guards found it before Maryam did, we would both be punished. But I decided it was worth the risk. The next morning, as we were eating our breakfast, I made a small cross from the foil top of a yogurt cup, which I then concealed in the washroom. My heart was overjoyed when Maryam found the cross I had made and left me one of her own. When I found out that Maryam's new cellmate was Fereshteh, Mahtab told me that she knew her and that she was a kind, gentle woman who would be a great companion.

During the long days, Munis, Mahtab, and I had lively discussions about faith and religion. They observed the Islamic traditions of prayer and fasting, which they tried to explain to me.

"The regime gives people a distorted version of Islam," Munis insisted, "and its actions have nothing to do with the real principles of the faith."

These debates helped to take my mind off my continuing sickness—a severe sore throat and chest infection, as well as the backache and headaches I had suffered off and on for weeks. A trip to the clinic in Ward 209—not actually a clinic, but just a room with a bed—yielded another round of ineffective antibiotics. The pills weren't even in a container. The "doctor" scooped a handful from the table behind her and handed them to me.

When Munis and Mahtab were praying a few days later, I asked them why they covered themselves to pray. "If you believe God is your creator, don't you believe He is closer to you than your skin? Why cover yourself up from someone who is already in your heart?"

"It's a sign of respect and part of our faith," Munis explained. "Otherwise we don't have to do it."

"But has God asked you to do this?" I said. "And has He asked you to speak to Him only in Arabic? Can God not understand you in Farsi? Do you really have to bow to Him five times a day? Can't you pray to Him whenever you want?"

Munis couldn't answer these questions, and they upset her. Seeing her agitation, I apologized and let the matter drop. That night, Mahtab came over to me and said, "Your conversation with Munis made me think a lot. You're exactly right, and I wonder why I never thought of these things before. You prayed to your Lord for me and it really made a difference: I felt much more relaxed. The routine, obligatory prayers I say as a Muslim are rituals, clichés, nothing but habits that have no benefit. I'm going to stop doing *namaz* prayers and pray with you instead."

Even though Mahtab's new routine made Munis uncomfortable, Mahtab was true to her word. She and I prayed together daily, sometimes skipping break time in order to pray instead.

| | | |

MARYAM

As the days passed, the guards in Ward 209 grew curious about Christianity, just as some of the guards in Ward 2 had. One of them surprised me one day by asking out of the blue, "Who is this Jesus, anyway? Some new fake leader who tries to convince people to follow him? It seems like there's another one every day. I heard a while ago that a man in a distant village claims to be in touch with ghosts and spirits and has attracted quite a crowd. Why have you young girls lost your senses and decided to follow some nut like that? It's a pity, is it not? In any case, whoever this Jesus Christ is, he's a very dangerous person to put you in this position." I knew that any explanation would fall on deaf ears, but I prayed that Jesus would open this woman's heart to the truth.

In our cell, Fereshteh spent hours every day reading the Koran and using her prayer beads. Her strict views of Islam prohibited her from accepting any new ideas about God. And yet she acknowledged an emptiness inside. "Our religious leaders have made a mess of Islam," she said. "Because of that, many people have deserted the religion and lost their faith."

She and I had already shared long conversations about Islam and Christianity. I had prayed for her, but now I decided to remain silent and let God touch Fereshteh's heart however He thought best. The next day, I made a foil cross and gave it to her. She put it next to her pillow. "From now on, every time I go to sleep, I'll pray with this cross in my hands," Fereshteh said. She also became keenly interested in the subject of baptism.

"Before you can do that, you must believe in Jesus as the Son of God and the Savior," I explained.

Fereshteh hung on every word and wanted to know more. "Could you sing your hymns louder?" she asked. This from an inmate who had flinched at the slightest word when I first arrived, fearful that the guards would crack down on us. "I hear them when you're praying and enjoy them very much."

I happily taught her "Christ Beside Me," "Come Down, O Love Divine," and others. Fereshteh was an eager student, learning the songs quickly and singing along with me. It was a wonderful way for both of us to keep our spirits up. Still, there were times when even singing couldn't distract me from the pain in my ear that had continued ever since my infection. My hearing was only partially restored, and headaches and dizziness still came on without warning. One afternoon, when I became too dizzy to stand, Fereshteh called for a guard to take me to the clinic. I put on my headscarf and a blindfold and went to the clinic.

After a cursory examination, the doctor said, "You have a ruptured eardrum. It will heal in time. Your headaches are caused by stress. I will give you some medicine."

The "medicine" turned out to be one of the prison clinic's all-purpose remedies: sleeping pills. After two days of this "therapy," I veered between a fog of semiconsciousness and deep sleep. One morning, when the guard came in with breakfast, I stood to take the plate and fainted, falling backward. Fereshteh later told me that the crack of my head against the wall was so loud that the guard put down her tray and rushed over to check on me. After that, the clinic sent even stronger pills. After taking them for only a day, I told the guard that I wouldn't take them anymore. The guard agreed, but made me sign a statement saying I had refused the medication.

The rules demanding quiet, coupled with the fact that prisoners always wore blindfolds outside their cells, created a powerful sense of isolation. The only breaks in the day were meals, trips to the toilet, and a one-hour period spent in the larger room with the clear skylight. Marziyeh and I kept up our clandestine communication, leaving tokens to each other behind the sink, and we deepened our friendships with our cellmates.

The next time I saw Marziyeh was on visiting day, about two weeks after our transfer to Ward 209. After being blindfolded and taken separately from our cells, we were brought outside to wait for a ride to the visitors' hall. Out in the courtyard, where we were allowed to remove our blindfolds, we discovered we were standing only a few feet from each other. We nodded, speaking only with our eyes, but one of the guards saw us and shouted, "No talking, you two!"

I was overwhelmed with joy at seeing and feeling the sun after being locked up in a six-by-six-foot cell for two weeks. It was so wonderful! The process of leaving Ward 209, waiting for the car, driving to the visitors' hall, and waiting again to be escorted inside, took hours. At last, we were allowed to spend fifteen minutes with our sisters. We sat in adjacent cubicles, with Shirin and Elena on the visitors' side, separated from us by a glass wall. We could see them only inches away, but could not touch them, and we had to use the cubicle telephones to talk. Guards stood close by to listen in on our conversations.

| | |

Marziyeh

When Elena saw me during the visiting time, she was shocked at my appearance. After two weeks in a windowless cell, I was as pale as a ghost. But at least I was clean and well fed, and had even managed to trim my eyebrows using strands of thread. Because we had so little time to visit, she and I talked at a furious pace. I told her only a little about the conditions in Ward 209, because I didn't want her to worry. And then I shared an amazing story with her.

"One morning about five o'clock, I was awakened by someone shaking my legs," I said. "I had a strange, vibrant feeling that it was the Holy Spirit. This had happened before and made me very happy. Because Mahtab and Munis were still asleep, I sat on my pallet singing songs of praise to the Lord for the peace He had given me. By the time they woke up, I had already arranged our breakfast of boiled eggs on the *softe* [a plastic tray about the size of a newspaper, which we used in place of a table in the cell]. They were surprised and asked why I was up so early. I said, 'I don't know. I just feel as if the Holy Spirit is with me.'"

As I told my story, Elena's eyes lit up. "Do you know what day that was?" she said with excitement. "Pentecost!"

I was completely astonished. It made me very happy to know that the Lord hadn't forgotten about me and that the Holy Spirit had filled me with a new sense of His presence on that special day.

Once I had given my brief report, Elena did most of the talking, bringing me important news.

First, our faithful and hardworking lawyer, Mr. Soltani, had not given up on us. He had continually tried to get inside Evin to visit us and to get our signatures, which would give him legal permission to represent us in court. For his dedication and commitment, he himself had been arrested and was now an inmate in Ward 209. How ridiculous! For defending the human rights of political prisoners in Iran, for standing up to the false arrest and widespread abuse of those prisoners, he had now joined their ranks! (He was sentenced to twenty years and forbidden to practice law. As of November 2012, he is still in prison.)

The second important news was that we were not the isolated, anonymous inmates we thought we were; thousands of people were praying for us and working for our release. The first indication we'd had of any of this was Mr. Mosavat's remark at our interrogation that one of our sisters had been interviewed by Voice of America. In fact, through the efforts of our friends, along with people we didn't even know, our case had been taken up by Amnesty International. A press release on April 8, 2009, identified us as prisoners of conscience, "detained solely on account of their religious beliefs."

The press release mentioned our illnesses and the crowded conditions in Ward 2 of Evin Prison. It also quoted Article 23 of the Iranian constitution, which says, "The investigation of individuals' beliefs is forbidden, and no one may be molested or taken to task simply for holding a certain belief,"[1] and Article 18.1 of the International Covenant on Civil and Political Rights (to which Iran is a party), which states, "Everyone shall have the right to freedom of thought, conscience and religion. This right shall include freedom to have or to adopt a religion or belief of his choice, and freedom, either individually or in community with others and in public or private, to manifest his religion or belief in worship, observance, practice and teaching."[2]

The Amnesty International document noted that "evangelical Christians . . . often face harassment by the authorities. Converts from Islam can risk arrest, attack, or the death penalty. Conversion from Islam (apostasy) is considered as forbidden under Islamic Law, which requires apostates to be put to death if they refuse to reconvert to Islam. There is no specific provision in the Iranian Penal Code for apostasy, but judges are required to use their knowledge of Islamic Law to rule on cases where no specific legislation exists in the Penal Code. A new version of the Iranian Penal Code is currently under consideration by the [Parliament] and prescribes the death penalty for those considered to be apostates."[3]

Amnesty International encouraged appeals to the Iranian authorities for our immediate and unconditional release, along with contact information for writing to the director of the Human Rights Headquarters of Iran, the head of the judiciary, and Ayatollah Sayed Ali Khamenei, the supreme leader of the Islamic Republic.

Elam Ministries, the London-based organization that sponsored the theology conference in Turkey where Maryam and I first met, was also publicizing our case. They had provided us with support and the New Testaments we had distributed before our arrest. Now they were trying to help us win our freedom.

Furthermore, friends and strangers by the hundreds had sent us cards and letters of encouragement in prison. Of course, we had not received a single one and knew nothing of their existence until this meeting with our sisters.

The world was watching how the Iranian government treated us, and it made the authorities very nervous. God had sent an army of Christians to help us, and we didn't even know it!

Elena was convinced that our transfer to Ward 209 was a sign that our case was about to be closed and we would be released. As the visit ended, my spirits soared. So much encouraging news! So much to be thankful for! Nothing could ruin the joy of the moment; not even being blindfolded, separated again from my sister and Maryam, and returned to my tiny, sunless cell.

OUR APARTMENT . . .

آبشار

BOTH PHOTOS

Exterior of the apartment building where we lived at the time of our arrest.

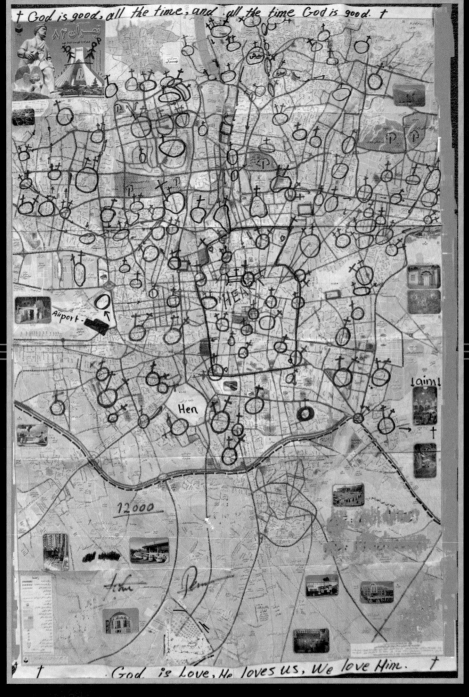

The map we used to keep track of our outreach in Tehran. The circles

The main door of Evin, used to transfer prisoners to court or other locations. This is only a short distance from our apartment; we lived in the prison's very shadow as we carried out our undercover ministry work.

▲ ABOVE

The door of Evin where families enter to visit someone inside. In this picture, you can see a woman and a small child approaching.

RIGHT ►

The walls of Evin, which we could see from the doors of our apartment.

This is not our cell from Ward 209, but rather a picture taken in 1986 from a cell in the public prison. Our cell in 209 was much smaller, with no windows and no light. Instead of being able to see out through the bars as in this photo, we were locked behind a solid steel door.

Very few photos exist from inside Evin's walls. In 2006, the government permitted a rare visit to media, showing a cleaned-up and sanitized Evin very unlike the one we would experience a few years later. After decades of restricting access, they wanted these photos to come out to give Evin a more positive image. The following photos are from that 2006 event . . . but contrary to what they expected, we can now share our insider view of what it was really like when the doors closed behind the journalists and no cameras were around.

We aren't sure which cell this is, but it is nothing like the one where we were held. We had no light or space, and certainly no clean, flowered sheets! When photographers are not present, the real-life cells are filthy, stinking of sweat, vomit, and backed-up toilets. Our cell in the public prison was also much more crowded than this one, packed with women sitting anywhere they could find a spot.

We suspect this press photo may have been taken in Ward 3, which is where guests are usually taken because there are fewer prisoners held there. You can see a female prisoner peeking out behind the guard, but this would not have happened where we were. We were guarded by other women, never a young male guard like this. This corridor is similar to the one in the ward where we were held . . . but it is much cleaner.

INSIDE THE WALLS **OF EVIN**

This phone is like the one we used, but most of the time there were many women crowded around us—screaming, fighting, and talking. We could hardly hear the person we were calling. We never saw anyone with the kind of quiet privacy shown in this picture.

Shirin Alam Hooli, our best friend in the public ward, who was executed by hanging on May 9, 2010, after two years in Evin.

The notorious Judge Salavati, known as "the killing judge," who sent Shirin to her execution.

Ayatollah Sadegh Larijani (head of the Iranian judiciary). We were told by Judge Pirabbasi in court that Mr. Larijani was called by UN officials and asked why we were still in prison.

RASTI

RIGHT ▶

After our release, we drew on our memories to create this image of Mr. Rasti (our first interrogator), using an online program. The result is very much like him, except he should appear older and more cruel. We never saw the real Mr. Rasti smile.

LOCKED AWAY, BUT NOT SILENCED . . .

◀ LEFT

Marziyeh as a child. These are some of the only childhood photos left of either of us. The reason? As soon as we were released from Evin, we purged our entire apartment. We threw away clothes we had worn, as well as pictures, mementos, and every personal item we could find. We thought that the police would be back for us, and in our fear we wanted to get rid of anything that might incriminate us or someone else. Experience has taught us that this is a normal reaction for survivors of trauma, but today we wish we had some of those things back.

A storm gathering over Tehran. Despite what the government did to us, we continue to love our country very much and pray for the freedom of our fellow Iranians, especially those still unjustly held inside Evin's walls.

CHAPTER 14

"EXECUTE US!"

Marziyeh

During our two weeks in Ward 209, we had not been interrogated a single time. That relatively peaceful period ended a day or two after our visit with our sisters when Maryam and I were called in separately for long, intense interrogations of six to eight hours each. Much of the time, the questioners, usually Mr. Mosavat and Mr. Sedaghat, asked us the same questions that they and others had been asking for months: "When did you convert to Christianity? Who do you talk to about it? Do you hold church services in your home? Where do you get your Bibles? Who are the people on this list? Who are the people in these photos? We're so sorry to have to keep you here; are they treating you well? Do you have any complaints?"

When I entered the interrogation room, Mr. Mosavat offered to let me take off my blindfold. "No, thank you," I said. "I am quite happy right now, and I prefer not to see your face."

I voiced my anger at being separated from Maryam when we returned to Ward 2 after our first interrogation, but added, "I must thank you for this kindness, because you have enabled me to talk about Jesus Christ with even more people."

"I didn't order you to be sent to separate floors, only separate cells," Mr. Mosavat fumed. "There must have been a mistake. Those people are so stupid!"

I sat silently for a moment before clapping my hands loudly in applause. "That was a very good show. Thank you for that, too."

"Miss Amirizadeh, it would be a complete waste of your young life and your beauty to remain in this prison. I advise you to stop insisting on your faith, recant your statements, get your freedom, and then go have fun and enjoy life." Clearly, he was used to having the upper hand, which was essential for making prisoners afraid and for making them say or do whatever he wanted.

"Thank you very much," I replied. "I was just waiting for you to order me to go have fun and enjoy life." I was determined to let him know that I did not believe his lies and was not falling prey to his manipulations. Humor and sarcasm were the defenses I had at hand, and I wielded them with confidence.

A few days later, I was interrogated again—hours and hours of the same questions, plus a few surprises. This time, there was a third man in the room, but he was a stranger to me. The room smelled of expensive cologne.

"Do you have relationships with men?" Mr. Mosavat asked me.

"What do you mean by 'relationships'? If you mean do I have a boyfriend, the answer is no."

"Are you saying you have no contacts with any men? Have you never gone to a coffee shop with a man?"

"Excuse me. I am a woman who has lived on her own for ten years. Of course I've gone out with men and may have sat with them in coffee shops as part of my socializing with other people. That is a really stupid question."

"Have you ever been in love?"

"That has nothing to do with any of this."

"You're right, it's irrelevant. I'm just curious."

| | |

MARYAM

When my turn came to be interrogated, Mr. Mosavat offered to let me remove my blindfold. "I don't mind it," I said. "I'd rather not see your face." I had no way of knowing that Marziyeh had said the same thing.

"You must take off your blindfold!" said another voice in the room. It was Mr. Sedaghat, the official in charge of Ward 209. I untied the blindfold and put it aside.

"Did you know you are now the subject of a website?" Mr. Mosavat asked. "Who are you using to write about your arrest?"

"No one. I know nothing about any website." This was true. The news was a total surprise.

"It's interesting you have never heard of this website," Mr. Mosavat said. "It's a Christian website. Ninety percent of its stories are lies. Now when someone logs onto it, the first thing they see is pictures of you and your friend."

"What did you expect?" I shot back. "That Christian organizations would praise you for arresting us? It's your own fault. Obviously, the church will react to this situation and publish news about it."

"We have no problem with people reading the Bible."

"Then why have you banned it from the bookshops?"

"Who is your pastor at the moment?" Mr. Mosavat demanded.

"Jesus Christ is my pastor."

The questioners again went over my statements from the police station when Mr. Rasti had written both the questions and the answers. When I was shown some of this information, I objected strongly.

"This says that the police found eight hundred Bibles and thirty thousand CDs in my house, all gift wrapped, and that I drove around Iran distributing them. When Mr. Rasti said I didn't need to read the answers he put down, he assured me, 'I'm not going to lose my life in the hereafter by writing lies on your behalf.' That man is a liar. I deny what he wrote."

Mr. Sedaghat positioned his body inches from mine, his foot resting on the leg of my chair. His huge beak nose made his sinister face even more unattractive.

"Look at me!" he ordered. I looked into his threatening, hate-filled eyes.

"What do you think will happen if we're forced to release you?"

I remained silent.

"I believe you know two people named Haik and Dibaj very well. You may have heard what happened to them." These two men, who had been held for years by the regime, died violently under mysterious circumstances after their release.

"So you're threatening me?"

"Not threatening you, just telling you what could happen later. Don't think you can be freed and go home just like that. Your apartment may catch fire. You could be involved in a car accident. Do you think these interrogations are the only power at our disposal?"

"I understand what you're saying," I said, my voice steady. "But I believe the times of our birth and death are in the hands of God alone. It may be God's will that we die in a fire or a car wreck. But it's good that you said what you did. Now if we're killed outside this prison, our friends will know you're responsible."

"You're not worth killing at the risk of our careers and reputations," Mr. Sedaghat snapped. "But there are fanatics out there prepared to spill your blood for the cause of *jihad*, and we cannot stop them. From the Muslim point of view, you are an apostate. They are free to shed your blood, and the court will judge their actions as justified."

"Then I'm happy I am not a Muslim. I believe in Jesus Christ, and one of His most important commands is to spread His message. The message of Christianity isn't what causes distress and chaos in Iran. It's your restrictions and bans. It's your bad laws. If everyone had the freedom to study and believe and share whatever faith their hearts called them to believe, Iran would not be in the mess it's in and I would not be sitting here being grilled by you."

Mr. Mosavat put on a big, brave, plastic smile. "Miss Rostampour, I agree with you to some extent. Worshiping God is not compulsory. But we live in a country that at this moment in time has these particular laws. Even I may not agree with all of them, but I have to follow them or I'll end up where you are. Why don't you let the churches in this country do the preaching and teaching about Christianity? Anyone who's interested can study them in depth there."

"What churches?" I fired back. I could feel my face growing warm. "The Assemblies of God have been closed to new people. Only one or two Farsi-speaking churches remain in all of Tehran, and they're under constant surveillance by your security forces. You threaten them and order them not to allow any Muslims or newcomers through the doors—yet you're telling me I should let these churches take the gospel to the city? Even church members are harassed trying to get in, never mind prospective visitors."

"Where were you baptized?" Mr. Mosavat interjected.

"Central Church, about five years ago."

| | |

Marziyeh

Two long, intense interrogations so close together made me feel depressed. I was physically drained, and I hoped that Maryam was able to bear up under the load as well. The isolation of the tiny, windowless cells, the nearly silent ward, wearing blindfolds everywhere, and being surrounded by other prisoners I could never see were hard conditions to endure. I knew the Lord was with me, but I desperately needed reminders of His love and care. In my weakness, I sometimes felt that He was far away. From the interrogators, I learned that a friend of ours on the outside who had become a Christian was questioned about us and denied knowing us. This woman and her daughter attended our home church regularly and eagerly learned Christian hymns and prayers. Of course, the interrogators could have been lying, but they wouldn't have known certain details about this person unless they'd talked to her. She had a heart condition, and her husband resented her for converting. I didn't fault her for lying to save herself; even so, it added to my dark feelings.

On the positive side, when Mahtab was asked if "the two Christians" had ever caused her any trouble, she replied, "Not only have they not caused me any trouble, they've constantly helped me and made me hopeful. They're far better than you Muslims who claim to be truthful and kind. I'd rather stay with them than with Muslims." The prison officials had hoped that Mahtab could convince me that Christianity was a mistake and that I should embrace the true faith of Islam. Instead, in a turn of events that only the Lord could have arranged, Mahtab was the one converted: eventually, she became a Christian.

The fact that we never left our cells without blindfolds compounded the oppressive atmosphere and sense of isolation in Ward 209. Another hard thing to endure was hearing the disembodied voices of other prisoners we had never seen, crying out in agony.

One night, I heard the voice of a young boy crying, begging for help, and screaming, "I can't stand it in here anymore! Please! Please!" He had reached the breaking point. He started pounding on the metal walls of his cell.

After a few minutes, I heard several guards go down the hall and open the door to the boy's cell. I heard the sound of blows from a club and the boy screaming in agony. Sometimes, the club would miss its target and boom against the wall like a cannon shot. They hit him again and again and again until his cries died down to pitiful, heartbreaking moans. Then silence. I never knew who he was or whether he stayed or left, lived or died.

Another woman in a nearby cell moaned and cried so much that I thought she must have been put near us just to keep us awake at night. She, unlike the boy, seemed to be completely ignored by the guards. This was strange, considering the rules demanding silence at all times in 209.

"I'm so afraid! I'm so afraid! Please help me!" she moaned day after day. She begged for sleeping pills, which they gave her; but as soon as she woke up, she started moaning and begging again. I put my hands on the wall nearest her cell and prayed for her peace of mind. Sometimes she would get quiet for a while, but then the yelling would resume.

One night, I dreamed that the guards let this woman out of her cell. She had the face of a ghost and went running up and down the corridor. In the dream, she came into my cell and put her head in my lap. When I started praying for her, all her sorrows and problems were transferred to my shoulders, so heavy and unbearable that they made me collapse. But the woman found peace. Then she cried and said that she wished she had known there were Christians next to her in prison.

I woke up shaking and told Mahtab and Munis about my dream. I saw it as a sign that the woman would be released. A couple of hours later, the guards came to the woman's cell and we heard her say, "Thank you! Oh thank you!" From the conversation, it was clear she was getting her freedom.

"Behave yourself if you want to stay out of prison," one of the guards said.

"Yes, yes, thank you!" the woman said over and over. It was wonderful to see how my prayers had been answered even for someone I'd never seen.

| | |

A few days after our interrogations, Maryam and I were taken again to Security Bureau 2 of the Revolutionary Court. We were handcuffed together, warned not to talk, and driven through Tehran in a black, unmarked car. We hadn't seen the city since arriving at Evin two months before. The sight of so many people, so many shops, so much light and space was astonishing. I had the impulse to shout, "Hey, all you people! Look at us! Look at how your corrupt government has locked us up on phony charges! Look at how the regime imprisons young mothers and tortures teenage girls in order to stay in power!"

At the same time, there was something genuine about the pain and suffering and the fight for truth inside Evin that was entirely absent from the scene on the street. The outside world seemed so superficial and lifeless by comparison. We passed the street that led to our apartment. That life and that world seemed like twenty years ago.

We arrived at the court and went into Mr. Sobhani's office. He was reading and barely looked up when we entered. After a moment, he sat straight in his chair. "You have been making a lot of noise," he began. "The satellite channels are talking about you around the clock. You are receiving hundreds of letters and postcards every day. Everyone's accusing us of interrogating you about your beliefs. What do they mean, 'interrogating you about your beliefs'?" He got more agitated as he spoke, his voice rising. "We have nothing to do with people's beliefs!"

This statement by Judge Sobhani of the Revolutionary Court of Iran is our nominee for Lie of the Century.

Mr. Sobhani glared at us across his desk. "You thought all this publicity would stop us from doing our jobs and carrying out our religious duty. They can broadcast all they want. I don't care. You are criminals, and I will perform my religious duty."

"Then why don't you allow our case to be broadcast on Iranian TV, so people will understand that doing what we do is a crime?" I asked.

Mr. Sobhani changed the subject. "Do you have any complaints about prison conditions?"

"We object to our conditions, and also to being kept in a state of suspense about the charges against us," Maryam said. "We object to the fact that we've never seen an official complaint against us in writing."

"You are accused of apostasy and insulting sacred beliefs of Islam. Do you accept these charges?"

"No."

"You are regarded as apostates and your sentence is death. Do you still have a complaint to make?"

"Do you really believe what you're saying?" I interjected.

"Of course I do."

"Then do us a favor and execute us as soon as you can." I might be in prison, but I would not be intimidated. Far from frightening me, Mr. Sobhani's threats inspired and energized my resistance.

"Of course I will."

Judge Sobhani angrily ordered us to write down our final defense statements. We still had no legal assistance. We had answered the charges against us so many times, both orally and in writing, that we had lost count.

"I have not changed my religion, because I did not have a religion before," Maryam said. "I found my path in Jesus Christ and will share my experience about Him with anyone who asks about it."

I ended my written statement with a prediction: "If the court and the judge ignore the principles of justice and truth and deliver an unjust sentence, they will face the wrath of God, which will one day engulf them in its flames."

Another man came in while we were talking to Mr. Sobhani. He was younger than the judge, and well dressed. His name was Mr. Heydarifar, and he had been assigned to our case by the regime because the publicity was starting to worry them. Too many eyes were watching our case now for us to simply disappear or be the victims of a "tragic accident." We were not recanting our statements. The regime was faced with justifying its charges against us to the world, and they were beginning to realize that it was an impossible task.

| | |

MARYAM

Throughout our time in prison, the presence of the Holy Spirit had been our rock, the one assurance we always had that the Lord loved us, would never forsake us, and was using us for some great purpose. There were times, though, when I was so weary and exhausted that I allowed that assurance to slip.

For several days during that period, I couldn't feel the Lord's presence. The loneliness that crept into my heart was frightening. I reached a point where I couldn't eat and felt an emptiness I'd never known before as a Christian. I prayed, walking around my tiny cell, asking the Lord to make Himself known in a special way. When Fereshteh woke up, I started singing hymns, and my voice filled the entire corridor. Fereshteh was afraid the sound would attract the guards. I expected the guards, too, but kept singing. I sang nonstop for hours. No more silence! No more following oppressive, inhuman rules! I sang at the top of my lungs until it was nearly dark.

Finally, exhausted, I lay down in the middle of the floor and closed my eyes. And there it was. The Spirit of God flowing over me, embracing me, reassuring me. I knew that He had never left my side. I was now free from sadness and pressure, completely happy.

"I'm amazed no guards came all day!" Fereshteh said. "You know your voice had to reach the men's corridor, and the guards there would complain to the guards in the women's section." She could feel the presence of God too.

At dinnertime, the guard we called the Ghost came with our food and said, "You did whatever you wanted today, and your voice carried all the way to the other side of the building."

"But I didn't do anything," I said. "I just sang." Though the Ghost was never very expressive, I thought she looked sad.

"What's happened?" I asked. "Why are you upset?"

"I'm tired of working here," the Ghost admitted. "I don't think I'm cut out for it. Would you pray for me?"

"I will be happy to." And so I prayed for my captor, secure in the presence of the Lord that washed over me in waves, in the deepest recesses of the most feared ward of the most notorious prison in one of the most oppressed nations of the world. Surely I had never felt more blessed.

CHAPTER 15

A LESSON IN FAITH

Marziyeh

Maryam and I heard more news of the growing interest in our case during the next fifteen-minute visit with our sisters. They said that our story was becoming bigger every day on satellite TV and the Internet. Churches, Christians, and members of organizations around the world were praying for us. We were lifted up as part of a spiritual family that circled the globe. Some of the stories also highlighted other religions, such as Baha'i, whose believers are also severely persecuted in Iran. We had met a Baha'i woman in prison, a kind, gentle, open-minded person who very quickly became a friend.

Our sisters also talked about the upcoming presidential elections. The media were full of background stories and predictions. The incumbent, Mahmoud Ahmadinejad, was very unpopular with the people. Many citizens thought he would lose the election to Mehdi Karroubi, Mohsen Reza'i, or especially Mir-Hossein Mousavi. Our sisters had written letters to Mr. Mousavi and Mr. Karroubi, petitioning on our behalf. Mr. Mousavi, a reform-minded leader who had been Iran's last prime minister before the office was abolished in 1989, seemed the clear favorite, according to media reports. If he won, we had high hopes we would be released.

A few days later, we had another long round of interrogations. Though we went on separate days, we again had similar experiences. Mr. Mosavat explained that our defiant attitude toward Mr. Sobhani during our last court appearance had made the judge angry and complicated the resolution of our case. Also present at these sessions was a university lecturer in Islamic theology who had come to coach us on how to express ourselves in order to have our case resolved. The court seemed less worried now about what we believed than about how we described it. The regime was evidently desperate for some face-saving way to turn us loose.

The theology professor asked all the familiar questions about when I had become a Christian, why I would "abandon" Islam, details about my activities, friends, travels, and so forth.

I described for him the experience that had brought me to Christ. "One day, as I was praying for wisdom and clarity in my faith," I said, "the Holy Spirit came to me, and I began to pray in words I didn't know, but I could still understand what I was saying to God. I had a vision of Jesus so close I could touch Him. The middle of my forehead burned as if someone had stamped it with a branding iron. I prayed until four in the morning. I had met with God through the Lord Jesus Christ. I will never deny Him, because by doing that I would deny my very existence."

Tears welled up in Mr. Mosavat's eyes as I spoke. As soon as he noticed them, he quickly wiped them away.

The professor spoke for an hour about the evils perpetrated by Christians during the Crusades. "What kind of Christianity is this that would commit such atrocities?"

"Professor," I replied, "I can't match your knowledge of history. But there's no need to dig into history books to find as many examples of Islamic atrocities as you care to hear about. They're here, right now, in this prison. In my cell at this moment is a teenage girl, named Mahtab, who has been here for three months for the 'crime' of being born among the *mujahideen*. I have come across countless girls who have been tortured and beaten by your collaborators. What can you call these except atrocities?"

"I don't know what you're talking about," the professor replied. "I have come here only to deal with you, and I know nothing about the other prisoners in 209."

"All it takes is a look around."

"In any case, I've come here to tell you that your insistence on your faith is going to cause you a lot of problems. Those whose friends and loved ones have martyred themselves for the glory of Islam will not allow you to misguide our young people. If we allowed everybody to promote their own personal beliefs and opinions, we would face anarchy and a collapse of the system.

"I think you had better go and think about this again. We've done our best to assist you and close your case, but your defiance in court has created more problems. If you keep this up, there's nothing we can do to help you."

"All the others we've arrested," Mr. Mosavat chimed in, "have eventually cooperated, and by changing their opinions and their language, they bought their freedom. Stop being so stubborn. We want to let you go, but you're making it difficult for us to do so."

| | |

MARYAM

When my turn came to be interrogated, the professor tried to suggest that maybe I didn't fully understand Christianity. Because I had converted at a young age, he suggested, I might not have understood what I was doing.

"Research and study will only give you information," I replied. "To learn about the Lord, you need more than that. I experienced Jesus Christ. I lived with Him. Touched Him. If I deny Him, I would be denying myself. This is what you don't understand. And you'll never get it from your research."

"We have books that help us interpret the Koran," the professor said. "A wise person can recognize that he should not abandon a complete religion."

"And what particular quality of Islam highlights this completeness?" I asked. "Wars? Power mongering? One-hour marriages?"

"All these were necessary," the professor interrupted. "God sent them in line with the needs of mankind at the time to prevent chaos and corruption. What is it about Christianity that is more complete and forces you to leave Islam?"

"First of all," I replied, "Christ said, 'I am the first and the last.'[1] There is no one before Him, no one after Him. Christ's completeness is evident in His love. Even the most sinful people on earth can feel God's love through Jesus. He was the perfect man, who sacrificed His life on the cross for our sins. By paying the price we could never pay, He gave us the priceless, holy gift of freedom—freedom from sin and freedom from religious laws we could never perfectly follow as imperfect mortals.

"Religious law brings condemnation and death, not forgiveness and freedom. I know a precious young woman named Zeynab who was executed in retribution for defending her life against a brutal husband she was forced by religious law to marry and prevented by religious law from escaping. Compare that with the story of Jesus hearing about a woman accused of adultery and condemned to death by stoning. He said, 'Whoever is without sin may throw the first stone.' Not a single stone was thrown. I prefer to follow Jesus.

"He teaches us that if we're slapped, we should turn the other cheek. He tells us to be kind to our enemies. These words strike a chord with me much more closely than the Islamic cry for revenge. I would rather follow Christ, even if His religion were incomplete."

The professor shook his head. "I prefer Allah's choice of forgiveness or demanding revenge. Why should I be kind to my enemies? I much prefer the Koran. In fact, if I were your family, I wouldn't wait for a court verdict before giving you what you deserve."

"I'm sure you'd kill me yourself," I said. "You would be rewarded for *jihad*."

"You're right!" The professor turned to Mr. Mosavat. "Do you remember when Ayatollah Khomeini returned to Iran? Remember our enthusiasm and happiness at the idea he had come to save us from the assaults of foreigners? Did you ever imagine the children of this very revolution would one day turn their back on Islam?" His eyes filled with angry tears. "I am prepared to give my life for the imam and his ideals!"

He turned back to face me. "Jesus was a prophet from God, not His son. Imam Husein was also a savior. Why don't you believe in him?"

"Jesus is different from every other figure in the Koran," I explained. "He was born of the Virgin Mary and the Holy Spirit. He was without sin. He rose from the dead. There is no one else in history like Christ. No one did what He did. All the other prophets were sinful, mortal humans, and therefore could not be the savior of anybody."

"It's one thing to believe this privately," the professor said, "but why do you have to evangelize?"

"Jesus said that if you know a good deed and don't do it, you have committed a sin. His greatest commandment was that we talk about Him. I believe everyone should know about Christ and have the freedom to accept or reject Him according to their own hearts."

The professor countered, "The Koran says anyone can become a Muslim, but Muslims cannot turn their backs on their faith. A Muslim who abandons Islam is an infidel."

"But the Koran also says religion is not compulsory," I replied. "I see you didn't mention that verse. Christ came to free the world from the condemnation of religious law. Because humankind is imperfect, we will always fail to follow these laws exactly. Jesus took the blame for all of our sins and shortcomings in order to free us from the consequences of failing to follow the law. And now Islam is trying to bring those laws back in a different form. Don't you think that's senseless?

"Jesus said that if we don't open ourselves to God's Kingdom, the way a child would, we will never understand it. The truth of the Lord is revealed only to those who trust Him like children and have a receptive heart.

"Yes, we have paid a price for our faith," I concluded. "We have paid it gladly. Jesus Himself said, 'If you wish to be My followers, you must pick up your own cross and follow Me.'[2] He paid the price for being true to His Father, and He expects no less from us. Prison conditions are very difficult, but it's nothing compared to Jesus' sacrifice. It's the least we can do to show our love and faith in Him."

Mr. Mosavat spoke up. "I've made inquiries and also watched the two of you. You don't behave in any sort of overtly religious way—no special diet, no special dress, no special language. Your faith is on the inside and you stand firm for your beliefs. I respect your faith because I've never seen people like you. You must have discovered something powerful to defend it like this. But I want to ask you not to discuss it with others. And don't hand out Bibles, because it's against the law."

"We won't be handing out Bibles, because you've taken them all away,"

I reminded him. "But God brings His truth to the world in a variety of ways. He doesn't depend only on two girls giving away New Testaments in secret. If someone is eager, God will show him the truth. He doesn't need books, and He doesn't need Marziyeh and me."

"Miss Rostampour," Mr. Mosavat said, "we hope by next week your case will be closed and you will be back home. We don't wish to persecute you. We're just waiting for the election to be over and for the appointments of court officials to be reconfirmed. If Mr. Mousavi wins, it will have a positive effect on your case. Only please, if you're summoned to court again, keep silent and don't even smile. If they think you're happy, they will come down harshly on you."

"I wish you success," the professor said. "I've thought a lot about why God has chosen the two of you. There are hundreds of people who distribute Bibles and promote Christianity in Tehran, but none has received the publicity you have. Everybody talks about you. They've made heroines out of you. Your pictures are on TV every day. Why hasn't this happened before?"

"I know the answer to that," I replied. "Think about it."

"I will," the professor said. "Good luck."

"And to you," I said as the professor left the room.

| | |

Marziyeh

After these sessions, Mr. Mosavat told us that these were our last interrogations. Separately, Maryam and I had the same reaction: If that's the case, then there's no reason to keep us separated any longer. At our request, I was allowed to move out of the cell with Munis and Mahtab—leaving with hugs and tears of farewell—and in with Maryam and Fereshteh. In the four years Maryam and I had been friends, this was the longest we'd ever gone without seeing each other. At the doorway to Maryam's cell, we fell into each other's arms, sobbing with happiness. "Come on, come on," the guard said curtly, "get on with it and get inside the cell." We also asked for a Bible and a television in our room. We got the TV, but not the Bible.

We had stopped trying to hide the flowers and crosses we'd been making for each other. When I entered the cell, the first things I saw, decorating the whole space, were the crosses and other tokens I'd left for Maryam. Along with Fereshteh, we kept up our handicraft once we were back together, and taught ourselves to make flowers out of disposable teacups to add to our collection.

These diversions helped pass the endless hours. The television was a help as well, though we had no satellite channels, only government-controlled stations that spewed propaganda and regime-approved Islamic programming. Of course, we didn't have access to any of the coverage of our case that our sisters and the professor had spoken about. We would have liked to see what the TV was reporting.

Because the only people we saw regularly were the guards, their attitude toward us had a big effect on how we felt. Some of the guards were friendly. They confided in us that they didn't like what they had to do but were desperate for a job to support their families. Some asked about Christianity and asked us to pray for them, which we were always happy to do. Others, though, were mean. There were times when the rudeness and petty cruelty wore us down and made us angry in spite of ourselves.

One afternoon, the guard we'd nicknamed Grumpy said she was taking us to make phone calls. After we put on our blindfolds and followed her to the telephone, she handed Maryam a number and said it was the only one she was allowed to call. The number was for my sister, Elena. When Maryam tried to explain the mix-up, the guard shouted at her, though eventually she let her call the right number.

When my turn came, the guard played the same game, handing me the number from our apartment and saying it was the only number I could call. "That's our apartment," I said. "There's nobody there."

"You're lying to me!" the guard scolded.

"I'm not a liar," I answered back. "I'm in prison for telling the truth."

The argument escalated into a shouting match, though finally the guard realized her mistake and let me call my sister. But the argument triggered a physical reaction in me and I started to feel very uncomfortable. After speaking to Elena for only a moment, I had to cut short the call and go back to the cell. There, I tried to rest, but my head was pounding, my back was on fire, and I started shaking and gasping for breath. Maryam and

Fereshteh called for the guard, who was suddenly afraid she would get in trouble for causing this attack. They took me to the clinic, where the doctor gave me a shot and put me on oxygen. The shot stopped my shaking, but the oxygen was only partly effective because the flow was restricted in order to conserve the oxygen supply.

| | |

A few days later, just before lunch, Maryam went to the toilet room to wash her hands. Usually, the windows in the corridor were closed, but this time one was open and it protruded into the hallway. Blindfolded, Maryam slammed into the window full tilt, the corner of the frame striking less than half an inch from her eye. The force knocked her flat on the ground. Her guard, the woman we had nicknamed Ghost, rushed over to see what was wrong. "You should be more careful in the corridor!" she snapped. "You should have looked through a gap in the blindfold."

That remark infuriated me. "That's ridiculous!" I said. "The corridor is so narrow that two people can barely pass with the windows closed. Then you open the windows and blindfold us!"

The Ghost was so upset and distracted that she didn't realize that Fereshteh and I had come running at the sound and were in the corridor for the first time ever without our blindfolds.

The three of us helped Maryam back to our cell. Her eye and lip were already swelling and discolored. In a few minutes, the side of her face and head were one massive bruise. When the Ghost offered to take her to the clinic, she declined. The Ghost was one of the better guards, and Maryam didn't want to get her in trouble. Besides, based on past experience, the clinic wasn't likely to do her much good. Fereshteh and I put ice on the injury instead.

We wrote to the head of the prison, asking to be returned to Ward 2 in the public section. We said there was no reason to keep us in 209 if our interrogations were finished. We complained about Grumpy and about Iron Woman, who was also hateful.

The prison warden soon had bigger concerns than our letters. On June 12, 2009, the Iranian presidential election took place, with Mr. Mousavi favored by many to win. Yet as the day went on, Iranian TV reported that Mr. Ahmadinejad had taken the lead and held it, reminding viewers all the while that the regime was dedicated to truth and accuracy in the election. Hours later, the ministry of the interior announced that Mr. Ahmadinejad had been reelected. Even the filtered and distorted news we were allowed to see made it clear that the people would challenge the results and there would be protests. Both Mr. Mousavi and Mr. Karroubi denounced the election process, accused the Ahmadinejad government of massive election fraud, and vowed to contest the results. Angry citizens flooded the streets and their peaceful protests soon turned into fiery demonstrations.

A couple of days later, we were told we were leaving Ward 209. Whether the immediate reason was our letters, outside pressure, or something else, we never knew. It was probably due to the fact that, within hours, hundreds of people arrested in the election protests overran the cells of Ward 209. We knew that the Lord was ordering events according to His will.

We weren't sure whether we were being released or simply going back to our old cell in Ward 2. Fereshteh was happy for us that we were leaving, but sorry to lose our company, as we were sad to lose hers.

When the time came, a guard walked us across the yard to the public section and back into Ward 2. It was the first time in two months we'd walked outside without blindfolds. As we were being processed back into the ward, an elderly guard asked if we were political prisoners.

"We came from 209, but we're not political prisoners," Maryam told her. "We're accused of being Christians."

"Really? I didn't know that was a crime."

"We converted."

The guard's face puckered in disapproval, like she'd just bitten a lemon. "Shame on you! Couldn't you commit a better crime?"

We went through the security search and changed back into our own clothes, leaving behind the baggy men's prison uniforms that looked so hilarious. Then we ran up the stairs to Ward 2, eager to see the many dear friends who had been absent from our lives but held fast in our hearts and prayers. The thirty-eight days we'd been gone seemed like two lifetimes.

CHAPTER 16

A DIFFERENT FREEDOM

Marziyeh

It was a joyful homecoming. As soon as Maryam and I walked through the barred door into Ward 2, we met Vida in the corridor. She hugged us excitedly and announced our arrival to the rest of the ward. Our friends surged forward to welcome us: Shirin, Silva, Sepideh, Tahereh, and others crowded around with hugs and greetings. After the isolation of 209, returning to the public area of Evin Prison felt almost like being free. The noise and commotion were wonderful.

"How pale you look," someone said. "How tired."

"Your faces seem swollen," said another. "Did they beat you?"

"No," we assured them, "no one beat us. They only asked lots of questions."

There had been changes in the ward during the five and a half weeks we'd been away. Mrs. Pari had been paroled. Our friend Arezoo had been freed. She told Rozita that her freedom was the answer to my prayers for her. Dear, mixed-up Mercedeh had been released as well. The plaintiff against her, who had seemed so unmovable, had come to the prison one day and waived her complaint. Mercedeh danced and screamed with joy at the news, and then ran around telling everybody it was a miracle that happened because of our prayers to Jesus. Her friend Setare and her former lover, Nazanin, were also free. We worried about them, wondering where they were and what they were doing, how they were coping with the wounds on their bodies and the even more painful scars on their hearts. Our comfort was in knowing that God was looking after them.

Mercedeh had been desperate to get out of prison. Some days she had screamed at God, demanding, "Why can't I get out of this hellhole? Why can I see only a little square of sky in the courtyard? Will I ever see the whole thing again?" It is the universal lament of prisoners everywhere: seeing only a little square of sky reminds them of their isolation from the world and makes them long for more.

We had always told Mercedeh that getting out from behind the prison walls wasn't enough. She also had to escape the inner prison of her meth addiction. Now that God had delivered her from the first prison, we kept praying she would also be released from the second one.

The leader in Ward 2, Mrs. Mahjoob, who had welcomed us on our first day at Evin, had been transferred to Ward 3, where the psychological prisoners lived. Her replacement was Mrs. Ghaderi, a quiet, capable woman whom most of our friends considered an improvement. Mrs. Imani, always arguing about the telephone, was in a different room. The guards had agreed to move her once a month because she was so disruptive. Our friend Rozita was now the telephone monitor, and she spent most of her day in a chair beside the phones, trying to keep other prisoners from arguing and fighting over who could talk and for how long.

We had our old bunks in Room 1. As we settled in, we learned about prisoners who'd arrived while we were away. Some had been arrested for associating with the opposition during the election—the aftermath was still stirring up lots of controversy. This "association" could be nothing more than receiving an e-mail from a person or organization who had supported Mousavi, the candidate many Iranians thought had rightfully won. Some prisoners took Ahmadinejad's reelection very hard, because they had hoped a new leader would mean their freedom.

One of our new neighbors was Sousan, a quiet, older *mujahideen* woman with white hair and a dry sense of humor. Her offense was being a member of the *mujahideen* and proudly announcing that fact to anyone who would listen to her. "I talk about the *mujahideen* everywhere I go, and I'm not afraid of anyone!" she proudly told us. "They have no right to stop me." The regime had falsely accused her of being a computer expert exchanging illegal information on the Internet. After forcing a false confession from her, they sentenced this mild-mannered, elderly lady to eight years in prison. She had been in solitary confinement for fifty days before coming to Ward 2.

Another recent arrival was a young, thin girl with a badly bruised face. She and her fourteen-year-old brother had been at a political rally after the elections. When security forces waded into the crowd and started beating her brother, she had tried to defend him. They turned on her, kicking and punching her, and arrested them both. When their father complained to the police, the court dismissed his complaint and ordered the two children to apologize to the soldiers for filing charges against them. They had refused, and the judge sentenced the girl to prison.

"My father told the judge that on the day I'm released, he will personally take me to church and convert me to Christianity," she said. "He told them, 'We detest this Islam of yours, which is just an excuse for injustice and repression. There's no point in allowing my daughter to remain Muslim for even one more day of her life.'"

The court ordered her to be held in custody until she apologized. This is a common demand; otherwise it would be clear that the government had been wrong to arrest her.

It reminded me of my discussions with Fereshteh in 209. When she insisted that the regime's actions had nothing to do with genuine Islam, I had disagreed: "This regime's Islam *is* the true Islam, written in the Koran. But most people never read it for themselves because the text is in Arabic and because they're afraid of being fined or punished if they drop it accidentally or handle it with impure hands or question anything it says. Islam does its best to keep people away from God and a personal relationship with Him because that direct connection threatens the power and control of the religious leaders. They want to keep people in the dark, trusting in religion, so they will continue to depend on them. The criminals who run Iran are running it in accordance with Islamic statutes."

||||

MARYAM

During our weeks of isolation, we had often thought about the children, and now we were anxious to see them. I asked Rozita about Pouneh's son, Alfi, who had been born not long after we arrived at Evin, and a few minutes later she brought him in to see us. His features had changed so much in so short a time! We hugged him happily, and then went down the hall to the room where all the mothers and their young children lived. They were delighted to see us, eager to know where we'd been and what had happened, piling on their questions one after another. We quickly noticed that Aboubakr and his mother were missing. When Aboubakr turned three, the authorities took him away and sent his mother downstairs to live with the other drug addicts. Her heartache must have been almost unbearable—worse even than being in prison. Would she ever see her child again? There was no way to know. Now that he was in the hands of the authorities, they could do whatever they wanted to either one of them without being accountable to anyone.

We always enjoyed visiting the children, especially when we were worn out from thinking and talking about the hardship all around us. Their room seemed peaceful, a separate world from the tense, oppressive atmosphere of the rest of the ward. The little ones were too young to know they were being cruelly punished for crimes they hadn't committed. Nobody asked them, Why were you arrested? Do you have bail? When will you go to court? How long is your sentence? Their only crime was being the children of women on the wrong side of Sharia law. They lived with few toys or little luxuries of any kind, bad food, poor medical care, scant sunshine, no fresh air, no trees or birds or flowers to spark their curiosity, no grass to run through barefoot, no sense of family, surrounded by adult prisoners who were as likely to despise them as pay them any attention.

Later, when we went to visit Alfi again, he was lying on his mother's bed, and she was on the floor in front of him, crying. I sat next to Pouneh and asked what had happened.

"When I phoned my mother today, I learned that the court might sentence me to life in prison as an accomplice to the murder my husband committed. I was angry and terrified and wasn't myself. I put Alfi down for a nap and left the room. When I came back, he'd fallen out of bed. In my anger at the court, I forgot that my son is too young to look after himself. Instead of picking him up and cuddling him, I beat him for falling out of bed. I'm so sorry!"

"You should have asked me to watch him," I said angrily. "I've told you before that whenever you're tired, give Alfi to me and get rid of your anger another way." Alfi seemed fine now, smiling at me and waving his chubby little arms in the air.

When I returned to my room and my own bed, I dissolved in tears at the thought of that poor baby's suffering. I felt helpless at such a sad, frustrating situation. I often walked Alfi to sleep at night after dinner, singing hymns to him and praying for him. Pouneh was happy to turn him over to me because she had started romantic relationships with several women downstairs and would rather spend her time with them.

Pouneh seemed truly sorry for losing her temper, but that didn't keep her from lashing out again. One night, after we were in bed, we heard Alfi crying. A little later, Rozita brought him into our room with a very concerned expression. Pouneh had slapped him so hard we could still see her red fingerprints on his face. I calmed him and got him to sleep. The next morning, I confronted Pouneh about what had happened.

"Maryam, I'm so stressed out that I don't know what I'm doing," Pouneh insisted. "God isn't helping me at all. I don't have anybody on the outside to follow up on my case. I'm so tired! And what am I doing with this child in prison anyway?"

"Dear Pouneh," I said sternly, "I understand your situation. I have prayed with you about it, and you promised to leave your difficulties to God. In practice, though, your attitude hasn't changed. There has to be change in your heart in order to see God's presence in your life. If you're forgiven, God will help you, and your problems will be solved. Being frustrated with God won't help you. Besides, the way you treat Alfi makes God angry. You have to be more careful with your son."

We prayed together again. All I could do was hope for the best and keep praying that God would work in Pouneh's heart.

| | |

Marziyeh

Inmates typically arrived at Ward 2 with few possessions, often little more than their clothes and a handful of grooming items. Tahmasebi was a different story. She moved into our ward from downstairs with so much stuff that the guards gave her three beds to store it all. She must have had connections in high places to get that much space when others were sleeping on the floor.

Tahmasebi was only thirty, but had already served thirteen years of a life sentence for smuggling drugs. She was a muscular, masculine-looking woman with the calloused hands of a manual laborer. She was from Tabriz, famous around the world for its handmade carpets, and had a strong Azeri accent. Tahmasebi worked as the stockroom clerk at Evin and had taken samples of everything that passed through her work area over the years, including a collection of dolls that attracted lots of attention. She lined them up on one of her beds and carefully covered them with a satin sheet. Though at first other prisoners resented her for taking so much room, the dolls, hangings, and other decorations she put up made the place more attractive for everybody. Tahmasebi had a miniature forest of potted plants and flowers that transformed part of the room into a pleasant little garden.

She was a hard woman to get to know at first. She got up very early and was away at her job all day. She returned at night, made a cup of tea, watched television, and talked only with Rozita and Mrs. Ghaderi. Longtime inmates like Tahmasebi claimed special privileges and tended to mix only with other long-timers. After a few nights, Rozita introduced us to her as the "faith prisoners."

"You're lucky to have God on your side," she said.

"God is on your side too," I replied.

"I don't think so, my dear. God doesn't like me at all."

"Tahmasebi, God loves you and has not forgotten about you."

Tahmasebi practiced the daily Islamic prayer ritual of *namaz*, kneeling on her white mat and wearing a long, white *chador*. Yet for all her display of piety, it seemed routine, without any feeling or love of God.

One day when I was washing clothes, Tahmasebi came in to talk with me. "I don't think you value freedom," she said. "Why do you insist on defending your faith and giving these people an excuse to keep you here? All you have to do is tell them what they want to hear and you'll be free. If you were in my shoes, you'd know how precious that opportunity is! I've been here for thirteen years, and day and night my only dream is to be free. You can have freedom anytime you want, yet you stubbornly refuse."

"I understand your position," I said. "Thirteen years is almost half your life. You have every right to feel tired and hopeless. But my life and Maryam's life are dedicated to God. For us, freedom makes sense only in the context of our relationship with Him. If I can't live and act according to the principles of my faith, then I'm not free, whether I'm in prison or outside. Real freedom means being allowed to follow the faith you choose, not having to lock it up or hide it in a cage. In here, I'm free because the regime can't force me to abandon my faith for theirs."

This answer got Tahmasebi's attention. "I don't understand," she said. "What kind of faith is it that erodes your freedom and forces you to spend your young life locked away here?"

"It's pure love," I explained. "When you are in love with God, when you live with Him and He becomes your world, the problems of this world become unimportant. The only thing that matters is to be with your love—with God—even inside a prison. They have imprisoned only our bodies; they can't imprison our souls. My faith and beliefs are still mine. As long as I have God, I am free."

"I still don't understand," Tahmasebi said. "You are so lucky to have such faith. At least you're sure God loves you."

"I believe God loves you, too, Tahmasebi. More than you can imagine."

A few nights later, I dreamed that I was handing out fish to all the prisoners, and Tahmasebi wanted the biggest one. I wasn't sure what the dream meant, but I thought it could mean that Tahmasebi was in for a big surprise. At breakfast that morning, I told Tahmasebi about the dream and announced to the whole room that it meant she would be released within six months.

Prisoners were transferred both from prison to prison and from room to room within a prison. I told Tahmasebi, "This room is the last one you will be held in before you have your freedom."

Everybody was astonished at such a bold and outrageous prediction. "I appreciate your sympathy," Tahmasebi said, "but I've heard this sort of thing many times before. I'm serving a life sentence, and I will not be freed."

Rozita turned to Tahmasebi. "You had better believe Marziyeh," she said. "I have every confidence in her dreams and her faith. She's predicted the release of several prisoners, and every one of her predictions has come true." Then to me she added, "In fact, it's high time you had a dream about me!"

"My dear Rozita," I said, "I'm not a fortune-teller. God reveals these predictions to me. It isn't my word, it's God's. All I can do is pray for these people and for you."

"Why does God answer your prayers and not ours?"

"God hears the prayers of the faithful and always answers. But only according to His plans, not ours."

Thirteen years behind bars had given Tahmasebi the physical strength and resilience to survive and endure. Others didn't withstand the conditions as well, and their spirits were broken by threats and abuse from the government.

Kianoosh was a young woman who had saved some antigovernment news reports on her office computer after the elections. She had not subscribed to the stories and didn't know where they had come from. But because the security forces found them on her hard drive, she was charged with using the Internet to spread the word about postelection protests.

When she first arrived at Evin, all she did was sit in a corner and cry. She finally opened up a little, but remained very quiet and kept to herself. The authorities told her that if she wanted to be released, she had to make a video confessing that she had sent e-mails to friends and relatives asking them to take part in the protests. She did as they ordered but told me she regretted doing it.

"Why did you confess?" I asked. "They'll surely use it against you later on, and they may not even release you now, despite their promise."

"I couldn't refuse," she said, shaken and angry. "They scared me to death. They said if I didn't cooperate, they'd keep me in prison and pass a heavy sentence on me. I had to repeat what they told me to say."

I was afraid she might also have "confessed" to other crimes that she didn't tell me about. She was newly married and worried that her husband would leave her. She spoke to him every day and came back from each call red-eyed from crying. She had overheard some of our conversations about Christianity, and she asked us to pray for her. "Your prayers calm me down," she said.

| | |

MARYAM

The conversations Kianoosh heard were some I'd had with Mrs. Arab, whose bed was next to mine. We sometimes talked late into the night. I had met Mrs. Arab before Marziyeh and I went to Ward 209. She was an unusually generous person who bought food for the poorest prisoners. She was also expert at knitting. Though we had tried to resume our friendship with her when we returned to Ward 2, she seemed to avoid us.

One day, I asked Mrs. Arab to teach me some knitting patterns. As she demonstrated the designs, she said, "I've heard that you and your friend talk a lot about Christ. I've seen you praying for other prisoners and being kind to them, but I've avoided getting close to you."

"We noticed that," I said. "We figured you hated us because we were Christians. Many people here consider us unclean and *najes* [untouchable], and so they shun us."

"I never hated you," Mrs. Arab insisted. "On the contrary, I was envious of your faith. Yes, I heard that you are untouchable because you abandoned Islam, but I always defended you and asked your critics how they can be so sure of their own piety. In my view, you two girls have more faith than those of us who consider ourselves Muslims.

"To tell you the truth, I knew that one day you'd talk to me about Christ, and that's why I was avoiding you. I was afraid you would influence me, and I didn't want that to happen."

"Why?" I asked, genuinely puzzled. "I've heard you are a pious woman. If you have genuine faith in the path you've taken, why should you be afraid to talk to me?"

"I come from a completely Muslim background," Mrs. Arab said. "I can never turn my back on that. But I also respect Christians and believe everyone should be free to practice their own faith. Islam has special meaning for me. Even so, I would like for you to pray for me and my problems. I think God hears your voice. But please don't speak to me about Christianity. I don't want to have any doubts."

"Don't worry," I said with a smile. "I'm sure that if God has chosen you and wants to reveal His truth to you, He doesn't need me to do it. But if you lose your Islamic faith by talking to others or reading the Bible, then that belief is not through faith but through fear, and you're better off without it." I prayed as we walked together in the courtyard. When I finished, Mrs. Arab was crying.

"I'm afraid because I feel Christ wanting to talk to me," she admitted. "Years ago, my son was kidnapped and held for millions in ransom. After several months, the situation seemed hopeless. One rainy night, I passed by a building where a man stood at the door. 'Do you have a problem?' he asked. I told him I was desperate and didn't know how to pray so that God would hear me.

"The building was a church. The man said, 'You can ask Christ to help you. He will hear your voice. We will pray for you too.' That night, I promised Christ that if my son was released, I would light candles and make charitable donations to the church every year, and I would call my son by the name 'Christ' when we were in private. Three days later, the kidnappers reduced their ransom demands and my son was released.

"I have kept my promises to the church, but have told no one about any of this. When I heard you and your friend were here for your faith in Christ, it made me shudder. To me it was another sign from Jesus."

Sometime later, Mrs. Arab stopped me in the courtyard during a break. "I've thought about it, and I want you to talk to me about Christ. Who is He? Why should I know about Him? What does He want from me?"

I shared my Christian testimony with Mrs. Arab, and she and I agreed to pray for each other every day. As her understanding of Christianity deepened, Mrs. Arab got more worried. "I don't feel worthy of getting close to Christ," she said. "I have committed many sins. I'm afraid of meeting Jesus."

The idea of God as a benevolent Father who forgives all our sins is entirely foreign to many Muslims, who've been taught all their lives that

God is a God of retribution and punishment. Over time, more prayer and discussion helped Mrs. Arab understand. She promised she would find a Bible when she was freed and was very excited about taking part in a church service in the future.

| | |

As the postelection protests intensified, the prison became more crowded than ever. The rate of arrests skyrocketed, while the number of women released on parole slowed to a trickle. Women were jammed so tightly into the cells that there was scarcely room to move at night. The air became even more stale, and the smell of so many bodies in close quarters was sickening. Many new prisoners, especially young girls, were sent to our room because we'd gotten a reputation for being able to calm newcomers down and make them less afraid. When other prisoners didn't want to hear their crying or answer their questions anymore, they sent them to "the Christian girls." Marziyeh and I liked meeting new arrivals because they brought the latest news from outside. Since the protests had intensified, our TV and newspapers had been cut off. Even telephone privileges were restricted. We were always eager for updates.

One night, after lights out, Shirin Alam Hooli rushed into our room and said that two girls had just been transferred from Ward 209. She wanted us to come introduce ourselves. We followed her through the dark hallway to a cell where the young women sat in a corner on the floor, still dressed in the Islamic covering they'd had to wear on their walk from 209. A knot of women crowded around, pelting them with questions.

We worked our way through the cluster and introduced ourselves. The girls said their names were Maedeh and Magda. Maedeh immediately asked, "Are you the Christian girls?" We said we were. "I've heard a lot about you from Fereshteh."

"Were you in Fereshteh's cell in 209?" I asked excitedly. "How is she? Does she still have her TV? What happened to her court hearing?" I was so happy to hear about my dear friend and former cellmate that I rattled off questions faster than Maedeh could answer.

When I finally gave her a moment's reprieve, she smiled and said, "Yes,

Fereshteh told me she was cellmates with you. She was very upset to be separated from you and talked about you day and night. And yes, she still has her TV.

"Before I was with her, I was in a different cell in 209, and I saw the messages you had written on the walls—your names and the charges against you. How did you do it?"

"We marked in the fresh paint with yogurt lids."

Maedeh went on, even more animated than before. "Were you also at the Vozara Detention Center? Magda and I spent a few days there, where the walls and even the ceiling had messages like 'Christ is the Savior,' and 'God is love.' They gave us a feeling of peace during some very frightening days, and we wondered who'd left them there."

"Yes, we did that," Marziyeh said. "We spent fifteen days at Vozara." Maedeh was very interested in Christianity and asked a lot of questions. She had visited a church and felt joy listening to the prayers and hymns, even though she didn't understand the language. Eventually, we shared some stories of our lives and our faith journeys with each other, and we prayed together. After a while, Maedeh and Magda were released.

Maedeh was a great example of God's love and power even in situations that seem hopeless. If we hadn't been in prison, we wouldn't have had the chance to leave our messages at Vozara and Ward 209. If Maedeh hadn't been in prison, she never would have seen them and we never would have met her. What looked like a failure by worldly standards was a great victory for Christ: His message proclaimed under the very noses of a regime desperate to stop it.

CHAPTER 17

A WATCHING WORLD

Marziyeh

Our conversation with Maedeh was another reminder of how God had moved us on from what we *thought* we should be doing to what He wanted us to do. We had hosted two home churches and distributed twenty thousand Farsi New Testaments, evangelizing while avoiding the regime. It was a slow process. Now that we were in prison, we could talk openly about our faith. Whereas before we had searched for people to speak to, now they came looking for us: "Go see the Christian girls!" The very prison system that tried to silence us was now our megaphone: Our arrest, our story, and our message of faith were news around the world. Our interrogators were helping us share the gospel!

As remarkable as that situation was, God never seemed to run out of new surprises. When we got back to Ward 2, the gossipy old woman we called Mommy had been moved to a new spot in the room, away from the door and into a back corner, to try to keep her from stirring up trouble. It didn't help much. She kept telling stories about inmates, spreading rumors, and trying to turn one prisoner against another. It seemed like this was her way of feeling important.

Her big mistake came from crossing Tahmasebi, whose stature as a long-timer made her fearless in standing her ground. A new girl, named Mahnaz, was in on drug charges. For some reason, she came to live with us on the second floor instead of downstairs with the rest of the addicts. Encouraged by Mommy, she bullied the other women, the way the addicts were used to treating one another.

One day, Tahmasebi, who was very fastidious about cleanliness and about her big stash of personal belongings, saw Mahnaz leaning on her bed. That caused an argument that later grew into a full-fledged fistfight. When we heard a lot of yelling and ran into the hallway, we saw Tahmasebi holding Mahnaz by the throat with one hand, like a cat holding a mouse, and furiously slapping her face with the other. She was so angry and so strong that the rest of us were powerless to stop her. Finally, her anger spent, Tahmasebi let go, saying, "No more bullying from you. This is it! One more step out of line and I'll deal with you permanently."

She knew that Mommy had encouraged Mahnaz's behavior. Walking to the door of Mommy's room, Tahmasebi added, "Let me warn everybody who fans the flames of these troubles: Stop it. Immediately. I don't care how old they are, or how long they've been here. From now on, I will deal with them the same way."

The rest of us in the room discussed whether we should complain directly to Mrs. Rezaei, the warden of the women's prison. Many of us had tried to reason with Mommy; we had tried to befriend her and had endured her lies and slander countless times. Furthermore, we had seen her one night walking briskly and easily in the hallway when she thought no one was looking—her whole "I can barely walk" routine was just an act! Another way of getting attention! When we shared the idea of a formal complaint with Rozita and a few others, they were ecstatic.

When Mommy caught wind of our plan, she rushed to give Mrs. Rezaei her side of the story first, hoping the warden would make a decision on the spot and refuse even to see us. But we got our appointment anyway. Inmates waited hours in the hall outside the warden's door for a meeting that might last ten minutes at most. When our turn came, we entered a large, comfortable office decorated with plants and carvings. There was a big desk with several large leather armchairs in front of it. Mrs. Rezaei was a tall, slim woman with a welcoming face and a calm manner. We knew from experience that prison officials were more careful with political prisoners because they were more likely than others to spread the news of how they were treated. Our recent notoriety on TV and on the Internet made our treatment even more important.

Mrs. Rezaei invited us to sit down, pretending not to know why we were there. She was a very good actress.

I explained that the woman we called Mommy constantly caused disturbances and breakdowns of peace and calm in our room. She was addicted to talking behind other people's backs and turning women against each other. "We're sure you have heard of the fistfights she has caused recently in our ward," I said.

"She also has a habit of telling new prisoners all about the other inmates," Maryam added. "We don't actually mind that, because she always tells them we're here because we are Christians. This makes the newcomers curious, and they always want to know more about Jesus and Christianity." This was true. We knew many of the guards didn't like the fact that we talked about Christianity and were very sensitive about the issue. Privately, we knew that Mommy, as irritating as she was, was also helping us. In spreading her gossip about us, Mommy spread the word to every newcomer about "the Christian girls" and made them want to know more about our message.

Mrs. Rezaei thought for a moment. "You are absolutely right about this old woman," she said. "She's too old to change her behavior. The only solution I can see is to move her to another room. I will order the change."

Later that evening, someone came in and said to Mommy, "You are moving to another room immediately."

Mommy was incredulous. "Never!" she sputtered. "Who has ordered this?"

"Mrs. Rezaei."

Mommy bolted for the warden's office, but the order stood. She would be moved away from the political prisoners and in with the murderers.

Mommy's next tactic was to delay the move as long as possible, but the guards would have none of it. Miraculously, by the end of the day, Mommy was gone for good. Everyone in our section was happy, and they showered Maryam and me with thanks for doing what had seemed impossible.

| | | |

Our friend Mrs. Arab returned from her parole. It was normal for women who had been locked up for a while, and who had families, to get a temporary parole to visit their relatives. As strongly as Mrs. Arab had defended Islam, she was getting more and more interested in Christianity since her son had been released by his kidnappers after she prayed to Jesus. She told me she was still in prison partly because her husband, an Islamic fanatic she had left years before, was jealous of her success in the rice trade and was using his government connections to keep her behind bars until she agreed to go back to him.

One night, not long after she returned to Evin, Maryam and I had a long talk with Mrs. Arab about Jesus. The next morning, she said she had dreamed about Him. Later that day, when she came back from the cultural center, she said she had a secret to share with us after lights out.

When the guards closed the cellblock for the night, Mrs. Arab called us to her bed. From underneath her pillow she pulled out a book of short excerpts from the Bible. With tears streaming down her face, she said she had found it in a stack of unused books in the cultural center library.

"When I opened it, I couldn't believe what I had," she said. "The sentences were talking to me. I felt like this was God's way of answering my questions about Him."

It was another amazing reminder that God has His own way of doing things. Mrs. Arab hid the book under her pillow and read from it every night from then on.

| | | |

MARYAM

We had now been imprisoned for nearly six months, including two weeks at the Vozara police station and thirty-eight days in isolation in Ward 209. We still had not met with a lawyer who was in a position to represent us in court, and still had not seen the charges against us in writing. We had come to terms with the fact that there was nothing else we could do to gain our freedom. Christian activists were calling for our release, faithful believers around the world were praying, and (we later learned) influential people were working behind the scenes to help us. But it was all in the Lord's hands. We had to trust the next step to Him. Rather than worrying about our release, we focused on getting through each day and reaching out to our fellow prisoners with encouragement and compassion.

In the outside world, our story had become international news and seemed to get bigger every day. We'd heard about this during our most recent interrogation. New arrivals now recognized us from TV and Internet reports. Some greeted us like entertainment personalities. We didn't care about the celebrity; the advantage to us was that it made new prisoners seek us out and ask us questions about our faith. In an alien environment where they were disoriented and afraid, our familiar faces attracted them.

One example was a woman who came into our room one night after lights out. The area was packed with bodies as usual, so that she had to find a spot on the floor. We heard her crying and saying, "I don't belong here with all these criminals!" Later, she started crying again, making an irritating noise like she was trying to get attention. We made a sign to Rozita that we'd like to talk to her. When Rozita signaled her response, Marziyeh and I went to sit beside the woman on the floor in the dark.

As we sat down, I took the woman's hands in mine. Her face was swollen, probably from a beating. She grasped my hands in return and said, "I'm so afraid, I'm losing my mind! I can't sleep. I'm in here because of a mistake. If my husband could have paid my bail, I wouldn't be spending the night with these prisoners. I'm afraid of them."

"All prisoners are not criminals," I said softly. "Many of the people here are political prisoners or have been arrested on financial charges. They're normal people. You don't have to be afraid of them."

"Are you a political prisoner?" the woman asked. "I like you."

I laughed. "No, my friend and I have been jailed because of our belief in Jesus Christ."

The woman sat up straight with a start. "You're the two girls on Voice of America TV! I thought I'd seen you somewhere. My husband and I follow the news about you on TV and the Internet every day. I never imagined I'd be seeing you in person. I didn't think they would keep you here with the regular prisoners. Do you know you're famous?"

"Yes," I said, laughing again, "we've heard something about it. So, now do you feel better? If you hadn't come to this prison, you would not have had the chance to meet us." I added, jokingly, "So you see, being in prison isn't all that bad. You're in here with famous people. You don't have to be ashamed of coming to prison and cry about it. In fact, if you keep crying, the long-term inmates will get angry and send you down the hall to sleep with the murderers. This room is the best one in the prison, so you'd better keep quiet."

The woman held on to my hand like a child. "Do something to calm me down," she begged. "I'm so afraid." I prayed for her and told her to try to go to sleep.

As it happened, she was held for only a few days. On the morning of her release, she said, "As soon as I get out, I'm going to tell everybody I saw you in person!"

A few days later, Marziyeh and I were visiting with Shirin Alam Hooli in Room 2 when another new inmate sat down beside us and asked excitedly, "Are you the two Christian girls who are supposed to be executed?" We all laughed at the question, but then we asked how she knew about us and that we were supposed to be executed.

"I saw your photos in the news and on the Radio Farda website. [Radio Farda is the Iranian Farsi language service of Radio Free Europe.] Now here you are, just like in the pictures: one with short hair and one with long hair. I heard there were two Christian girls here, and when I saw you, I realized you're the ones on the news." Then her tone sharpened. "I've heard you will be executed. You'd better think about this. It's not worth it." The woman's comments made Shirin angry, but we decided not to get into a conversation.

Another prisoner, Mrs. Pari, came back from parole with news that her daughter's home church was praying for us. Her daughter was happy that she knew us and hoped we would encourage her mother to open her heart to Christianity.

"I think on some Islamic celebration day you're going to be forgiven," said Mrs. Pari, "because there are lots of campaigns going on saying you should be free. It will be hard for the government to convict you. On the other hand, if they set you free, they will lose face. It would be admitting they were wrong. Therefore, they will issue an official forgiveness." Seeing all the reports about us on the outside had convinced Mrs. Pari to treat us with more respect.

| | |

In my wildest dreams, I never expected to celebrate my twenty-eighth birthday in prison. Yet here I was, and it was a wonderful party. Shirin Alam Hooli had knitted a beautiful bag for me; others made gifts in the craft center or bought them from other inmates. Silva and our friend Marjan sang for me, and Shirin even danced, which no one had seen her do before. Marziyeh's sister had sent her some jewelry to give to me, and my sister had sent a beautiful cross for me to wear as a necklace. Since we had not yet been allowed contact visits, these gifts were smuggled in by families of our friends in prison, who secretly gave them to Rozita during one of her contact visits.

At our meeting with the warden, we had told her that we had not been allowed any contact visits, even though we should have, and she arranged for them after that.

My cross necklace was yet another way to attract the attention of new prisoners. One of a group of new girls stopped me in the courtyard during a break and asked if I was a Christian.

"Yes, I am. Why?"

"I noticed your cross, and I thought you and your friend must be the two famous Christian girls everybody's talking about. Is that right?"

"Yes, that's right. How do you know about us?"

Without speaking, the girl took me by the hand and led me over to the rest of her friends. There were ten girls, all still in their party clothes from when they had been arrested for improper social contact under Sharia law.

"Hey!" the girl shouted to the group. "This is Maryam, the Christian girl we prayed for in church. Can you believe she's here in person?" Her friends crowded around, hugging me and shaking my hand. Shirin Alam Hooli and I sat down to visit with them.

"Most of us are Christians," the girl explained. "We live in Dubai. We were baptized a few months ago and go to church there. We came here for vacation and were invited to a garden party where there were both boys and girls. An hour after the party started, officers came and arrested us all. We're waiting to find out how much our bail is, but nobody knows we're Christians. Please don't tell anybody," she added quietly.

It was exciting to see so many young girls enthused about being Christians. Their biggest worry at the moment was that there were pictures of their baptisms in the cell phones the police had confiscated. If the authorities saw the photos, the girls would be in serious trouble.

"There are two girls in our group who are not Christians," the young woman said. "Would you talk to them?"

Both of these girls recognized me and asked some questions about Christianity. Then one of them said, "Seeing you here is a sign for us. We feel ashamed because we actually are Christians, but are afraid to say so openly, and many things inside our hearts still haven't changed."

I spoke to them and encouraged the whole group. The next day, they paid their bail and left. As they were going, one of them said, "It seems like the only reason for us coming to prison was to meet you."

By now, our case had been mentioned in several official reports that were circulated by Amnesty International, the United Nations, and the European Parliament about the brutality of the Iranian government. On August 8, 2009, online petitions were launched on our behalf. On August 14, Jubilee Campaign USA submitted a formal petition to the United Nations Working Group on Arbitrary Detention, requesting help for us. In their petition, Jubilee referred to a May 27 declaration from the European Union condemning Iran's discrimination against Christians in general and us in particular.

We knew the Iranian judges were much more lenient when accused prisoners begged them for mercy and made them feel important. Our elderly friend Sousan, sentenced to eight years, had had her term reduced to one year after her sister went to court and begged the judge on her knees for help. Marziyeh and I agreed that we could never humiliate our faith in that way. We had absolutely nothing to apologize or ask forgiveness for. Now God was honoring our steadfastness by sending the whole world to help us.

CHAPTER 18

WAITING FOR NEWS

Marziyeh

Ever since the postelection protests, the whole country was in chaos. The rest of the world had no idea how angry the Iranian people were at being cheated, because foreign reporters were banned from showing the crowds in the streets or documenting any of the opposition. A few brave citizens made videos with their cell phones and broadcast the truth to the world. The security police tried to keep a lid on the uprising by cutting off communication inside the country and censoring the news even more than usual.

Within the walls of Evin Prison, the overcrowding went from extreme to unimaginable, with prisoners packed in so tightly that guards couldn't even enter our rooms. Many women had no bed and nowhere to store their belongings. We had to stop using windowsills as storage shelves and drying racks because new prisoners had to have the space. Their blankets completely covered the floors; at night it was hard for everyone to find room to stretch out. The heat and stench of so many bodies was worse than ever. We heard that hundreds of young girls arrested in the streets were downstairs in the drug addict ward, and that hundreds more were being held in schools because the prisons couldn't take any more.

We used to read the *Hayat-e No* and *Etemad-e Melli* newspapers every day, but now they were banned. The only hint we had at the time of the scope of the protest, other than the prison filled to bursting, was through the censored stories on state TV. It was such big news that even they had to show some of it. For a while, we also got news from phone calls: friends on the outside told of hundreds of protestors, especially young people, being murdered by the regime. Then all the prison telephones were disconnected; our last source of information was cut off.

Many prisoners accused of fraud and other nonviolent crimes had expected to be released under the newly elected administration. They had started packing their bags and waited for the prison doors to be opened wide. Instead, the investigation of all charges ground to a halt. No one was getting out; no cases were being moved through the courts.

Our friends Tahereh and Kamila were experts at ferreting out bits and pieces of news. They were the first ones to learn that the Ashraf camp in Iraq, where so many *mujahideen* prisoners had friends and family, had been attacked by Iraqi soldiers, killing or injuring many of the refugees there. Tahereh, a kind, elderly woman with serious eye problems, had no word about her children. She felt sure that the Iraqi and Iranian government officials had worked to distract the attention of the world from the internal political demonstrations by slaughtering innocent people in this Iraqi camp.

After a while, Tahereh learned that her children were safe, but the Iraqi government was now demanding that the refugees leave the country or be sent back to Iran by force. Some refugees, including Tahereh's sister, started a hunger strike, hoping to get the attention of the United Nations or some other international body that could help them. The Iranian government was now claiming that the *mujahideen* themselves were behind the protests all along. It was all part of the regime's plan to arrest *mujahideen* and their supporters without any evidence and send them away to be tortured.

As the crisis in Ashraf played out, the authorities told Tahereh she was being transferred to another prison with a reputation even worse than Evin's. She had appealed her five-year sentence, and though the appeal had not yet been heard, she was being transferred anyway. The doctors had warned that she needed eye surgery right away or she might go blind. Moving was a hardship for her, and there was no reason for it. Maryam and I joined a large number of Tahereh's friends who complained to Mrs. Rezaei about the order. Even enormous Mrs. Soraya waddled down to the office to show her support. She liked Tahereh, and she would never miss an opportunity to complain to Mrs. Rezaei. The women's warden made a call, but the person in charge at the other prison was at lunch. She spoke with our head warden, Mr. Sedaghat, who he said he knew nothing of any orders to transfer Tahereh. We helped her pack, then hugged her and cried at the thought that we might never see her again. That afternoon, officers from the other prison arrived with a written order and took her away. We lost a kind and faithful friend, and the children down the hall lost a substitute grandmother who loved them very much. The little ones missed her as much as we did.

| | |

To balance out this sad departure, there was some rare good news for a couple of our friends. The first was Tahmasebi, who had served thirteen years of a life sentence and thought I was crazy for predicting she would be free in six months. Now she was free! When word of her pardon came, no one could believe it, especially her. She ran into our room sobbing. Everyone on the ward remembered my dream and the prediction that Tahmasebi would have her freedom.

"Now you can rest assured that God does love you," I said.

One of the other women asked, "Why is it that the Christians' prayers and dreams lead prisoners to freedom?"

"It isn't us," Maryam explained. "This is a victory for the Lord. He is only using us to do His work." God was showing Tahmasebi a miracle in her own life. She was convinced that her freedom was impossible, but for God, nothing is impossible.

Once a prisoner knows she will be released, the final few days seem as long and agonizing as all the years before. The paperwork for Tahmasebi had to come from another city; in the meantime, her mother had gone into the hospital with a serious illness. Tahmasebi was desperate to see her mother before she died. After several more days of delay, the prison agreed to let her go with a prison escort to visit her mother in the hospital for a day. The trip made her very happy, and after that she seemed more able to bear the wait.

A few days later, her mother died. Now she hoped to be out in time to attend the burial, but that didn't happen either. Maryam and I decided to hold a memorial service for Tahmasebi's mother in our room. Many of the women were surprised that two Christians would organize a memorial service for a Muslim and conduct it so sincerely.

With her mother's passing, Tahmasebi wondered what she would do once she was free. She had no skills, no money, and a criminal record. She expected her brothers and sisters to sell their mother's belongings and divide the money between them without giving her a share. She had an Islamic temporary marriage with a man who had promised to help her when she was released, but now he said he couldn't because of financial problems. He also had another wife and children who knew nothing about his relationship with her.

She applied for a loan of two million tomans ($1,000) to help her start a business, but her request was denied. We prayed for her, and many of us gave her what little money we could to help her begin her new life. For her years of work in the warehouse, she had earned eight thousand tomans ($4) per month.

As the day of her release approached, the women on the ward threw a party for her, with singing and dancing. Marjan made a cake, and we all signed a card and gave Tahmasebi little presents to remember us by. At last, the great day arrived. Her name was announced to report to the office to be released. We made a double line for her to walk through, showering her with candy and other little treats, singing and dancing with happiness. Maryam and I had also given her a cross some time back. Now she said, "I will keep this cross forever!" We walked her to the door with one last prayer for her safety and success. "I don't know what awaits me," she admitted. Then with a last smile, she turned and was gone through the doors of Evin Prison to the blue skies and fresh air of freedom.

| | |

Only a short time later, our dear friend Silva was the fortunate one. Because she had served only one year of a three-year sentence, she was not optimistic that she would be out anytime soon. Then one day she whispered to Shirin

Alam Hooli, Maryam, and me that she was going to be released after all. A few hours later, her name was called from the loudspeaker. The regime had set her free!

We all shouted and cried with joy. It was a bittersweet time, because as much as we wanted her to go, we would miss her so much. She and Shirin had been cellmates for a year, so parting was especially hard for them. We all sang a song to her, and Soraya honored our tradition of breaking a plate, which symbolized the farewell message of the lyrics: "Go, go, and never come back!"

After Silva left, Maryam and I spent more time than ever with Shirin to help her get over the loss of her closest friend. Shirin, too, heard her name over the loudspeaker from time to time, but it was never good news. All of her close friends hated to hear her name called because we were always afraid it meant more hard questioning. Sometimes she was taken to Ward 209 for a day of interrogation, as we had been, though she was often beaten as the authorities constantly pressured her to turn over names of other members of PJAK.

Even though Shirin had been through some of the most severe torture we'd heard about—hung by her heels, whipped on the soles of her feet, kicked in the stomach until she vomited blood, beaten unconscious for days—she had the will of an ox, and her pride in her Kurdish heritage and loyalty to the PJAK political movement were unshakable.

Shirin's attitude got her in trouble with the guards over the smallest matters. One time, the pipes in the toilet became blocked. It took three days for the plumbers to make repairs. After the repairs were finished, the guards told us we had to take some pills to make sure we didn't get sick from the backed-up pipes. Because our medical care was so incompetent, a lot of us didn't want to take the pills, because we didn't know what they were. Everyone pretended to swallow them, but hid them in our hands and threw them away later. Everyone, that is, except Shirin. She openly refused to swallow the mysterious pills. The guard reported her to the warden, and Mrs. Rezaei summoned her to the office.

Shirin already had a long history of defying prison rules. That, plus the charge against her as an enemy of God—punishable by death—added weight to the smallest incident. But Shirin didn't care. She was a radical, stubborn girl who believed the struggle against Kurdish injustice should be fought in the open. She never considered any other approach. Her tough attitude was a stark contrast to her sensitive personality and big heart.

When a top judge was murdered in Kurdistan, the regime interrogated all the Kurdish prisoners associated with PJAK, including Shirin. They also asked her again if she was ready to repent of her opposition and cooperate with them. Instead of answering their questions, she grilled them about the torture she had endured and demanded they answer for it. Nothing could stop brave Shirin. With her eyes weakening and her hair falling out because of malnutrition, she looked ineffective and helpless. But inside she had the heart of a lion.

We talked with her sometimes about the similarities and differences between her standing up for Kurdish rights and our standing up for Christ. The key difference was that Shirin's fight was personal, while ours was God's will. We didn't oppose her fighting, because her battle was important, but we did oppose her tactics. It was painful to see a young woman so kind and full of life make such a hard sacrifice in pursuing her goals of freedom for the Kurdish people and especially Kurdish women. We encouraged her to stand for the dignity and freedom of her people but not get caught up in politics.

| | |

MARYAM

Every so often, we had groups of official visitors at Evin Prison. Beforehand, the guards would nervously shout at us to clean our rooms, take down our clotheslines, put on our veils, and not eat anything to avoid dropping food on the floor. We had to sit silently on the floor while a herd of strangers walked through, looking at us like we were a museum exhibit or animals at the zoo. Sometimes they were government officials; other times they were foreign visitors or celebrities. They were always taken to the newest, cleanest parts of Evin, which meant that most of them didn't come into Ward 2. Typically, they saw only the cultural center and Ward 3. Still, we had to sit on the floor wearing our veils for hours before a guard would come through shouting, "Finished! The veil is finished!" and that would be the end of it.

New prisoners kept pouring in, even after we thought our cells couldn't possibly hold another body. One new arrival was Zari, a former professional basketball player at least six feet tall, who had been arrested for fraud. Of course, we immediately nicknamed her "Little Zari." Despite her size, she was a simple, sensitive, frightened lady. She had been married only two months and was afraid her husband would divorce her now that she had been arrested; his parents didn't know about her situation, and she was worried what would happen when they found out.

Another new inmate was Shahla, who soon became friends with Shirin, Marziyeh, and me. Shahla was an amazingly happy person, always saying funny, nonsensical things and making jokes. She did hilarious imitations of the different guards, of soldiers marching, and of other people in the prison. She was even entertaining when she cried. She shed so many tears that she had to wipe her face with towels because tissues were soaked in no time.

We also welcomed Mrs. Yadolahi, who said she was a well-known news anchor on one of the satellite TV networks. She actually lived outside the country and had been arrested when she came to Iran to visit. She loved to dance and took it very seriously, closing her eyes and moving in wide, sweeping motions, running across the break area and assuming artistic poses with her hands reaching up to the sky or wrapped around her body.

So many women and girls came and went during our stay in Evin. For every one we've mentioned, there are many more whose stories should also be shared with the world. But it would take another whole book just to tell of their lives, courage, and sacrifice. We hope one day we will have the opportunity to write it in their honor.

| | |

From the earliest days of our imprisonment, we both had serious health problems. Marziyeh had a backache, sore throat, kidney problems, and infected teeth; I had headaches, a terrible earache, and stomach trouble. We were severely undernourished and had almost no exercise and not enough sunlight. At its best, the clinic was no help; sometimes it even made us sicker, and visiting the doctor was always a major ordeal because it required so much bureaucracy and waiting. We felt sick or in pain every day of our imprisonment. At one point, Marziyeh was in bed so much that the ladies teased her with the nickname Sick Saint. Though we tried not to let our infirmities bother us, there were times when we hurt so bad that we had to go to the clinic again in hopes of getting some relief.

For me, one of those times came during the holy month of Ramadan, when devout Muslims must fast from sunup to sundown every day. The morning call to prayer, which had been at 5:00 a.m., was moved to 3:30 a.m., when it was still pitch black. Few prisoners observed the fast, but for the entire month, the meals were served only before dawn or after dark. We continued to avoid the smelly, chemical-laced prison food and bought canned food, jam, and cheese (which we could save for breakfast the next morning) from the shop. The canned food was always some horrible brand sold only in prisons.

Lesbian activity continued at a high level. The government secretly encouraged these relationships to help maintain control and to give the guards leverage: a threat to separate two lovers carried a lot of influence. Some guards themselves had lesbian encounters with the prisoners. This also seemed to be unofficially approved, because their behavior was visible to the security cameras. Relationships and tensions caused fights almost every day. Some altercations were so violent that the guards were afraid to enter the cells to stop them. When a lesbian mother got into a screaming, punching, hair-pulling fight, her children were terrified. Some of us would always try to move the children to a safer place until the fight was over.

| | |

I had never recovered from the terrible stomachache I'd had in 209 or from my burst eardrum. Stomach pains interrupted my sleep nearly every night. I made an appointment with Dr. Kashani, a slim, bad-tempered woman, to ask if my sister could bring me some vitamin tablets. When I arrived for my appointment, the doctor paid more attention to the papers on the desk in front of her than she did to me.

"So what's wrong?" the doctor asked curtly. When I started to explain my problems, the doctor interrupted. "Make it short!"

I told her that the warden had said we could have vitamins in the prison with a doctor's approval.

Dr. Kashani looked up. "What are the charges against you? Which other doctor has seen you?"

"I am in prison because of my belief in Christianity. Dr. Avesta and a few other doctors in Ward 209 have seen me."

"Are you here for your belief in Christianity or for your conversion from Islam?"

"I converted to Christianity eleven years ago."

Dr. Kashani looked back down at her desktop. She never examined me or even touched me. "About your ruptured eardrum, it will get better," she said. "We can't do anything for your stomach here because we don't have any equipment. The issue of bringing vitamins into prison has nothing to do with Mrs. Rezaei. The clinic will decide on such matters. Your condition is not so serious as to need vitamins." Then she yelled to the clerk through the doorway, "Next!"

Our health crisis took an even more dangerous turn when a prisoner came in with a case of swine flu. The crowded cells, poor air circulation, and terrible sanitation gave the virus perfect conditions for spreading. Before long, half the ward had the flu, including Marziyeh. She became so weak she couldn't sit up in bed. The sound of coughing rang out up and down the halls day and night. None of the sick prisoners received any medicine or treatment. I was one of the few who were well enough to try to help the others. I bought milk and asked a friend who worked in the kitchen to warm it, then passed it among the flu victims. I also made tea and honey. That was all some of the women could eat; even those who usually ate the prison food couldn't stomach it when they were this ill. Eventually, the epidemic passed. As far as we know, by the grace of God no one died.

| | |

One week melted into another as we waited in vain for some news of our case. Our lawyer, Mr. Soltani, who had seemed so capable and dedicated to defending our rights, was still in prison. We didn't know when or if we would have a trial. No one seemed to know anything, and no one seemed accountable to anyone. We kept hearing conflicting reports—some questioning whether we'd even broken a law, and others suggesting we would be condemned as apostates and executed.

Iran's civil law specified that religion was a personal decision and that everyone was officially allowed to observe their religion openly. However, it was an offense punishable by death to convert from Islam or to induce someone to convert. To further confuse matters, the part of the national penal code calling for execution of apostates was currently in draft form and not officially approved by the Guardian Council, the Islamic elders who ran the country. Judges were directed to use their personal knowledge of Sharia law to decide matters that weren't specifically covered in the penal code. So if a judge personally thought we were apostates, he could condemn us to death, whether the law was officially approved or not. Or he could keep delaying action on our case until the law was passed and execute us then.

We had to have a new lawyer and decided to try to get Mr. Aghasi, a famous lawyer in Iran. Our sisters met with him, and we talked with him by phone. He agreed to take our case, but as before, he had to get our written permission to represent us. With all the interference from the prison and the court, it had taken poor Mr. Soltani months of fruitless trips, calls, and cajoling to try to complete even that simple step.

Marziyeh asked the social worker at Evin exactly what the procedure was and who should be involved. She told us each to write a letter giving our permission, sign and fingerprint it, and give it to her. A social worker would pass it to Mr. Aghasi in the prisoners' visiting hall. He couldn't visit us to get the letters because without the letters he couldn't visit us. (This, we later learned, is what Americans call a "catch-22.") It wasn't even clear if the court would let us have a lawyer. The "investigations" were still going on, and the intelligence ministry had still not given permission for us to be represented in court.

Also about this time, we had our first contact visit with our sisters since our arrest. Usually, only prisoners who had close ties with the authorities or spent time in the cultural center were allowed these visits, and we had been banned from the center by the director. Even so, we had asked Mrs. Rezaei for permission to have contact visits, and they were approved.

It was so exciting! The morning seemed to drag by more slowly than ever as Marziyeh and I put on our veils, waited in one line after another, and finally got to the visitor area. The few prisoners who were allowed contact visits met their guests in a different place than where normal visits occurred, a big room downstairs furnished with tables and chairs. The guards did what they could to intimidate us and make themselves feel important. One gruffly told us that if we talked to anyone except our visitors, he would cancel our visit. They criticized our *chadors* and said other things to make sure we remembered how important they were and how unimportant we were.

None of that mattered as we entered the room and ran to our sisters—we wrapped our arms tightly around them and never wanted to let go. "Be strong!" we said. "Don't cry!" But we all cried with happiness anyway. We had just sat down together, the four of us, when another self-important guard came over and told us we could only sit in pairs. So we split up, Marziyeh with Elena and me with Shirin. They told us the good news that they had received our letters of permission for Mr. Aghasi and everything looked fine. We should expect to hear from him soon. Knowing that our contact visits would only be once a month for ten minutes each, we talked like crazy.

A guard walked up and stood beside my sister and me. After listening for a moment, he looked at Shirin and said, "If your sister did no wrong, she would not be in jail now."

Shirin stopped talking long enough to look him in the eye and say, "I take pride in my sister!"

This guard had been extremely rude to us in the beginning, but he had softened his attitude over time to the point where he was almost friendly. He looked at Shirin and then said to me, "Well, it wasn't so bad for you to come to prison. You're famous now! A few nights ago, I saw you on the Voice of America, and that was the first time I knew what your charges were." He leaned in a little. "I hope you will get your freedom. Good-bye." Then he walked briskly back across the room.

How many other guards and officials felt the same way, but never had the courage or opportunity to say so? How many have a heart hungry for Christ right now as we write this? O God, keep them safe and reward their longing with Your loving presence in their lives.

CHAPTER 19

BEYOND COMPREHENSION

Marziyeh

There was one other kind of visit available by special request from prison authorities. A *shari'a* visit was a private meeting between a prisoner and her husband. If they could show a marriage certificate, or had a *sigheh* temporary marriage, they were allowed to spend the day together in a large suite in a separate building near the main visiting area. Little Zari, the towering ex-basketball player, missed her husband terribly and was very afraid he would divorce her for being arrested. When she learned that she could have a private meeting with him, she was very happy. She hoped it would make their separation easier and that he would be less likely to leave her.

Too often, unfortunately, a private visit also gave the husband a chance to criticize or threaten his spouse. Naseem had become our friend before we left for 209, and we had grown even closer after we came back. She had been to private visits with her husband, and she explained to Little Zari how the process worked. She had a private visit the same day that Zari did, but hers brought her to bitter tears. Afterward, we saw her sitting in the corridor, crying. We knew she had been imprisoned for murdering her mother-in-law, but we hadn't heard the whole story.

Naseem sobbed, "Everybody tells me, 'You are a simple, stupid woman. Can't you see your husband is betraying you?' But I love him and will do anything for him, even if he's the worst person in the world."

"Dear Naseem," I said, "why do they say that? What has your husband done?"

"He's the real murderer—he killed his own mother! I confessed for his sake because he can't stand prison. He promised to get a pardon for me from his family."

"How could this happen? How could the police not know the truth?"

"One day, he got into an argument with his mother. In a rage, he picked up a kitchen knife and stabbed her, then ran out of the house like he was crazy. The police investigated us both and forced a confession out of us by torture. My husband had always quarreled with his family. Because he had a bad relationship with his brothers and sisters, he knew they would never pardon him, but he was sure they would pardon me. So I took the blame. Now I've been in prison for two years.

"Recently, the police decided to reopen the investigation, because by the way I described the crime scene they suspected I wasn't really there and that my husband was the murderer. I changed my statement so that they know I didn't do it. My husband wouldn't visit me or take my calls for a year. Now that the police suspect him, he visits me every week, and we have a private visit as often as possible so that I won't tell them he's actually the guilty one."

Maryam and I prayed for her and from then on tried to be close when she was lonely and upset. What seemed like an obvious solution to everyone else was hard for her. She couldn't bring herself to accuse her husband, believing it would mean certain death for him.

| | |

So many of the women of Evin were imprisoned unfairly. There were countless stories of women who were only trying to protect themselves, who had been pushed to the breaking point by the ruthless laws that gave men unlimited control over women or who, like Naseem, were locked up because of a convoluted family situation that pressured them into sacrificing their freedom to protect the guilty.

Even some murderers didn't belong there. In any civilized country, these women would be recognized for what they were: mentally ill people who had no idea what they were doing and could not be responsible for their crimes. In Iran, they were treated like animals. They should have been somewhere where they could do no harm and where they could get help for their sickness, not condemned for behavior they couldn't understand or control. Of all the murderers we met at Evin, one is burned into my mind and heart like no other.

Maryam and I heard one night that Soheila Ghadiri had been taken to a solitary cell. This was standard procedure on the night before an execution. It wasn't the only reason for going to a solitary cell, but when anyone went to solitary, we all held our breath. Sometimes one friend from the cell block was allowed to accompany the accused, and sometimes not. Would she come back? Or would we hear of her death the next morning?

Soheila was a disheveled woman who wore filthy rags. Everyone assumed she was insane. She had come to Tehran when she was fourteen with a man who promised to marry her. Once they arrived in the city, he abandoned her. Afraid to return home in disgrace, she lived a vagabond life on the streets, supporting herself by prostitution. After accepting the offer of a seventeen-year-old customer to live with him, she got pregnant and decided to move back onto the streets.

The police arrested her for vagrancy and took her to a health care center because she was pregnant. When the baby was born, Soheila felt she could not allow him to live a life of miserable deprivation as she had, but she saw no way of offering him anything better. She told the health center nurses to keep the baby away from her because she might hurt him. Tragically, they ignored her warning.

When her baby was five days old, Soheila stumbled into the health center office, her hands and arms streaked in blood.

"See," she said in a flat, expressionless voice, "I told you you shouldn't have left him with me." Opening her palm, she handed them her infant son's tiny heart.

Because the boy's father was not available to give his consent that Soheila should live, the court sentenced her to death. She had no family and no one to defend her. In some cases, the court assigns a public defender to help indigent prisoners, but this was not done for Soheila. Finally, the organization One Million Signatures provided her with a lawyer. He found the drug-addicted father, who gave his consent for a pardon. However, Soheila had been with so many men that the court ruled it wasn't possible to know whether the young man was actually the father.

Her lawyer advised her to claim she was insane. Instead, she told the court about living on the streets since she was fourteen, the many men who had abused her, the health care workers who had ignored her warning not to leave the baby with her.

"I'm not insane," she declared. "But I could not stand the thought of my child suffering as I have suffered, enduring the misery and pain I have endured. I was relieved when they put handcuffs on me and took me to prison, because at least now I had a roof over my head and food to eat. I wish I were a turtle. He always has a roof over his head and food for himself. In this world, I've never had a roof. I have nothing to live for."

The morning after Soheila was taken away, we learned that she had been hanged before dawn. Her nightmare of a life was over. She was twenty-eight.

| | |

Farah was an unrepentant murderer of a very different sort. She was a short girl of twenty with a round face, large dark eyes, and a beautiful smile.

"I killed my husband," she said matter-of-factly. "And I do not regret what I have done. I'm just happy that he no longer lives in this world."

At fifteen, she had been forced to marry a wicked cousin that no one liked, in order to get him out of his parents' house. After sex, he regularly beat Farah, leaving scars and broken teeth. She put up with his abuse until he made plans to sell her to one of his friends as a prostitute. On their way to his friend's house, she jumped out of the car, trying to escape. Her husband stopped the car, caught her, beat her unconscious, and left her by the side of the road.

She told her mother that her husband was a psychopath and that she had to have a divorce. "Women have to bear with their husbands," her mother declared. "All married couples have disagreements, but that's no justification for divorce."

She then went to her mother-in-law, who was also her aunt, to beg her for help. "He beats me every day, and one day he's going to kill me!" Farah warned.

The aunt realized that if they divorced, her violent and despicable son would be back in her house. She didn't want that, so she told Farah that her husband was still young and immature, and that with time he would turn into a good family man.

Once the husband heard that Farah was asking for a divorce, he beat her worse than ever. The next time he attacked her, she stabbed him to death with a knife.

"He was lying in a pool of blood in the kitchen," she recalled. "I neither regretted what I'd done nor feared the consequences." She was in prison waiting to see whether her family would agree to forgive her.

Her eyes filled with tears as she finished her story. "Do you believe I'm a murderer?"

"Dear Farah, I don't think you're a murderer," Maryam said, stroking her hair. "You just tried to defend yourself. You are a strong girl who can smile even though she has been so badly tormented."

We told her about Jesus and how He could help her in these hard times. Hers was one of the stories that made us ask hard questions about God. Why should a sweet-spirited, innocent, fifteen-year-old girl have to suffer so much and be driven to murder to save her own life? God's wisdom is always right, always greater than our own, but sometimes it is beyond our comprehension.

| | |

MARYAM

A steady stream of prisoners came and went through Ward 2 at Evin Prison. The courts had resumed their work—even seemingly hopeless cases like Tahmasebi's were resolved—yet our case went nowhere. We knew that there was an international outcry against our arrest and demands from Amnesty International, the United Nations, and other groups that all charges be dropped; that the government of Iran would not risk losing face by acquitting us; that, unlike most other defendants, we refused to change our story or retell it in a way that would give the government an excuse to let us go. The result was an impasse in the courts that had now gone on for months.

One night, with no warning, our names were called on the loudspeaker and we were told to be ready to go to court the next day. Shirin and our other friends worried that we would be convicted or sent back to Ward 209. Marziyeh and I did our best to console them, telling them not to worry and that we were happy to be doing something at last. We still had no assurance that a lawyer had been secured for us, so we assumed we would have to defend ourselves.

The next morning, we reported to the office at 6:00 a.m., wearing our long *chadors* and the silly slippers prisoners had to wear to court. We weren't allowed to have shoes because they were another place to store contraband and also because wearing the oversized, goofy-looking prison slippers was humiliating. We waited in a small, filthy building with other prisoners on their way to court that day, including one who clearly had a bad case of swine flu. The stale air was made even worse by the stench of dried vomit from where drug addicts had thrown up on the walls and by the smell of cigarette smoke. Prisoners didn't all go to court in a group. Instead, we were handcuffed to guards one at a time and driven across town to the courthouse. Marziyeh and I went together because our hearing would be with one judge. We had called our sisters to tell them about our court appearance, and as we pulled out from the prison gate, we saw them waiting in the street to follow us.

We went to the same place as before, Revolutionary Court, Bureau 2, which heard national security cases. As we waited on a bench, wearing our handcuffs, a man with a thick mustache came toward us. We recognized him from photos in the news.

"Are you Miss Rostampour and Miss Amirizadeh?"

"Yes, we are."

"I am Mr. Aghasi, your new lawyer. I'm sorry we haven't met yet, but I'm still trying to get the judge's permission to visit you in prison. Today you will probably only hear the charges against you. The actual court hearing will be another day. I will go in and speak privately with the judge first."

He disappeared into an office and came out a few minutes later. "You don't have a court hearing after all," he explained. "You're here because the deputy prosecutor, Mr. Haddad, wants to speak with you. I told him I was defending you and said I wanted permission to visit you in prison. He said I had to put the request in writing, and I told him I had already done this. He told me I could get the authorization paper for a visit tomorrow. When you go in, be sure to insist that you want a lawyer and that you have given me permission to represent you." Mr. Aghasi then wished us well, said good-bye, and left the building.

Shortly after, Marziyeh and I were called into an office with a sign on the door reading "Deputy Prosecutor." It was a huge room. Like other rooms we'd been to in the courthouse, it was lined with photos of bloody soldiers in battle, martyrs for Islam. Not a good spot for two Iranian girls accused of following Christ. It was a frightening place that knocked the wind right out of our bodies; we could scarcely breathe.

An old man seated behind a desk on a raised platform—the place of power—told us to sit down. We recognized Mr. Haddad from television, with his long gray beard and mustache and penetrating eyes. Like all other government officials, he had a circle marked on his forehead from touching it to a clay tablet for long periods during Muslim prayer. Beside him on the desk were what looked like hundreds of files marked "Post-Disturbance Cases." Evidently, every person in the country had been arrested during the demonstrations following the sham elections.

Mr. Haddad asked us if we were Christians. We said that yes, we were.

"I believe in Jesus Christ, too, but I am not a Christian," he said. "Do you still insist on your beliefs?"

When we said yes again, he went on, clearly perturbed. "I wanted to see you today to warn you that if you continue with your resistance, you will have a terrible future. Two prosecutors have issued indictments for your execution, and they are insisting that these sentences be carried out. They have forced me to confirm the sentence and send it to the court for a final order. I can't help you much or others will pressure me. You can simply write down that you renounce your belief in Christ, and I will be able to sort the situation out for you. Otherwise, I will send the case to Mr. Salavati in Bureau 15, and then I won't be able to help you at all."

Without hesitation, we both answered, "We will never renounce our faith."

"But how can you be so sure you're right?" Mr. Haddad asked. "We Muslims believe in Jesus, too, but we do it without renouncing Mohammed or the other prophets. No one changes his or her religion just like that."

"I personally met with Jesus, and the Lord revealed this truth to me," Marziyeh said.

"God never speaks to people!" Mr. Haddad roared, his voice filling the room.

"Do you believe that God is the ultimate power?"

"Yes, of course."

"Then He can speak to anyone He chooses."

"Yes, but you are not worthy of this gift! God speaks only with His chosen prophets!"

"The Lord determines who deserves this privilege, not you."

Mr. Haddad tried another tack. "You Christians do not have a religious law to separate good from evil. You can sin anytime you wish."

"Yes, Jesus has done away with Sharia laws, but He doesn't allow us to sin whenever we like. He tells us that our salvation comes only through belief in Him. To believe in Jesus doesn't mean disregarding rules and obligations. We are guided by the Spirit of the Lord."

Mr. Haddad shook his head. "I have no quarrel with your beliefs. But your file says you've been promoting Christianity and that a large number of Bibles and other religious literature was discovered at your house. You have been found as apostates and sentenced accordingly for promoting Christianity. Mr. Sobhani, the chief prosecutor, and Mr. Heydarifar, his assistant, both regard you as apostate. If I pass judgment contrary to their conclusion, they will sue me."

He waited for a reply, but Marziyeh and I said nothing. He waited some more. "Well, you can go think it over now and let me know when you want to see me again."

Just then, his telephone rang. He listened briefly, scanned the mountain of files on his desk, and then looked at us. "What should we do with all these people?" Another pause while he listened. "I can't deal with it now!"

As we stood to leave, we told him that we wanted Mr. Aghasi to be our lawyer and would sign whatever papers were necessary for him to represent us.

"Oh yes," Mr. Haddad said reluctantly. "Here they are. Come and sign them. But I don't know why you bother, because he can't do anything."

We signed the papers and left. As we opened the door, we saw Mr. Heydarifar waiting outside, desperate to know what took place in our meeting. We passed him without a word. Our guard was waiting to escort us back to our bus. We had no idea what would happen next, or when. At the moment, we were too tired to care. We returned exhausted to our cell, where everyone wanted to know what had happened. We gave them a quick version of the day's events, fell into our beds, and were asleep in an instant.

CHAPTER 20

GOD AT WORK

Marziyeh

Only a few days after our appearance before Mr. Haddad, we heard our names on the loudspeaker again. Our lawyer, Mr. Aghasi, had been granted permission to see us! After about six months in prison, this would be our first meeting with any legal counsel—and we still had not seen the formal charges against us. A guard walked us about two hundred yards across the courtyard to a separate building where prisoners and their attorneys met.

The building was a small, crowded place where guards and soldiers milled around and lawyers waited for their clients to arrive. There was a row of glass cubicles with a table and four chairs in each, and a window between the lawyers and the inmates. Armed soldiers walked back and forth between the cubicles. Our escort turned us over to the security officer, saying he would be back for us in half an hour. Our actual time with Mr. Aghasi was limited to fifteen minutes, and the conversation would be recorded.

When our names were called, we stepped into one of the cubicles, where Mr. Aghasi was waiting. "Mr. Haddad finally allowed me to see you after playing games for a few days, but I've still not been given access to your files. Therefore, I have no idea about your background, the circumstances of your arrest, previous interrogations, or what stage your case is in. I'm told I will have them a couple of days before your trial so I can prepare my defense. So tell me exactly what happened. What about the interrogations? And what exactly are your religious beliefs?"

Knowing our time with Mr. Aghasi was limited, we briefly recounted the story of our arrest, the search of our apartment, and the various places we had been held. We also told him about our Christian beliefs and our activities.

"I need to know your current stance so I can defend you accordingly," he said. "What have you decided now? Do you still insist on being Christian? Do you still want to defend your faith?"

"Yes!" we both said without hesitation. "Otherwise we wouldn't have spent six months in prison! If we were willing to compromise, we would have done it long ago. We certainly will never change our minds now. We will defend our faith."

Mr. Aghasi thought for a few moments and then said, "Mr. Haddad has given me a message. He told me that if you continue to repeat your position in the courtroom, a heavy punishment awaits you. The punishment for apostates and for promoting Christianity in this country is death. The only way to avoid this is to deny the charges and admit you made a mistake. Whenever you come to this decision, Mr. Haddad will be willing to meet with you again."

"If we wanted to change our minds," I said, "we would have done that six months ago and not spent all those days in prison! We've been threatened with death. That's no problem. We're not afraid of death. What we're afraid of is life without faith, life without our Savior, Jesus Christ." I could feel my anger rising at the very thought that our lawyer would be suggesting this now.

Mr. Aghasi went on, "In Islam, we have a loophole called *taqiyya*, the lie of convenience. If you are cornered in a dangerous situation, you can get out of it by telling a lie and still keep your own true belief. Do you have this in Christianity?"

"No," Maryam said. "There's no such thing as *taqiyya* in Christianity. And even if there were, we wouldn't use it to save ourselves. We will never renounce our belief, even for the sake of momentary convenience."

"Well, in this case, women stand a better chance of being acquitted than men," he told us philosophically. "In Islam, women are given more leniency and more time to repent because according to Islamic law, a woman's wisdom is half that of a man and there's always the likelihood they will choose the wrong path. Since, according to Islam, men have a full-size brain, they are not given a second opportunity but must be executed right away.

"I personally respect your religion and believe, myself, that choosing a religion is a personal matter. No one else should be allowed to interfere. However, according to our country's laws, you are guilty of an offense, so we must do our best to get you out of this situation."

The armed guard outside our cubicle said we had five more minutes. In that brief time, Mr. Aghasi asked us about our prison conditions and the other prisoners in our ward. We then went to an office together to sign and stamp the forms to officially appoint him as our lawyer. And then our time was up.

As Mr. Aghasi walked away, a young woman approached him. We had seen her talking to other lawyers and prisoners, and had caught her looking at us several times from across the room. She spoke briefly to Mr. Aghasi and then came over to us.

"Is Mr. Aghasi your lawyer?" she asked.

"Yes."

"Could you tell me some more about your charges? Are you political prisoners? Or were you arrested in the street disturbances?"

"We are being prosecuted because we are Christians."

"You are Marziyeh and Maryam! How long have you been in prison now? Have you had access to a lawyer from the beginning?"

"We have been in prison six months, and this is the first time we've talked with a lawyer."

"I'm very happy to see you in person. I'm here today gathering the latest news on the cases of political prisoners. Have you heard that Mr. Heydarifar was dismissed from his job? It just happened this morning. We heard it when we were in Revolutionary Court."

Heydarifar was the prosecutor who had insisted we be executed. We asked what happened.

"Heydarifar, Sobhani, and another man, Saeed Mortazavi, were implicated in the unlawful arrest and transfer of protestors. Some have said they were responsible for the torture and murder of prisoners at the Kahrizak Detention Center. We are very happy to hear this news."

This was surely God at work! The three people who were responsible for our court case, the three who had indicted us for apostasy and demanded we be executed, were now accused of torture and murder and would themselves be tried behind closed doors. This good news was tempered by the fact that replacing the three court officials would mean another delay in our case. All we could do was wait.

The whole process was nothing but a show put on by the regime. These three were likely no more guilty than many others. But the regime had to blame somebody in order to take the spotlight off the illegal elections, the public unrest, and the worldwide outcry demanding our release. It was another renegade decision by the rulers, designed to stifle legitimate dissent and keep the powerful in power. This also was a stark reminder that prisoners are not the only ones who are captive in Iran. Everyone who lives under this repressive regime is—and will remain—a spiritual captive as long as these leaders maintain their iron grip.

Along with our dear friend Shirin Alam Hooli, we set up a daily activity schedule to keep ourselves busy. We tried not to think about the slow progress in our case and what might happen next. We were still roused before daylight by the call to prayer. Then came the scratchy, raucous wake-up music at 6:30 for morning roll call, followed an hour later by breakfast, the one prison meal per day we could stomach. When many people were at the cultural center—where we weren't allowed at first because we were unclean apostates and where we didn't want to go later when Mrs. Rezaei insisted we be allowed to—we sat on our beds and knitted. We spent the next part of the day reading and memorizing poetry, and gathering around to read our favorites aloud and discuss them. Iranians love poetry of all kinds: romantic poetry, history, humor, protest, politics, anything. We enjoyed listening to each other read, and we often teased Shirin about her Kurdish accent, which was actually beautiful. In the afternoons, we walked in the prison yard for an hour. After that, we went back to the ward to read some of the official newspapers (we were getting them again), listen to the radio news, and hold political discussions with other women who were interested. Shirin had started to learn English, and we helped her with her lessons. Our English was not good, but it was enough to help her.

Word spread through the ward that some political prisoners from Ward 209 were going to be transferred over to our hall. The first thing we thought of was whether or not dear Fereshteh would be coming. Maryam and I went to the store and bought some food and snacks to welcome the newcomers. Then we went downstairs where they would be brought in, and as the door opened, there stood Mahtab, Fereshteh, and Setare! We squealed with delight and hugged them tightly. There was a fourth girl, Arefeh, very shy and quiet, with a sad look on her face. We welcomed her, too, and I told her that just because we didn't know each other yet, there was no reason we couldn't celebrate her leaving the horrible environment of 209.

Despite the fact that there were already thirty-five women crammed into Room 1, we convinced Mrs. Ghaderi, the woman in charge of our ward, to send all four of the newcomers to our room. We explained to our cellmates that we would like to have these friends with us and that the new arrivals should stay together rather than be split up as was usually done. We helped them move in quietly and take up as little space as possible. Maryam sat next to Fereshteh and held her hands. They could not believe they were together again.

The news from 209 made it sound as if the place was worse than ever. With all the arrests after the election, there were four or five people in each tiny cell, where three had been a crowd. No more delicious kebabs or other decent food, but the same mediocre meals every day. Some of the new inmates there were prominent officials and politicians, now living under the same conditions as the people they once condemned.

The flow of prisoners in the public wing had also picked up, and many women came and went in the ward. Maryam and I took on the task of greeting new prisoners, introducing them to other inmates and explaining the rules and traditions of the ward. This gave us an opportunity to spend some time with Arefeh, who had been arrested during a demonstration and held because her family members were *mujahideen*, even though she herself was not. She was curious about our faith, especially when she learned that we refused to renounce it in order to be freed. She told us we were "silly" and added, "I think it is sheer stupidity that you two can buy your freedom by renouncing your beliefs and just walk out of this terrible place. You could do that and still continue with your religion outside, instead of wasting your life in here."

I tried to put our feelings into words. "Our insistence on our faith is not out of stubbornness. You may not be able to understand, because you haven't been through what we have. I have lived with God for many years, during some lonely and difficult times. He is the only support I have. He is my all. We are inseparable. My life has no value without Him. I love God so much that denying Him would be denying my own existence. How could I ever deny something that is in every cell of my body? I would rather spend the rest of my life in prison if that's what it takes to stay close to Him. I would rather be killed than kill the spirit of Christ within me.

"This is a struggle, a test of our beliefs and our strength. Holding on to our beliefs means rejecting injustice and inequality. Even if you think our beliefs are wrong, maybe you can see that we must not allow others to impose their beliefs on us. After all, what has landed you here in prison? Is it not your pursuit of justice and your protest against oppression? To have the right to think and speak as you choose?

"This regime tells its people that the regime knows best and that we should all do as we're told. Its message is, 'Shut up, say nothing in protest, do what we say.' You and I are struggling against the same oppression and censorship."

"I agree with everything you say," Arefeh replied. "But if I were you, I'd still renounce my religion so I could get out of here and continue the struggle. You're a lot more useful outside than in here. I don't have that option, because they're not going to make it so easy for me. But you do."

Her point of view was different from ours, and her struggle was a different kind—a struggle of politics and ethnicity, not of faith; a struggle of the world and not of the spirit.

| | |

MARYAM

My stomach trouble had grown worse than usual. The pain woke me up in the middle of the night and kept me awake for hours. One night, after dinner in Room 2 with Marjan and Shirin, I thought my stomach was going to explode.

An hour after going to bed I started feeling nauseated. At first I thought it was my usual stomach trouble, but soon I was running down the hall to the toilet, where I vomited again and again. It was the tuna I had eaten for dinner, low-quality canned food from the prison store. Shirin and Marziyeh came to help me back to the cell, but I was so weak I could hardly stand. They put me in a bed close to the door in case I had to go back to the toilet. The vomiting continued throughout the night, and the pain got so bad that I thought I might pass out. Even after my stomach was empty, I kept heaving. Finally, completely exhausted, I sat on the floor in the hallway and Shirin covered me with a blanket. Someone called a guard and after a few minutes convinced her to take me to the clinic.

Marziyeh wanted to go with me and argued with a guard while I leaned against the wall, barely able to stand. The guard made me put on a *chador* and carefully cover my hair. She was a lot more worried about my hair being covered than she was about getting me to a doctor. Marziyeh was forced to stay behind. The guard went down the stairs in the direction of the clinic—fifty steps in all. I followed slowly behind, afraid I would faint at every step.

"Come on, hurry up!" the guard barked. "I can't wait all night."

When we got downstairs, a guard told me to wait until he could coordinate with the doctor. I sat on the floor and closed my eyes. Every time I opened them, the room started moving.

"Quit pretending to be sick," the guard ordered. "There's no need for all this. I don't see you puking."

I was too weak to answer. As we started down the hall, I began to heave again. I grabbed a trash can from a doorway and threw up into it.

"Okay," the guard said, "I know you're not feeling well. Just control yourself and hurry up."

When we reached the clinic, the doctor on duty gave me a quick glance and asked the guard what had happened. "Couldn't you have waited until morning?" the doctor complained.

The doctor put me on an IV, put a trash can beside the bed, and left. I threw up again. When the IV container was empty, a nurse took me into another room, larger and very cold. "If you need to get up, you can use that little toilet in the corner," she said. "But be quiet, because the doctor and I are trying to sleep."

When the nurse came back later to change the IV, I was shivering with cold and asked for a blanket. The prison's hilltop location made for chilly nights, even in the summer. For some reason, I had the fleeting realization that my once-cozy apartment was only about five minutes away.

"We don't have any spare blankets tonight," the nurse answered brusquely. "They're all at the laundry." Then she added, "Why did you do something wrong and end up here anyway?" I said nothing.

The next morning, my hand was swollen and sore where the IV needle had been inserted. The IV drip had stopped; the fluid was completely gone. About ten o'clock, a nurse opened the door and was startled to see me in the bed. "Who are you? What are you doing here?" she demanded.

"Please take this needle out of my hand and let me go back to my ward," I said. "My hand is completely numb, and I'm completely frozen."

Shirin Alam Hooli and Marziyeh were waiting for me in the ward. They had stayed awake all night in case I needed them and there was any way they could help. Faithful friends are a great blessing any time. But in a place like Evin Prison, they mean even more because the prisoners have so little else to encourage them. There is nothing we wouldn't do for each other.

I was still recovering a few days later when Shirin's name was called on the loudspeaker. As usual, hearing her name was stressful for all of her friends. She had been sentenced to death and was waiting for a final ruling from the court as to whether or not she would get a pardon. Every time her name was called, we were afraid it could be a summons to the isolation cell where she would wait out the last day before her execution. The thought brought Marziyeh to tears.

| | |

Marziyeh

Before Maryam and I had gone to Ward 209, I'd had a dream about Shirin that I had never shared. In the dream, Shirin was sitting on a bed and I received a message that "the government will kill this girl." I couldn't bear to tell Shirin about it, or anybody else. It was something I desperately did not want to happen, yet I felt the Lord's message to me was unmistakable.

Shirin went to 209 for further interrogation. An agent from the Ministry of Intelligence was with the interrogator this time. They said if she would answer their questions and betray her friends, they would commute her death sentence. They accused her of giving them false information before and said they would have to transfer her back to 209 and start interrogating her all over again. Returning to live in 209 after two years in prison would be a very bad sign. If only she would "be a good girl," they would help her.

"I have no information to give you," Shirin said, her head held high. "Go ahead and execute me."

As long as she had been in prison and as often as she had been questioned, she sensed that her situation was different now. She felt somehow—with the indefinite intuition of a person who knows something but can't tell you how she knows it—that the court had already decided to execute her, and now was only trying to coax as much information out of her as possible before killing her. She was worried more than ever, and because she was worried, Maryam and I were worried. We encouraged Shirin not to quarrel with the guards over minor issues, but instead to rethink her attitude and stay out of trouble.

A little while later, she brought us a notebook. "If I'm going to be sent back to 209, I want to give you this diary to write in. If you're released before I get back, leave it with another inmate to return to me." She also gave us her books and other things to look after once she was transferred. We waited day after day for her name to be announced again, but the call didn't come.

Shirin said she was not afraid to die. That didn't keep her from being nervous about the news of a fresh round of persecution against the Kurdish people. One reason for her latest interrogation was that a judge had been murdered and the Kurds were suspected. The authorities were grilling Kurdish prisoners to see if they could get any clues in the case.

A few days later, we saw the news that several Kurds had been executed, including a boy. When Shirin came to our room for tea that afternoon, Maryam asked her if she knew him. She said she did not. She wasn't feeling well and left early that evening. Later, we went to check on her. The lights were out, and several inmates were watching TV. Shirin sat alone on her bed in the dark, knitting.

Maryam said, "You know the boy who was executed today, don't you?"

Without looking up, Shirin nodded and began to cry. She dropped her knitting and leaned her head against Maryam's chest.

"Yes, I knew him. He was only twenty years old."

We had never seen Shirin like this before. She cried her eyes out, as if she'd hidden a huge sorrow inside until she couldn't hide it anymore and now wanted to let it all go. Our unshakable Kurdish heroine, who had endured months of torture and years of imprisonment without flinching, suddenly seemed broken and defeated.

"If they take me back to 209, I'm going to make them execute me, too," Shirin said through her tears. "I'm sick and tired of the whole situation. I've seen so many people I love executed, lost so many of my friends at the hands of a merciless regime that has no compassion toward anyone, even a twenty-year-old boy. Please pray that they will now execute me, too. I can't stand this life in prison anymore."

Nothing they had done to her had ever made her hesitate. Now, though, it was clear that seeing her friends murdered by the government over the years had chipped away at her resolve.

After a long cry, she finally calmed down, but she had a splitting headache. During her past interrogations, they had hit her in the head so many times that her head still hurt most of the time, and she sometimes had dizzy spells and nosebleeds.

She took some painkillers, and Maryam massaged her temples to help her relax. That night, lying in bed, we prayed for our dear friend. We couldn't imagine how she felt. All we could do was ask God to be with her, to comfort her, and to give her strength for whatever was ahead.

CHAPTER 21

A CHANGE OF SEASON

MARYAM

The summer of 2009 was coming to an end. As the weather turned cool, inmates without warm clothing began to suffer when we were all herded out into the courtyard for the morning roll call. Most prisoners still went out before sunrise for Muslim morning prayers, too, and everybody had to go out to register at 6:30.

It was announced that prisoners could receive new clothes from their families. However, no linings or second layers were allowed, and no coats. If these items were found, they would be confiscated. Evidently, the idea was to make it harder for inmates to hide any sort of weapons or contraband.

In spite of the rules, we asked our friend Shamsi to help us get some warm clothes from our sisters. Shamsi was in charge of Room 2 and had become a friend, even though she had been a tough gang member on the outside and most prisoners were afraid of her. She later admitted that she'd hated us in the beginning for being Christians. But when she learned what Christians were really like after being around us for a while, she'd had a change of heart. Now we were happy to have her as one of our best friends. Because she had a good relationship with the guards, they never opened packages sent to her. She agreed to let our sisters put clothes for us in her packages if she could receive some extra clothes for herself as well. She also organized a system for bartering and buying clothes among the prisoners, and got clothes for the poorest prisoners, who couldn't afford their own. For a week afterward, we enjoyed modeling our new clothes for each other, complimenting and commenting on the various styles and combinations. It was our version of a shopping spree.

The clothes arrived just in time to help us with a crazy change in our daily routine. We seldom knew why the prison administration changed a policy. A new rule would simply be announced—or enacted without any announcement—and we had to go along; all we could do was guess at the reason. In the wake of all the protests, the arrest of some of the judges, and the overcrowded conditions at Evin, the guards became much stricter about prisoners going outside for morning roll call. In the past, old and sick prisoners had been excused. Because of the poor medical care and crowded rooms, there were always several women who had the flu, and others who were coming down with various maladies, who stayed in their cells, under the covers. Soraya, the huge woman with a cell and a shower of her own, never went out for roll call because it was so hard for her to walk. The guards knew that the women who weren't in the courtyard were still in their cells, so there was no practical reason to have everybody come out in the cold to be checked off a list. But now they began to enforce the rule— perhaps only because they knew they had the power to do it and because they knew it was uncomfortable and inconvenient. Who knows?

The guards also introduced a new wake-up routine, playing deafening music through the loudspeakers at 6:30 in the morning and screaming, "Get up! Get up! Hurry! Out of bed and into the prison yard for roll call!" Anyone who disobeyed was denied access to the cultural center, lost her phone privileges, and wasn't allowed visitors or parole. Some of the sick prisoners shivered with cold just getting out of bed, never mind going outside. There were women in their seventies who especially suffered from this treatment. For Marziyeh and others weakened by long illnesses, the trip outside made their symptoms worse and no doubt prolonged their sickness. Typically, we had to stand in the weather for up to an hour. After that, everyone except for Marziyeh and me and a few political prisoners had to face Mecca and recite in Arabic the *omalyajib* prayers.

Sometimes the guards didn't even take attendance, but made us stand outside just to harass us. Another mean trick was to threaten all of us by insisting that everyone would be punished—denied phone privileges, for example—on account of the slowpokes and slackers who refused to come out. The guards were hoping to make the old and weak prisoners out to be the enemy, getting us to blame them instead of the guards for the inconvenience, and causing disagreements or even fights among the prisoners.

The bad situation was made even worse on days when we had to go back outside a second time for the guards to search our personal belongings or when they came through occasionally spraying disinfectant. Marziyeh and I always took our diaries with us so the guards wouldn't find them, and when they sprayed we had to wash all our utensils and everything else because of the smell.

One morning, we had just come inside from another bone-chilling roll call and were eating breakfast when we were ordered back into the courtyard. Once we were all assembled, everyone who used the cultural center was ordered to go there, and everyone else was ordered to remain outside for the rest of the day. Even the old and sick inmates were forced to obey.

Though a number of women went to the cultural center, the yard was packed with prisoners. It looked like a crowd on market day, only much more of a crush. There were 150 women or more jammed together so tightly that most didn't have room to move. Even those of us who had warm clothing were soon uncomfortable; some women wrapped themselves in cardboard trying to stay warm. A group started dancing to lift their spirits and keep the circulation going, which irritated another group. The two factions started yelling and swearing at each other.

After a while, some of the prisoners started sitting and lying on the ground, which made the crowding even worse. Marziyeh's backache was aggravated by the cold and all the standing, and the chilly weather also caused a spike in my earache pain. Soraya, whose kidney problems were familiar to everyone, called out that she had to go in and use the toilet. The guards ignored her. When she started yelling louder, other women yelled too. Finally, after three or four hours, the guards opened the doors and we all rushed back into the warmth of our rooms. The women in the cultural center had heard the yelling and were very happy to know we had stood together for even so small a thing as the chance to go back inside. Such an expression of defiance was very rare and very exciting. Some of our guards warned us angrily that our voices were reaching the guards in the men's prison and making them sexually excited. If the sound of a woman's voice was enough to tempt these men, they must have been weak and unfaithful little boys indeed!

For all the encouragement our brief protest gave us, it didn't make any difference. Word soon spread that from now on, everyone had to spend the day either at the cultural center or outside. The reason, we believed, was that the prison warden, Mr. Sedaghat, was under some kind of pressure to show that his prisoners were happy, well cared for, and being educated at his cultural center, where they were all behaving like nice Muslim women. If the security cameras showed rooms full of women left on their own and not participating in cultural center activities, this would be a problem for Mr. Sedaghat. However, if the cameras showed a full and busy cultural center and the rest of the women's area empty, it must mean we were all down at the center being rehabilitated.

It was curious to think they couldn't have done this in the spring or summer when the weather was warm. It all started as soon as the cold temperatures hit. Because the cultural center held only about fifty people, there wasn't nearly enough room for everybody now that we were so terribly overcrowded. On top of everything else, the prisoners who were drug addicts were allowed into the cultural center for the first time, making it harder than ever to get a place there. Most of the women there had no interest in cultural activities; they just wanted to stay warm, and they whiled away the day singing and dancing. Therefore, the women who actually wanted to use the center couldn't do much because the room was so overstuffed with people. Everyone being out of the ward all day also wrecked our carefully planned schedule of shower times, which was essential since there were more than 150 women and five available showers.

| | | |

Any sort of coordinated prison protest was almost unknown in Evin. On the eve of an execution or after a major event was reported in the news, our phones were cut off and we were locked in our cells until it was clear we had no plans to react. There was also always the threat of punishment: We heard many stories of women considered troublemakers who were taken to a building next door and returned swollen, bruised, and bleeding.

Marziyeh and I had been banned from the cultural center since the beginning of our imprisonment. When we told Mrs. Rezaei, the women's prison warden, about it, she had said we should be allowed to go. But we never went, out of quiet protest against the way the director there had treated us. In the face of the new rules, we decided we still wouldn't go to the cultural center and that we wouldn't spend the day outside in the courtyard anymore either, even if it meant they would beat us.

The next morning, when we were all ordered outside, Marziyeh and I were the only ones who stayed in the ward. The guards came through, but they didn't step inside our cell and didn't notice us under our blankets. After the other inmates returned, everybody wanted to know how we had managed to avoid the mandatory trip outside. We explained that we simply refused to go. The following morning, a few others decided to stay in with us, but at the last minute, they changed their minds because of threats from the guards.

We knew that someone would soon complain to Mrs. Rezaei that we were being allowed to skip the morning roll call without any consequences. We figured the best way to deal with that was to go see Mrs. Rezaei ourselves first. Because Marziyeh was still in bed with her backache and flu symptoms, I went alone to wait in the long line to see the women's warden. When my turn came, Mrs. Rezaei ushered me inside.

"Mrs. Rezaei, my friend and I do not go to morning register," I explained. "The reason is because Marziyeh has a severe backache and chronic cold and flu symptoms and has been in bed for many days. You are aware that the prison clinic doesn't provide proper medical care. As for me, I can't stand in the cold for hours because I have a serious ear infection. Many other inmates suffer from various illnesses and disabilities that make it impossible for them to stand outside. We would rather go to solitary confinement than tolerate this inhumane treatment."

"Miss Rostampour, I am as unhappy as you are about this new routine," Mrs. Rezaei replied. "I've already registered my protest with Mr. Sedaghat, but he is adamant that the new orders be obeyed. Defiant prisoners will be sent to the security section. Enforcing these new rules is a problem, and I will do my best to resolve the matter as soon as possible. In the meantime, you should go out for the roll call like everybody else, because Mr. Sedaghat won't make any exceptions."

"Maybe Mr. Sedaghat should deal with the problem of the worthless prison clinic and its outdated drugs," I replied, "or the lack of proper hot food on these cold autumn days, before he decides to make these new rules about the morning count. Everybody in the ward is sick."

"I'm not happy about the situation either," said Mrs. Rezaei, "but we have no other choice. I'm not the one who makes the decision."

I could see there was no point in continuing the conversation, so I thanked the warden and returned to my cell. The next morning, Marziyeh and I stayed in our room again while everyone else went out to register. That same day, Shirin Alam Hooli came into the room when she should have been in the cultural center. She had gotten into an argument with the cultural center manager over the terrible overcrowding. There were so many people and so much commotion that it was impossible to do anything. Shirin said going to the center was a waste of time. Though her complaint was justified, it was yet another example of her resisting authority, which looked bad, considering her case and the latest round of interrogations.

Marziyeh and I didn't want to start any kind of demonstration; we never incited others to do what we did. Most prisoners were afraid of the guards and obeyed their every word. However, political prisoners like Shirin were different. Because some of them had already been through so much, nothing the guards did or threatened to do frightened them. But even some of the prison staff were now saying that the crowding situation was impossible and that the cultural center could no longer function. Prisoners needed to stand up for their rights.

After a week, the new rules were scrapped and we went back to the old routine of people being excused from morning roll call if it was hard for them to get out. Of course, none of the prison administrators would admit that our actions had made any difference. Whether they did or not, we were happy to have the old rules back.

| | |

Marziyeh

Other small acts of defiance sometimes made a difference as well. Reihaneh came from Ward 209 to the public ward and was assigned to our room. We'd heard a lot about her case from radio and television. She was a well-known journalist and blogger who had campaigned for Mr. Karroubi, and also with Mr. Khatami, a former president. Reihaneh was arrested after the elections for supporting them and being a member of the Green Movement. She had been in 209 for about fifty days. While she was there, she went on a hunger strike, refusing to take anything but tea and a few dates every day. She was transferred from 209 because the media were less likely to hear about her strike in the general ward than in the ward for political prisoners. When I first met her, she was pale and weak from physical and psychological torture; her malnutrition made her look even worse. She was nothing like the healthy, robust woman in the news photos.

Soon after Reihaneh arrived, Mrs. Rezaei called her to the office and said that her hunger strike was breaking the law. She must stop it immediately or be severely punished. Reihaneh ignored the threat.

Within a few days, Maryam and I got to know her. "I've heard a lot about you two Christians and your resistance," she said. "Did you know that Christian prisoners are given asylum more easily now since you've been arrested and put in prison?"

"How could this be related to us?" Maryam asked.

"Since your arrest, foreign governments are more willing to accept Christians seeking asylum. They now believe that most of the Christians in Iran are under oppression, and that as soon as the Iranian government finds out about them, their lives are in danger."

We had no idea our situation had made this kind of difference. We thanked God for His mercy and kindness. Reihaneh wanted to write the story of our lives and our Christian experience. Because I still spent most of the day in bed, it wouldn't raise any suspicions if Reihaneh sat beside me for long periods of time. Thanks to her training as a reporter, she could take my story down in shorthand. The more we talked, the more interested Reihaneh became in Christianity, until finally she put aside her pen and notebook and wanted to talk about faith. She knew a priest and his family in London who turned out to be an acquaintance of mine. How incredible that she and I would have a Christian friend in common halfway around the world!

"If this preacher is your friend," I said, "I'm surprised you haven't wanted to learn about Christ before."

"I have my own personal beliefs," Reihaneh answered. "But I've never heard anything like your experience with Christ. It's very interesting to me."

"I've told you so much about myself," I said. "Now it's your turn."

Reihaneh explained that she had studied journalism and media, and had completed a course on human rights in England. She was active in defending human rights, especially rights for women. She wrote articles for reformist newspapers and began to attract a following. She was arrested and accused of taking part in illegal rallies, disturbing the peace, propaganda against the state, and insulting the president. Because she had been a faithful supporter of Mr. Karroubi, the authorities forced her to confess that she was having an affair with him in order to fabricate a corruption case against him and tarnish his reputation.

Reihaneh wanted to write a complete report of the plight of women in prison, an exposé of the abuse, corruption, and evil that made up the fabric of the Iranian prison system. With help from some other prisoners, I listed the names of every inmate, their charges, the year they were arrested, and all the details of their stories. Reihaneh made notes about the terrible medical care, the bad food, and the predatory lesbianism that was so widespread— and that, before the security cameras were in place, had routinely led to the rape and beating of new prisoners. In one especially gruesome case, a young woman had been raped in front of her child.

The first step in Reihaneh's project was an article she wrote in the form of a letter to her interrogator in Ward 209, which she titled, "Doctor 209." She read it to Maryam and me. It was a scathing yet hilarious letter condemning him in a sarcastic way and exposing things about him. She planned to get it out to a friend during a contact visit so it could be posted on her website.

Whether that letter made it to the outside world or not, we never knew. A few days later, Maryam and I had a mysterious visitor whose presence began a whole new chapter in our story. Without warning, the pace of our lives suddenly moved much faster, the danger suddenly much closer at hand.

CHAPTER 22

MYSTERIOUS VISITORS

MARYAM

It was visiting day. We weren't due for our monthly contact visit, so this would be a regular visit sitting across from our sisters, a piece of glass between us, talking with them on the phone as our conversations were recorded by the guards. But this time, Marziyeh had told Elena not to come, because Marziyeh felt too sick to put up with the hours of standing and waiting required for the fifteen-minute visit. My sister and I would visit while Marziyeh stayed on the ward and rested in bed.

The trip to the visitors' center—the long wait at the women's prison, the minibus ride, another wait at the visitors' center, the ride back, and still another wait to be frisked before returning to Ward 2—took even longer this time than usual. Word came around that the electricity in the visitors' center was off, and we had to wait for it to come back on. After a long delay, the decision was made to let everyone with visitors that day, about thirty women, have a contact visit. This was a wonderful surprise! I walked down the stairs to greet Shirin, and we fell into each other's arms, thanking God for the unexpected opportunity. We talked nonstop for my allotted fifteen minutes and then said our good-byes.

Back at the women's prison, in line waiting to be searched, I leaned against the office wall, exhausted from hours of standing. Suddenly, the door flew open and two men and two female guards walked briskly in. It was very unusual to see men in the women's prison unannounced. The guards immediately ordered the prisoners to cover their hair completely.

These guys must be from Ward 209, I thought.

One of the visitors, a middle-aged man with a round face, looked at me. "Are you Miss Rostampour?"

"Yes, I am."

"Do you have any idea how long we have been waiting for you?" I was too surprised to speak. "You have caused a great deal of trouble for us with these letters of yours. Every day, we have to open and read letters about you and your case."

"You have to read letters about me?"

"Yes! At least forty or fifty letters a day that have been sent to you from all over the world."

"If the letters are sent to me, why should you be reading them? Perhaps this is another example of the abuse of human rights in this country—that you open and read other people's mail."

"Did you really expect us to give them to you so you could get more encouragement to defy us?"

We don't need to read the letters to be encouraged by them, I thought, my heart filled with joy. *The world is watching you. We have a family of faith that loves us and cares for us. We are not alone!*

"Besides," the man added gruffly, "unless the judge in your case permits it, we're not allowed to give them to you. How long have you been in prison?"

"Seven months."

"And are you still a Christian?"

"Yes, I am a Christian."

"What have you decided to do? Are you still insisting on your decision, or have you changed your mind?"

"I've already gone through my interrogations and have nothing more to add to what I've told you already."

The round-faced man looked at his companion. "She says she's already gone through her interrogations."

"Let's go," the other man said. Just like that, the two men left the cellblock.

During the entire exchange, the rest of the prisoners waiting to be searched had been absolutely silent. As soon as the visitors left, they all started talking at once.

"Do you know who those men were?" one of them asked me.

"Not really," I said. "Who were they?"

"They're from the security section of the ministry of intelligence." To the other inmates, it was a case of famous security officials coming to visit a famous prisoner.

"So what? I'm not accountable to them, no matter who they are." I did my best to sound confident and defiant. Inside, I was afraid of what could happen to me and Marziyeh. We knew all about the security section's reputation for being particularly ruthless. Had they come to beat us? To torture us at last?

| | |

When I got back to the ward, I learned that the men had come there earlier. They had tried to speak with Marziyeh, but she had stayed in bed with her head under the blanket. The men had instructed some other prisoners to get Marziyeh up to talk with them. When one of the women poked her head under the blanket to pass along the directive, it was all she and Marziyeh could do to keep from laughing.

"I can't come out. I'm not feeling well. I'm trying to sleep," Marziyeh had said weakly, adding a couple of convincing coughs for good measure.

"You heard her," the friend told the visitors. "She isn't feeling well and she can't talk to you."

The men had then waited two hours for me to come back from the visitors' area. No one, not even the inmates who had been at Evin the longest, could remember officials waiting two hours to see anybody. This kind of behavior was absolutely unprecedented.

It looked as if somehow, miraculously, the regime was starting to feel serious heat about keeping us in prison. We weren't going to change our story. They couldn't execute us as originally planned because too many eyes around the world were watching them now. Yet if they let us out while we still proclaimed our Christian faith, they would lose face with the radicals who kept them in power. The tipping point was coming closer.

| | |

The next morning, after roll call and breakfast, Mrs. Mujahed, one of the ward monitors, ordered Marziyeh and me to put on our *chador*s and report to Mrs. Rezaei's office immediately. When Marziyeh took longer to get ready than Mrs. Mujahed wanted, I went ahead by myself to take the pressure off. Three men were waiting for me—the two from the day before and a third man, who was older and had gray hair. At first, I assumed they were there to take me for punishment because of my behavior the day before. When I said hello, they all replied with looks of surprise.

"These gentlemen are from the security section of the prison," Mrs. Rezaei explained. "They are here to see you."

The older man with the gray hair asked, "Are you well?"

"Yes, thank you."

The middle-aged man with the round face said, "She's the one from yesterday who said she had already had her interrogations."

"Yes indeed," added the third visitor, a man in his thirties named Mr. Ramezani. "She's the woman who mocked us yesterday."

When Marziyeh came in and stood next to me, the men asked us to sit down.

"You were not feeling well yesterday, were you?" Mr. Ramezani asked Marziyeh.

"No," Marziyeh said. "I've been sick for months."

Mr. Ramezani turned to Mrs. Rezaei, who was sitting nervously behind her desk. "Doesn't your health clinic look after these people?"

"Of course they do," Mrs. Rezaei answered defensively. "I think we've sent her to the clinic several times."

"Then why isn't she better?"

Marziyeh spoke up. "Because they give all sick prisoners the same medicine, no matter what's wrong with them, and it has no effect whatsoever. We're not allowed to bring in our own medications from the outside."

As Marziyeh and Mr. Ramezani continued to criticize the medical treatment, the other authorities left the office. After a momentary silence, Mr. Ramezani began a rambling speech that was rather hard to follow. Clearly, he was distressed and uncomfortable speaking to us, uncertain of what he wanted to say. As he spoke, his face grew pale and he began stuttering, looking at the floor like a nervous boy trying to propose marriage. Somewhere, someone was under pressure about our case, and the government was more desperate than ever to let us go without actually acquitting us.

"Someone had a dream about you," he began, nodding toward me. "He was in prison in another city at the time, but told me about it. In the dream, Jesus encouraged him to meet you. That's why I came to see you both yesterday."

He turned his eyes toward Marziyeh. "Unfortunately, you, Miss Amirizadeh, didn't want to see me, though I did have a polite encounter with your friend here. I told her that Evin receives dozens of letters for you every day that we have to read. I think you get more mail than the administration office. I've heard a lot of news about you now that you've become famous." He paused awkwardly, then continued, "Let me say that I have nothing against your faith. In fact, to some extent I also believe in Christ, and there are a lot of verses in the Koran that confirm the things about Christ that you believe in." He lowered his voice. "But maybe it's not right to speak of these things here. And nobody knows what I said about my belief in Christ—what I'm telling you could put me in danger."

Mr. Ramezani asked us some questions about our beliefs, and we shared a short version of our faith journey with him. "My beliefs are not like other Muslims," he commented. "I disagree with what they do. If I said a word about it, it would definitely get me into trouble." He asked us to read Surah 90 from the Koran and tell him what it meant to us the next time we saw him. "I interpret the verse to say that Jesus is a savior," he said. Marziyeh and I said we would look it up.

"Somebody has asked me to come to see you and find out about your needs," he stuttered, looking down at the floor again and back up. "I can help you get whatever you want from outside the prison—medicine, vitamins, blankets, clothes—just let me know."

We told him we'd been trying to get vitamins for months. He handed us a phone number. "Give this number to your relatives," he said. "They can call the security office directly and get permission to bring vitamins in." Marziyeh told him about the terrible food, the poor health of so many inmates—including herself—and the stupid early morning roll call. Though we had quit going outside in the cold ourselves, we still got threats and hassles from the guards, as did everybody else who wouldn't go.

"Unfortunately," Mr. Ramezani said, sounding genuinely apologetic, "I can't do anything about that unless you have a letter from the clinic saying you're sick. I'll do my best to have the guards leave you alone, but you really need a letter."

"But the clinic won't give us a letter," Marziyeh explained. "They don't even examine us. Why would they give us a letter? And the new rule is only making matters worse—the terrible health care combined with the requirement to go outside in the cold every morning is making the sick prisoners sicker, and the ones who aren't sick yet are going to catch something."

"I know these problems very well," Mr. Ramezani admitted. "But unfortunately, at Evin, they have their own special rules. Canceling the morning schedule must come from a higher authority. Until then, I will talk to Mrs. Rezaei about your needs and these conditions, and you try again to get a letter from the clinic."

I was shocked at this man's attitude and willingness to help us. Who was he really? And who had sent him? Marziyeh and I thanked him for his visit.

"No, no, I'm obliged to do this," he insisted. "I've been ordered to come and see you. I too believe in Jesus Christ. He was tortured and crucified. The people who imprisoned you say this wasn't so, but they're making a huge mistake. Jesus was beaten, tortured, and crucified, and then He rose from the dead."

Now I was even more shocked! We had been arrested, harassed, humiliated, and in prison for seven months for saying what this high prison official—seemingly feared and obeyed by everyone—was saying right in front of us in the office of the women's warden. I asked him to tell us more about what he knew of Christ's resurrection.

"I can't talk about it in here. It isn't allowed," he replied in a halting tone. "We can talk some more about it on the outside. But please don't mention to anybody that we've discussed Jesus like this. It will only make big problems for all of us." We promised to keep our talk confidential. Then our incredible conversation ended, and we went back to the ward, where our friends were waiting nervously for us.

In light of the visit we'd had the day before, and now with this high official coming to meet with us, they were worried we were about to be punished. We told them that everything was all right, that the authorities just wanted to know more about the letters we were getting from around the world. We didn't mention the likelihood of getting vitamin pills, because we thought it might raise questions or cause trouble. Some of the other women were already jealous of the attention we got for being in the news so much. We didn't want to give them any other excuses to resent us. Marziyeh called her sister, Elena, told her about our meeting, and passed along the phone number from Mr. Ramezani.

| | |

Marziyeh

A few days later, our new lawyer, Mr. Aghasi, came to visit us in prison again. He said our court date would be coming up soon, and at last we would have a chance to defend ourselves. He asked if we'd thought any more about changing our position, whether we might be willing to soften our stance on our Christian beliefs. We said, as we'd said so many times before, that there was nothing to think about. We would never turn from Christ, never water down our story, never deny our Savior. We asked him to prepare our defense with that in mind.

We also asked him if he could bring us some vitamins and proper medicine. He said it was not possible for a lawyer to do that. We had to ask the clinic or the welfare office. If our worldly hope for legal relief was vested in Mr. Aghasi, our hope for better health rested in the hands of the strange Mr. Ramezani.

Within a week, Maryam and I were summoned to the office and told to prepare for court the next day. Our friends assured us that this time around we would finally have our bail set and be released. Others said because of all the publicity surrounding our case we would be released unconditionally.

The next morning, we were up early, waited hours for the minibus to the court, and sat handcuffed together for the ride across town. As our bus pulled into the street, we saw Elena and Shirin and some of their friends waiting for us. They waved and shouted encouragement and followed us to the court building.

The last time we'd been to the Revolutionary Court, the judge had told us that if we didn't change our story, our case would be transferred to Bureau 15 for a final verdict. The judge there, who was also the judge in Shirin Alam Hooli's case, was famous for sentencing prisoners to death or to life in prison. Nothing else. But when we entered the building this time, we saw from the sign that we were going into Bureau 26. "This is good news," Mr. Aghasi remarked. "I know the judge in 26. He comes from the family court and is a very kind man."

We stopped outside the courtroom door. "I'll go in first," Mr. Aghasi said, "as I have not been given the opportunity to read your file yet. I was only informed about your court summons yesterday. Now I have fifteen minutes to read your file and prepare your case. After that, I'll call you in."

We had been in prison almost eight months. We had been threatened with a sentence of death. Yet this was the first—and might be the only—time we would ever appear before a judge with our lawyer present. And now he had fifteen minutes to read our file and prepare our defense.

As we waited, Elena and Shirin joined us. This was the first time they had been allowed in the building when we were there. They gave us some fresh fruit juice, which tasted wonderful. They also had food and sweets for us, but they were not allowed to give them to us.

A few minutes later, the clerk opened the door and called us in. We waved good-bye to our sisters and passed through a very large courtroom into another one that was smaller. There was a raised desk at one end where the judge sat. On the wall behind him was a large color photo of the Scales of Justice. The judge wore a gray suit and looked as if he hadn't shaved for two or three days. In front of the judge's bench was a table for the defense. We sat down and Mr. Aghasi took a seat next to us.

Looking up at the Scales of Justice, I knew that our faith and our lives were hanging in the balance. But I also knew that God's hand would guide whatever happened next.

CHAPTER 23

GUILTY AS CHARGED

Marziyeh

Our lawyer greeted the new judge. He was a middle-aged man with gray hair and beard. He wore glasses and had the familiar red spot on his forehead indicating many hours of Muslim prayer.

"We're fortunate to have Mr. Pirabbasi as our judge," Mr. Aghasi said, gesturing toward him as Maryam and I settled into our chairs.

"I'm rather busy these days, I'm afraid," the judge said. "But Mr. Larijani contacted me and asked me to follow your case." This was incredible news! Mr. Larijani was the head of the entire judiciary. Our lawyer asked him why Mr. Larijani was involved.

"Sources at the United Nations have telephoned him and asked him to sort out this case as soon as possible."

In time, we learned who had brought our case to the attention of the United Nations. To protect that person and preserve his ability to help others, we will not say any more about him here.

The judge turned from Mr. Aghasi and looked at Maryam and me with a stern expression. "Do you realize that, due to your perseverance, our enemies have taken advantage of the situation and run several negative campaigns against us? Maybe you don't know what kind of people are using you and your case for their own objectives."

There had been a vigil in front of the Iranian Embassy in London supporting our release—another reminder that Christians around the world were praying for us. As good as this made us feel, the publicity made things trickier for the Iranian judiciary, and the government's anger grew, along with its frustration over not resolving our case. We very much hoped their anger wouldn't boil over into harsh action.

The judge opened our file and sat reading silently for a few minutes. When he looked up, I had butterflies in my stomach. Mr. Aghasi's face revealed nothing about what he was thinking.

The judge said, "The charges of propaganda against the regime and insulting our sacred values are baseless. There is no substantiated evidence to support them." He leaned forward. "I don't suppose you've insulted any other religions or religious beliefs, have you?"

"No," we said.

"No," Mr. Aghasi echoed.

Judge Pirabbasi sat up straight behind the bench. "Therefore, I hereby acknowledge your acquittal from the charges of instigating propaganda against the system and insulting our sacred values." Just like that, without a statement or a word of testimony from us, we were cleared of these serious charges after months of interrogation, humiliation, and judicial stalemate. As the judge spoke, he made some notes. Then he looked at us again.

"Now we come to the charge of apostasy. This charge remains valid. And as you know, the sentence for this crime is the death penalty for men and life imprisonment with labor for women."

The judge looked at our lawyer. "I'm sure you've already briefed your clients about this issue."

"Yes, I have."

We had been told repeatedly that the maximum sentence possible for us was death. We knew of plenty of women who had been executed in Iran. However, this was also the second time we'd heard that we could not be executed because we were women.

Judge Pirabbasi turned to us again. "I wish to ask you a few questions, one person at a time. Miss Amirizadeh, are you a Christian? Are you called to follow Jesus? Explain to me what you mean by that."

As the questions hung in the air, I felt chills run up and down my body. They were the same questions, asked the same way, I had been asked during my baptism ceremony in Turkey. And as Maryam had reminded me the night before when our court date was announced over the loudspeaker, today, October 7, was the four-year anniversary of that day.

After I became a Christian, my friends encouraged me to be baptized because a baptismal certificate made some kinds of travel easier to get approved, but I hadn't wanted to take advantage of my faith or use it as an excuse for anything. I didn't want to use God; I wanted God to use me.

Furthermore, I'd had a dream in which Jesus Himself had already baptized me in a beautiful lake. "You no longer belong to this world," He had told me. "You belong to Me." At the time, I didn't think a "second" baptism was necessary or appropriate.

But during my trip to Turkey, when other believers were being baptized in the sea, God had prompted me to take part as well. I had never wanted to be baptized inside a church, but instead wanted the ceremony in a natural setting like the one in my dream. And so, seven years after becoming a Christian, I had been baptized in the sea on October 7 at 7:00 p.m.

"Are you a Christian? Are you called to follow Jesus? Explain to me what you mean by that." It was easy to say yes to those questions during a Christian ceremony filled with hope and promise. And though I was very afraid as I sat in this Islamic courtroom with my life on the line, it was just as easy to say yes now. I would willingly follow Jesus to a new life or to death. Though the situations were polar opposites, the promise of faith was equally steadfast for both.

In answering the question before the judge, I explained my faith in Christ and my personal relationship with Him. "I consider Jesus to be the Son of God and my Savior," I concluded, using the exact words I had used at my baptism.

The judge was visibly startled by such a bold statement from a prisoner whose freedom seemed so close at hand. He challenged my statements of faith, and soon he and I got into an argument.

"I am a Christian, and my faith is in Christ!" I declared.

"So you don't believe in Islam?" the judge asked angrily.

"Jesus said, 'It is finished.' He said there would be no more prophets after Him."

Mr. Aghasi became anxious at this turn of events, finally interjecting himself into the conversation. "This woman's belief in Christ must not be interpreted as an insult to other religions," he said, almost shouting.

The judge stopped talking to me, and I stopped too. "Mr. Aghasi, you may present your defense to the court in the matter of apostasy."

"My clients respect other religions in the same way they respect their own," Mr. Aghasi said hopefully. "In promoting Christianity, they have not tried to turn people away from the religious beliefs they already held. They believe in Christ in the same way other religions believe in Him."

This, of course, was not true. Mr. Aghasi was doing his best to have us acquitted of the apostasy charges. But Maryam and I had told him repeatedly that we stood by our belief that Christ alone was the Son of God and that there were no other prophets or historical figures to compare with Him in any way. The more he talked, the more he veered away from the Christian truth we were upholding, toward a religious position that was completely alien to us. He was no longer representing our position; he was talking for himself.

Unwilling to remain silent any longer, no matter what the consequences, I interrupted Mr. Aghasi's statement.

"Judge, our lawyer is wrong!" I felt all eyes in the room now fixed upon me. "We're not two children who need someone else to say what we think on our behalf. Jesus said, 'I give you the Holy Spirit and you don't need anything else. It is finished.' We don't believe in Christ the way other religions do. Jesus is the beginning and the end. He is everything. Any view that diminishes His perfect completeness is a false view. Jesus is the one and only true Savior of the world. Nothing you can do will make us deny that truth or water it down.

"We believe the Lord is our ultimate liberator, and we don't want to be released from prison under any circumstances if it means denying Christ. If we had wanted to be freed by denying our faith, we could have gotten out of prison months ago. Jesus is our Savior now and forever!"

Mr. Aghasi's face flushed with anger and frustration. He thought he was doing a heroic job to save us from life in prison, and here I was undoing all his effort!

"So you disagree with his statement?" the judge asked.

"Yes, we do," Maryam said. "We have to change some of the last sentences."

"That's fine," Judge Pirabbasi said. If he had any doubts about our position before, he certainly had none now. "I have no problem with changing them. I'll write down whatever you say. I've already told you what to expect if the charge of apostasy is proven. I will write that you say, 'We believe in Jesus Christ.'"

Our lawyer's face was still red as a beet.

"Mr. Aghasi," the judge said, "I'm going to write down whatever these women want me to write. And I say to them, 'Stand by your beliefs.' After all, everything in this world comes at a price. If they have reached this conclusion and believe in what they say, then they will have to pay the price for it."

Maryam and I stepped forward to sign some papers acquitting us of the political charges and reaffirming our belief in Jesus Christ. When we returned to our seats, the judge said, "I have made a note of all our conversations today. I have acquitted you of the political charges brought against you by the Court of Revolution. But with regard to the apostasy charge, it must be dealt with by another court, which is designed to look into these particular cases."

"Couldn't you handle this issue in your court, too, instead of referring it to another judge?" Mr. Aghasi inquired.

"No, I don't think so," Mr. Pirabbasi answered. "You can check the law, but I'm sure I have dealt appropriately with the first charges, yet can be no further help on the second charge."

Maryam asked the judge if we could have the letters that had been sent to us. The guards had told us we could have them only if a judge gave his permission. To our surprise and delight, he agreed and said he would order the letters to be released to us. We also asked about our laptops, identity papers, and other items that had been confiscated on the day of our arrest.

"None of that property is here," he told us. "Everything is probably at the Gisha police station where you were arrested, or in Bureau 2 where you came to court before." He called a clerk and instructed him to see if any of our belongings were there in Bureau 26. The clerk left the courtroom and came back in a moment with two Bibles.

"This is all we have here," the judge said. "But don't worry, everything of yours will be returned."

"What about the rest of our Bibles?" I asked.

"Oh, well, I'm afraid they cannot be returned to you. We kept these two in your file as evidence. The rest must have been shredded by now."

"Well," I said, "since you have these copies here, maybe you should read them. You've read the Koran; you might as well read the Bible, too."

Mr. Aghasi jumped to his feet. "Now then, young lady," he snapped, "you don't give up on your evangelizing even in here?" I had truly rattled him—he had to have a way out, and I wasn't giving it to him. The judge walked out of the courtroom, leaving us alone with Mr. Aghasi.

| | |

MARYAM

After Marziyeh's outburst, Mr. Aghasi was frustrated, embarrassed, and angry all at once. "Why did you have to do that?" he said to her. "I was only at the beginning of my defense! There would have been no problem if you had simply agreed to sign the statement I prepared. You are the first defendants ever to deny their lawyer's statement. It would have set you free! And so what if they weren't exactly accurate? They were only my words, not yours."

"We would not sign," I interjected, "because you know as well as we do that by signing that statement, it meant we agreed with whatever it said."

"Judge Pirabbasi is a friend of mine," Mr. Aghasi reminded us wearily. "He has been recently transferred to the Court of Revolution and is responsible for the political cases. I wish that today he would have tied up your case file so that the apostasy judge could deliver his ruling. Unfortunately, now your case will be referred to the Court of Justice."

The judge came back into the courtroom, and to our surprise he sat at the table with us and ordered his clerk to serve us tea. He had collected himself and was back in search of a solution. Mr. Aghasi said again to Mr. Pirabbasi that he wished the judge could resolve our case.

"In serious cases that normally end with a sentence of life imprisonment or death, this court, the Court of Revolution, does not get involved," the judge said. "Those cases go to the Court of Justice, where there is a three-judge panel. I'm afraid there's nothing I can do to change that."

He took a sip of tea. "As I'm drinking tea with you, it reminds me of a guest from Sweden who was also a Christian. To prove we don't regard Christians as unclean, I picked up her half-empty teacup and finished it. That really impressed her. I love the Christian people and respect their religion and beliefs. But you must not do anything that might play into the hands of the Western powers."

The judge left again and returned with a bottle. He asked about the conditions inside Evin prison, especially the medical care. Then he poured half the contents of the bottle into a smaller bottle. It was rosewater perfume. "I don't believe you have any perfume in prison. I give you this as a gift and hope it will also help with the hygiene there."

Marziyeh and I exchanged glances of half surprise, half amusement. It was hard not to laugh at the thought of carrying a glass bottle of perfume through security. "Thank you, but I don't think the prison staff would allow us to take this bottle into our ward," I said.

The judge called for his clerk and asked for his official stationery. Then he wrote a note saying that the perfume was a personal gift from Judge Pirabbasi and must be allowed into the prison. We took the bottle and the note and left the courtroom to find our sisters, who had waited outside. Mr. Aghasi was still griping at us for not accepting the statement he'd given. "Why did you have to say you disagreed with it?" he muttered.

Our soldier escorts interrupted us and said we had to leave. Shirin and Elena had brought us sandwiches, which they handed to us as we parted. Walking toward the waiting room to wait for the bus, I asked one of the soldiers if we could wait outside rather than in the filthy room that smelled like a trash dump. He gave us permission. When our sisters saw us going to the yard, they walked toward us, but before they got to us, a woman from the court building yelled at our soldiers. "What are they doing outside? Why aren't they in the holding cell?"

She made us go into that dreadful room, where flies buzzed around patches of dried vomit. We used our headscarves as breathing masks. The smell made me want to add my own vomit to the situation, but somehow I was able to control myself. Our appetites gone, we gave our sandwiches to other prisoners waiting for the bus. They wolfed them down as if they hadn't eaten in days.

| | |

Marziyeh

After an hour and a half wait, the bus took us back to Evin. During the ride, I played over in my mind what had just happened in court.

God wanted to put me to the challenge on the anniversary of my baptism. The first time I was asked the questions, I was free, happy, and surrounded by friends. Now I'm under the threat of death. God is asking, "Are you still a Christian?" The path to Christ is never the easy way. As Jesus said to His disciples in Mark 8:34, "If anyone would come after me, let him deny himself and take up his cross and follow me."

Today I renewed the promise I made to God on this date years ago. I promise to take up my cross and follow Christ. I want to die for God. I will follow Him forever. Sometimes God puts us in a difficult situation and tries us. This is the real test. "When you are in fear, will you still be true?" I decided in court to follow God even if it kills me. He is my lover, and I am faithful to Him. Life has no meaning without faithfulness to God. I'm happy I could confess under the circumstances.

When we went in to be searched and showed the guards our note and the bottle of perfume, they were flabbergasted. "The judge treats you like this!" they exclaimed. The guards' attitudes changed instantly, and now they treated us with respect.

Everyone in Ward 2 was anxious to know what had happened. "Maybe they'll offer bail," one of them said. Maryam and I agreed that we'd never accept bail now. The regime should apologize to us because they'd arrested and imprisoned us without reason. We were innocent and they knew it.

"If you're offered bail, you should praise the Lord," a voice in the crowded room declared. "If you think this government will ever apologize to you, you're crazy."

"We believe in our God," I said. "We're sure God can show His victory. We can't do it, but God can show His power."

They were astonished at our story of how the judge had served us tea and given us perfume. Nothing remotely like this had ever happened before.

"I *know* they'll apologize now!" someone said, and everyone laughed.

Our comments in court made big news, though we never knew how word of our statements before Judge Pirabbasi could spread so fast.

| | |

MARYAM

A few days later, Marziyeh and I were called to the prison office, where a grumpy guard named Izadi was on duty. She had glasses, a wrinkled face, always wore a black *chador*, and looked like a witch. She often swore at prisoners, especially when she was talking on the loudspeaker. She said Mr. Ramezani was waiting to see us again. "Are you girls blind?" Izadi growled as she walked with us to the office door. "Can't you see there is a strange man in this office? Put your *chadors* on properly!" Maybe we had a few stray hairs showing, but mostly she was trying to show off her authority over us.

Mr. Ramezani didn't seem to mind about our *chadors*. In fact, he snickered at Izadi's sharp comments. He handed us vitamins and medicine he'd received from our sisters.

"These items are for these two prisoners," he said calmly but with authority to Izadi. "They have been authorized by the judge. Please be sure they receive all of them."

Izadi had a sudden and dramatic change of attitude. Once she realized that our visitor was someone very important, she became a different person. Mr. Ramezani said he wanted to speak to us in private.

"Of course," Izadi said in a calm and polite tone that we'd never heard from her before. "There's an office right here you can use. I will bring you tea." We accepted the offer of the room but declined the tea. Izadi left us with Mr. Ramezani and a guard, closing the door behind her.

As we sat down, our visitor asked, "Did you read the verse in the Koran that I asked you to read?"

"Yes, but we didn't understand it," Marziyeh said. "There was nothing in it about Jesus. We think that most of the verses in the Koran that refer to Jesus are in the part known as the Nessa. Is that what you meant?"

"No, I gave you the right verse. Did you pay attention to it?"

"We could only read the Farsi translation," I said. "The verse is written in Arabic and we don't understand Arabic." It is said that the miracle of the Koran is in its original Arabic. True Muslims are supposed to read it only in the original language.

"I see," Mr. Ramezani said. "You should have concentrated on the Arabic text, which indicates that this is the verse in the Koran that refers to Jesus not only as the Son of God but also as the Savior of mankind. Furthermore, the Muslims have changed its meaning in Persian so that you don't get an accurate reading in Farsi."

I had never heard this before. "How do you know this?" I asked.

"The man who has asked me to visit you is the one who told me all about this."

"Who is this man? Is he a Muslim? Why does he want to help us?" The mention of this anonymous figure was a surprising and very mysterious turn of events.

"He is not a Muslim," Mr. Ramezani explained. "In fact, he does not believe in any religion at all. He can connect to all the prophets, and in one of his dreams, Jesus asked him to come and visit you. He and I have been ordered to help you out of your situation.

"This person says you will soon be freed and then he will personally tell you about his message. We are certain you will be set free soon." He shifted gears suddenly, leaving us to ponder the identity of this amazing mystery man. "When do you think Jesus will return?"

"No one has a definite date for it," Marziyeh answered. "The Bible makes that clear. I'm not a fortune-teller, so I can't know the day."

"The return of Jesus is very near," Mr. Ramezani said confidently, then added some confusing statements about dates and the calendar. When we asked him to explain more clearly, he said, "I cannot tell you everything right now."

His cell phone rang. He listened for a moment. "Can you guess who I'm with right now? Miss Rostampour and Miss Amirizadeh." He spoke for another minute before finishing the call, then said to us, "This is very interesting. That was the man who sent me here to bring you this message. He didn't know we were meeting now, but just called to ask how you were.

When I said I was with you, he was very pleased and asked me to give you his best regards. He also wanted me to tell you that you will soon be released from prison. The eight months you've been in here have been a blessing from God. He wanted to protect you from problems you would have faced if you'd been outside during this time."

Could he have meant the riots after the presidential election? Would we have been convicted on different charges? Killed? Something else? We had no idea.

"Now your prison term is over, and you must be freed," he went on. "This man lives in a provincial city and is traveling to Tehran to see you."

"Is he that confident about our freedom?" I asked.

"He surely is!"

Mr. Ramezani told the guard in the room that he must not say anything about our conversation because it would cause trouble. "Rest assured that I will not tell anyone," the guard answered.

Our visitor stepped out of the room for a few minutes to see another prisoner who knew him and had heard he was in the office. While our guard was alone with us, he asked, "Are you the two Christian prisoners who get all the mail?"

"Yes, we are. How many letters are there?" Marziyeh asked.

"There's a whole roomful of letters and postcards, with dozens more arriving every day. Several soldiers open and read them, and then report the contents to the authorities."

"What do the letters say?"

"Many of them are in English, and most of them say the same thing. They talk about the sheep and the shepherd, they say they are praying for you, they encourage you to keep resisting, they send you Bible verses, things like that. Some people send drawings."

"Since they don't give them to us, maybe at least you should read them and benefit from their contents," Marziyeh suggested.

When Mr. Ramezani came back, I reminded him that he had said earlier we could have our letters if the judge agreed. I told him that Judge Pirabbasi had ruled we could have them.

"If so, he should have sent a written order to the prison office. The judge knows perfectly well that words don't mean anything in prison; everything has to be done through official written orders. I think, in any case, he will order that you get the letters after you've been released, because there are so many of them, and prisoners aren't allowed to receive letters anyway."

By the time we returned to Ward 2, our meeting with Mr. Ramezani had already made headlines. Some of the inmates remained jealous of the attention we received, yet they all wanted to know about our discussion and what would happen next. We hid our vitamins and medicine in our bedcovers. We heard later that our visitor had stayed to talk with several other women prisoners after we left so as not to raise suspicions that he had come again only to see us.

This visit left our heads spinning. Who was this Ramezani character, really? Who was his mysterious friend? How could they be so sure we would be released?

It was all the more shocking and disappointing, then, when the next time we were summoned to the office by the raucous loudspeaker, it was to go back to the place we dreaded most and had hoped never to see again.

CHAPTER 24

WAITING ON THE LORD

MARYAM

"Maryam Rostampour! Marziyeh Amirizadeh!" Our names rang out over the loudspeaker. When we reported to the office, a guard from Ward 209 was waiting to blindfold us and take us to that miserable place. It was very unusual for prisoners to return to 209 after their cases had been heard by the Revolutionary Court. Fereshteh told us that it usually meant a prisoner's sentence was either going to be extended or applied.

Marziyeh and I walked to the other building, peeking out from under the bottom of our blindfolds to watch our escort's feet as usual, and waited in the hallway facing the wall. We heard a woman's frantic voice cry out, "I swear to God I'm innocent! There must be some mistake!"

I was taken alone into a room, with Marziyeh left facing the wall in the hallway.

After the guard had left the room and shut the door behind him, a voice told me to remove my blindfold. In front of me were two men sitting at a large desk. One of the men wore a gray suit and had only one hand. The other man was much older, with white hair. The older man invited me to sit. He asked how long I had been in prison.

"More than eight months," I answered.

"Why did you convert to Christianity? Didn't you know that those who renounce Islam are considered apostates and their sentence is death?"

"I met with Jesus Christ. My story is a long one, and I've told it many times since I've been here. Would you like to hear it again?"

"You are very decent girls," the white-haired man said. "You were also our guests here in Ward 209 for a while." Something familiar about him registered in my mind—I knew his voice! He had been one of the interrogators in 209 before, but this was the first time I had spoken to him without wearing a blindfold.

Now the younger man spoke. "Miss Rostampour, we have no problem with you and your friend being Christians."

Really! Then how to explain the past eight months?

"Everyone is entitled to his or her own beliefs. You chose to be Christians."

He made it sound as if becoming a Christian in Iran was as simple as buying a loaf of bread. *So they arrested and imprisoned us just for fun, and Christian converts don't really face the death penalty?* Obviously, he was trying very hard to offset the mess others had made of our case with some syrupy language. *Someone is really worried about what the regime has done to us and how it makes them look!*

"What can I do for you?" the man asked.

What can you do for us? Anything either of us requested would make us beholden to him, which no doubt he would desperately like to happen.

"I don't need anything from you, thank you."

"Do you know who this is?" the older man asked.

"No, I don't."

"This gentleman is Mr. Jafari Dolatabadi, Tehran's chief prosecutor. He is here to help you."

The chief prosecutor, here to help us? Most interesting!

"If you need anything, all you have to do is ask."

Mr. Dolatabadi smiled and said, "I have the power to let you go free or not. Are you sure you don't want me to help you with anything? I can set you free."

"I sincerely thank you for your kindness," I replied, "but my trust and reliance are with God. I believe it is the Lord's will that Marziyeh and I should be in prison, and that our freedom lies in His hands alone. If the Lord wishes to release us, no one can stand in His way. Of course, we don't like staying in prison and we would rather be free, but we prefer to wait for the Lord's decision on the matter."

I was irritated at Mr. Dolatabadi's attitude and his remark that he had the power to release us. It reminded me of Pontius Pilate's claim that he had the power to save Jesus.

The two men looked at each other and smiled. "Very well," the prosecutor said. "So you don't request anything from me. By the way, have you ever been to Rome?"

"No, never."

"Then why is the Vatican involved in your case? What's going on?"

"I have no idea. We've been in prison and have had no news of what's going on in the outside world. However, it's only natural for the Vatican to get involved with our case because we have been imprisoned on charges of being Christians and believing in Jesus." (We never learned any more about the Vatican's reported involvement.)

"In any case," Mr. Dolatabadi said, "you must have known that to convert to Christianity and then promote it the way you have in this country is quite dangerous and subjects you to execution. You must be very careful."

The door opened and Marziyeh came in. After being told to remove her blindfold, she took a seat. The men offered us sweets and treated us like honored guests rather than prisoners threatened with death. Clearly, the Vatican's involvement had brought the publicity in our case, and the need to resolve it, to a new level on an international scale.

Mr. Dolatabadi asked lots of questions about conditions inside Evin—food, medical care, our general health—as if he, the city's chief prosecutor, had no idea what went on in the city's prisons. Marziyeh gave him an earful about her sickness and the lack of decent medical care for herself and everyone else. I talked about my recent food poisoning and the careless treatment for that.

"How could they do this to you?" Mr. Dolatabadi exclaimed.

I started telling him about the ridiculous rule requiring every prisoner to go outside for the morning roll call, regardless of her condition. He picked up the phone and entered a number.

"Mrs. Rezaei, Miss Amirizadeh and Miss Rostampour are in my office and have complained about some prison problems." There was anger in his voice. "I ask you to sort these out as soon as possible."

Mr. Dolatabadi then launched into a long monologue, starting with his belief that everyone should be free to practice whatever religion they like, but that our problem was in generating so much publicity about Christianity and talking about it with too many other people. He advised us not to endanger our young lives by defending these beliefs so inflexibly. Beneath his words, we saw a completely different story.

Like everyone else we had talked to lately, he was scrambling for a way to avoid an international crisis by persuading us to change our story about what had happened to us—forget the mistreatment and relentless interrogations; overlook the inhumane treatment and injustice; believe that our mistreatment at the hands of Mr. Sobhani, Mr. Haddad, our anonymous interrogators, and everyone else was because of their personal actions and opinions, not because they were acting in the name of the kindly, compassionate, and accommodating Iranian regime. That's what they wanted the world to believe.

After Mr. Dolatabadi finished his speech, Marziyeh and I were blindfolded and taken back to our ward. As always, our friends crowded around to hear what had happened. When they found out we had met with Mr. Dolatabadi, they were convinced it was a prelude to our release and the final settlement of our case. We began to think they might be right, that we actually were going to be freed soon. As happy as the thought made us, it was sad to imagine leaving Shirin, Marjan, and our other wonderful friends behind. That night, we talked to them about our hopes for the future, feeling somehow that these might be our last hours together with them. We promised one another we would meet again as free people. We didn't concentrate on the sad feelings, but on all the happy times we'd shared together.

| | |

Within days, we found ourselves blindfolded once again, escorted to Ward 209, and seated before Mr. Dolatabadi and his white-haired companion.

"I have agreed to release you on bail until your trial begins," the chief prosecutor said.

We had heard this story before from Judge Sobhani, and it turned out to be a lie. Even so, the words made us hopeful.

"You will be released after posting bail of 200 million tomans [about $100,000] each."

"We don't have anyone who can help us raise that much money," Marziyeh said. "Besides, after nearly nine months in prison under these charges, we want to see our case resolved. We think the case should be settled instead of releasing us on bail while still under charges."

"You wouldn't actually have to pay the bail," the older man said. "Your sisters could stand as your guarantors. I can call them now and they can go straight to the courthouse to register their names on your behalf, and their guarantee will serve as your bail."

"I have agreed to your freedom," Mr. Dolatabadi added. "But please don't give any interviews to the press."

We said we would contact our sisters and talk it over. We were blindfolded and left in the corridor, waiting for our escort to take us back to the public ward. As we stood there, someone handed us each a takeout container of barbecued chicken and rice. We heard the old man's voice say, "Eat. These are for you."

I couldn't suppress a laugh. "We can't eat with blindfolds on." Instead, they allowed us to take the delicious-smelling food with us.

The sight of the food amazed the guards in the Ward 2 office, who were used to seeing prisoners return from 209 exhausted and worried, and sometimes bruised and bleeding. They didn't want us to go into the ward with our food, so they sent us into the kitchen to eat it. It tasted heavenly! But it was so rich and we hadn't had real food in so long that we couldn't eat it all. Marziyeh and I split one container of food and gave the other to some other prisoners who were in the room. After we'd eaten and were walking to our cell, Amiri, the guard who had been so mean to me the night I got food poisoning, called out to me. She apologized profusely for her rude behavior that night and also for forcing me and the others to attend the morning roll call outside. Right behind her came Mrs. Rezaei, who also

257

apologized. Mr. Dolatabadi's brief phone call had ushered in a new world inside Evin Prison, at least for the moment.

| | | |

Marziyeh

The very next day, our names were called again to go to Ward 209. Instead of fearing for our safety, our friends were now convinced this summons was moving us yet another step closer to freedom. Parvaneh, the prisoner who made a little money as the cleaner of our room, asked for our autographs to prove she had shared a cell with two such famous people. We said we would gladly write in her book, but that we weren't famous and our words were for her alone. Others teased us good-naturedly by shouting, "What's on the take-out menu today?" and, "Who's coming to apologize to you today?"

We were blindfolded and taken to 209, where we waited in the corridor, facing the wall, until we were led into a room. A familiar voice told us to remove our blindfolds. It was our old interrogator, Mr. Mosavat. Sitting silently next to him was a middle-aged, heavyset man with a dark mustache and a stone-faced expression.

"Welcome," Mr. Mosavat said, as if he were greeting two old friends. "Please take a seat." He had evidently been in an accident. The side of his neck was red and looked as if it had been burned. One of his hands was bandaged.

"I hear you are being freed," he said. "It took us nine months. I'm not sure whether you believe me or not, but I want you to know that my colleagues and I were heavily involved in pursuing your case and did our best to get you released. Those efforts have now borne fruit."

Oh, really?

"Don't you ever think that it was international pressure or the church that secured your freedom. You were just unlucky that your arrest coincided with the Nowruz holidays, and after that we had the election and its aftermath. All these events delayed the processing of your case. But anyway, when are you going to be released? Who is going to pay your bail or stand as your guarantor?"

"It's not clear yet," Maryam said. "Our lawyer is looking into it."

"Well, God willing, you will soon be freed! I heard from Mr. Dolatabadi the good news of your forthcoming release. He asked me to speak with you, as there are a few points we'd better tell you before you leave prison.

"You should know that, from now on, your lives will be under the spotlight. If in the past, as you say, you didn't know that such things as promoting the message of Jesus and his prophecies are illegal in this country, now you know it very well. If anything else happens to you, you cannot claim you didn't know about it. So you'd better not do anything that could cause you any problems or 'accidents.' Do not contact any sources outside the country. Do not attend any Christian gatherings at your home or anywhere else.

"Also, on behalf of the system, I ask for your forgiveness and hope you will forget the mistreatments you have been subjected to and will return to your normal life. And," he added a little defensively, "you must excuse me for not visiting you these past few months. I was sick."

He leaned back in his chair. "Now you can say anything you wish. You can even swear at us."

I answered Mr. Mosavat simply, "I can only reply with the last words of Jesus, who said, 'Father, forgive them, for they know not what they do.'"[1]

Dismissed, Maryam and I put on our blindfolds and left the room. "You know the way by now," Mr. Mosavat called after us lightheartedly as we started down the hall.

That afternoon, we received a phone call from the mysterious Mr. Ramezani. "I hear the chief prosecutor has been to see you and you're about to be freed."

"Yes. He has agreed to a guarantor for our bail until our trial," I said.

"Well, thank God for that. I told you that you would soon be free! I've called to offer my congratulations and to ask you to definitely contact me after your release. I must see you. I also want you to know I am very happy about your freedom."

We promised to contact him later.

The guard standing nearby said, "So you are to be set free?"

"Yes."

"What was your charge?"

"Believing in Jesus Christ."

"Well, thank God for that." She and another guard stared in amazement. It was probably the first time the head of the security section had called a prisoner to congratulate her on her release. When Maryam told another prisoner that Mr. Ramezani had called us, the woman joked, "Now it's President Ahmadinejad's turn to come visit you in prison!"

| | |

While the final chapters of our story were playing out, other prisoners were hearing news both good and bad about their charges. Reihaneh's case was also in Bureau 26 with Judge Pirabbasi, who had been so kind to us. The judge had encouraged her to end her hunger strike and had offered her something to eat in his courtroom. She was soon released on bail and joyfully reunited with her family.

Our sweet friend Marjan was sad at the thought that we would leave her. She became depressed and uncharacteristically argumentative. I reassured her we would always hold her in our hearts and be praying for her. "Our freedom must not be the end of our friendship with you," I said. "We shall never forget you. You've promised to get in touch with us whenever you are freed. No matter how long it takes, we will be waiting to hear from you and celebrate your freedom."

After the comings and goings of prisoners over the months, our closest remaining friend was Shirin Alam Hooli. Since her roommate Silva had been released, Maryam and I were the ones she had spent most of her time with. She was so gentle and had such a kind spirit, yet she had endured so much. Hearing of her friend's execution had been a terrible blow, and now we, her best remaining friends, were about to leave her.

The last big hurdle seemed to be arranging the bail guarantee. We were on the phone to our sisters every day working out the situation. Because they had no personal wealth, they had found two well-to-do businessmen who owned property and were willing to guarantee our bail. Our sisters went with these businessmen to see Mr. Dolatabadi and make the arrangements. They brought a big bouquet of flowers to give him. However, he was out and they were unable to see him. When they went a second time, the same thing happened. But this time Mr. Dolatabadi's secretary told them they could come back and see Mr. Ghotbi, another judge in the Revolutionary Court, and he would handle our case.

Elena and Shirin appeared before Judge Ghotbi, and the two businessmen offered their guarantee. However, because the judge didn't know the men, and because Maryam and I didn't know them, the judge refused to accept their guarantee and said they had to put the full amount on deposit. He said that, as an alternative, our lawyer, Mr. Aghasi, could sign our guarantee. We had already asked him to do this for us, but he had declined.

The judge then suggested that our sisters themselves could be the guarantors. Under the circumstances, they agreed to take the risk, even though they wouldn't be able to pay the bail if it became necessary. When they went to another room to sign and fingerprint the forms, the judge asked them if they were also Christian. They said that they were.

"Of course, you are aware that I am allowed by our religious law to cut you in half with a sword right now," he fumed at them, his voice rising. Then he regained control of himself. "But I prefer to leave it to the law to decide." He explained that he would now send a letter to Evin, instructing the warden to set us free. The charge of apostasy was still pending, but at least we could be on the outside until the trial. As we had learned from following our friends' cases, it often happens in Iranian courts that prisoners are released on bail but the charges are never settled or dropped. That way, the accused still have a case open against them and can be rearrested on the flimsiest pretext.

Every night, we wondered whether this would be our last night in Evin Prison. Our last night in these crowded, smelly rooms. Our last night in triple-bunk beds, lying awake looking at the ceiling or our cellmates who were already asleep. Our last night living on awful canned meat and other miserable food. Our last night surviving dangerously incompetent medical care. We wondered whether it would be the last night we would spend with our dear friends, especially Shirin, Marjan, Setare, and Mahtab. Our last night to do God's work behind bars.

We had always heard that the final few days before release were harder to endure than all the other time combined. Now it was true for us. The hours and minutes crawled by. Compounding our feelings were the hard choice our sisters had made and the risks they had assumed on our behalf.

And in the midst of anticipating our release, there was an indescribable feeling of terrible sadness at the thought of leaving our precious friends behind. Never in our lives would we form friendships as deep and rich as the ones God had blessed us with behind the high and foreboding walls of Evin Prison. The word *Evin* wasn't strange to us anymore; it was now as familiar as our own names. It was our university, in that it had taught us things we could never have learned anywhere else. It was our church, a place of sincere, deep faith and trust in Jesus Christ. For months, it had been our home and family. It had become a part of our lives, representing the worst days of our lives as well as some of the best.

| | |

MARYAM

Shirin Alam Hooli was trying not to show her emotions, strong and stoic to the end. Sometimes she would say, "I'll miss you," but that was all. Late in the afternoon, Shirin, Marziyeh, and I went for a walk in the prison yard, holding hands.

"I want to pray for you," I told Shirin. She laughed and said, "Go ahead!" But when I started, I realized I couldn't go on without crying. I cut the prayer short because I didn't want to cry then.

The day was gray, chill, and drizzling. As she had a thousand times before, Shirin looked up at the square patch of sky we could see from the courtyard. A flock of birds passed overhead, flying low in the bad weather. "I wish I were free like those birds," she said wistfully. "I wish I were free like them. I wonder if I'll ever see the whole sky again, instead of only a piece of it framed by a window or a prison wall."

She looked around the courtyard with the sad stump where the lone tree had been, the wet ground, the numbingly familiar walls. "I'm so tired of this place," she said. "I don't think I can stand it another minute. When do you think I will be free, Maryam?"

"I don't know," I said, surprised and concerned by my friend's somber tone. "But I hope it will be very soon."

"Don't forget our promises to each other," Shirin said, suddenly more animated. "You will go and prepare our green farm, because when I'm free, I'm coming there to you."

We had talked endlessly about Shirin's dream of living on a green mountain far away, in a wooden house surrounded by peace and quiet. Sometimes it seemed so real we could almost feel ourselves standing on that mountain in the pleasant breeze, calm, serene, and free.

"Be sure to keep in touch with us, so we'll miss each other less until you join us," I reminded her. It was hard to talk. I wished that Shirin's case could be settled before we left. Only God knew when we would see her again.

Later that night, our friends had a going-away party for us. After lights out, we all sang songs and they gave Marziyeh and me poems, notes, and little gifts to remember them by. Arefeh gave us a funny letter recalling her remark when we first arrived that we were stupid for insisting on our faith. She wrote, "I wish everybody in the world was as stupid as you!" We all tried to cover our sadness with laughter and joking, determined not to cry. Those of us who were closest decided to share a secret name so we would never forget each other. Besides Marziyeh and me, the group included Shirin, Arefeh, Kamila, Mahtab, Setare, Sousan, and Marjan. We were very different women, from different levels of society, with different faiths. But we were united forever in standing against the injustice that has destroyed the body and soul of the Iranian people.

We promised each other that one day we would meet again in a free Iran. Our greatest wish, our fondest dream, was that Iran would shake off the chains of its evil rulers and that the people of Iran would be delivered from injustice and dictatorship.

Though by now it was long past midnight, we were too excited to sleep. Tomorrow night we could find ourselves in a different world. Only God knew whether He was finished with us in Ward 2, Room 1 of Iran's most feared and brutal prison.

CHAPTER 25

NOT WHAT WE EXPECTED

MARYAM

The raucous sound of the loudspeaker woke me from a short and fitful sleep, ordering everyone outside as usual for the morning roll call. It was Wednesday, November 18, 2009 (in the Iranian calendar, Aban 27, 1388). This morning, for a change, Marziyeh and I went out for the attendance count. The weather at that early hour was bone-chilling, wet, gray, and depressing. After we were dismissed, most everyone went back to bed, but I couldn't possibly sleep.

I was so restless I went for a walk in the courtyard despite the cold and rain. I picked up a couple of wet leaves and a small rock from the pavement—reminders of a place I would likely not see again. Alone in the yard, I said a prayer for all of our friends. For an hour, I poured out my heart about my love for them, my concern for the future, and all the other thoughts that flooded my mind.

After breakfast, when inmates usually left for the cultural center, no one on the ward wanted to go because they were afraid to miss our departure. But because prisoners were never released before noon, we encouraged everybody to go to their morning activities. The ones who stayed behind were uncharacteristically tense and short-fused. Tempers flared hotter than usual over telephone time and careless remarks. Even women who were usually calm seemed out of sorts.

Marziyeh and I went to see some of the children, especially little Alfi. We would miss him so much. We tried to play with him, but he had a cold and was in a grumpy mood. I lay down on his bed with him and cuddled him for a while. If only we could take him with us! Into a world of fresh air and healthy food and safety and running barefoot across the grass. A world he had never known. What would happen to him? What would happen to all these people we had grown to love so deeply? If only they could all be freed before we were.

Midday, the women returned from the cultural center for lunch. Shirin Alam Hooli came to our room to eat with us. "What do you feel like now that you're being freed?" she asked.

"I don't know," I said. "But I know we'll miss you."

Shirin answered, "When you are free, run to our mountain and shout for joy at the top of your lungs. Think about your freedom and don't worry about me. I'll be free, too. Come to my house and arrange my hair."

"All right, Shirin," I said with a smile. "But I wish we were together. Promise to look after yourself and get out of here soon."

"I think I'll be getting out of here soon myself," Shirin said laughing. "I've been here two years, and I'm really tired of this place."

| | |

One o'clock came, then two, the minutes crawling agonizingly by. I was waiting for someone in the hall when Mrs. Alipour burst out of the office, beaming, waving a piece of paper.

"Your freedom papers have arrived," she shouted as she threw herself into my arms.

A few minutes later, our names were announced, and the whole ward burst into cheers. We had already packed our few belongings. Now friends from all over the ward swarmed into our room to hug us and wish us well. Many were crying. Someone began to sing "Yar-e Dabestani-e Man," the Persian folk song by Mansour Tehrani that has become popular at many protests against the Islamic regime.

Then the women began to sing the song we sang whenever a political prisoner was released: "Go, go, and never come back!" I heard the sound of a plate shattering on the floor in our honor.

There was nothing left to do but walk through the corridor and out of the ward, yet Marziyeh and I could scarcely bring ourselves to leave. We carried our things from the cell into the corridor, still hugging and kissing everyone we could reach. Finally, we couldn't hold back our own tears any longer.

At the end of the hall, the guards told the other prisoners they couldn't walk any farther. We gave them all one final embrace, Shirin last and longest of all. Seeing each other's tear-stained faces made us laugh in spite of our sadness. How we would have given anything to take Shirin with us on those few final steps to freedom.

We kept walking, waving to the sea of faces framed in the doorway until the office door closed behind us. We moved through a series of checkpoints to a spot near the main gate of Evin Prison. We signed and fingerprinted one last form.

The guard who walked us to the gate was one we had seen many times before, though we'd spoken very little. "Are you the two Christians?" she asked.

"Yes, we are."

"I've heard a lot about you. I'm very happy that you are finally released." She looked around to see if anyone was nearby. "Can I ask you a favor?"

"Of course. What is it?" I said.

"I've heard that your prayers are always answered. I have a problem in my life. Could you pray for me, too, please?"

"Absolutely. We will pray to Jesus that your problem will be solved."

A sentry led us to the main gate, opened it, and ushered us through. We were free.

| | |

Marziyeh

The first thing we saw was our sisters waiting with their arms open wide. We embraced them like we'd never let go, laughing and crying at the same time. The soldier told us to leave the area without making any noise.

Usually when prisoners are released, all their friends and family are there to welcome them. In our case, someone made sure there was no public display or celebration.

I couldn't believe we could go anywhere we wanted. Driving toward our apartment, I stared at the traffic and commotion all around me, not feeling at all like I had expected to feel. For months, I had dreamed of this moment, but now that I was on the outside again, something was out of kilter. Though my body was free, my soul and spirit were still with our precious friends suffering terrible injustice inside Evin Prison. This thought made it impossible for me to enjoy our new situation. I felt strangely indifferent to our liberation.

Our sisters had cleaned our apartment, except for our bedrooms, straightening the mess the *basiji* had made the day they arrested us. Our books, computers, and other property were still missing. From the window in our apartment, we could see the walls of Evin Prison in the distance. We would never look at it in the same way again. Everything seemed so strange—the view, the rooms, our belongings were all so alien and unfamiliar. Maryam and I walked around staring, as if we'd never been there before.

We took turns in the shower. How huge and immaculate our bathroom was! No crowd, no time limit, no smell, no toxic-looking walls.

We looked at our furniture, clothes, pictures on the walls, and stacks of music CDs that the *basiji* had left behind. We had so much stuff, and it didn't even feel like ours. Frivolous possessions mocked us from every direction. The two girls who once bought and used all these items were gone, replaced by two people with a different outlook on life. We were restless—pacing through the rooms, sitting on the floor, alternately crying and stunned into silence. We had never once cried for ourselves in prison. Now the tears came in a flood.

Without understanding why, Maryam and I both had a sudden, overwhelming sense that our things were closing in on us. Our apartment was oppressively cluttered, and we had to throw out whatever wasn't relevant to our lives anymore, whatever could get our Christian friends into trouble. We dashed to our rooms and started ripping photos and posters off the walls, tearing up papers and lists, cleaning out our closets, tossing everything into the living room. After an hour or more, our sisters helped us put it all in trash bags and throw it away.

Somehow that made us feel better. Elena and Shirin prepared dinner—fresh, sanitary, and delicious—and ate with us: two kinds of stew, pasta, fresh fruit, and cookies. Every time we slowed down, they said, "Eat! Eat!" The meal gave us stomachaches after so long without regular food. These were the dishes we'd dreamed of for months, yet all we could think of now was our friends back in Ward 2 choking down that horrible slop. When prisoners leave, the other inmates ask for their phone numbers in order to keep in touch. Their first question during the first phone call is always, "What did you eat?" Our meal made us wish somebody would call. The moment would have been so much more enjoyable if we'd had our Evin friends on the line to celebrate with us.

That night, we couldn't settle down. This was not what we had expected. We were apprehensive, deeply frightened somehow, after feeling so confident all of our months behind bars, though we didn't know why we were afraid. We asked our sisters to drive us around town for a while. It was as if we wanted to run away from the home where we were arrested and which we hadn't seen for nine months. The streets and the crowds looked the same as we remembered. The difference was that now we watched the people and thought of the terrible burden they live under, whether they know it or not—a ruthless dictatorship based on oppressive laws that in the blink of an eye can rob anyone of their freedom, or even their life. Someone might be watching them right now, tracking their movements, listening to their phone conversations, monitoring their e-mails, ready to spring a trap on the flimsiest of pretenses.

We had tried desperately to give the people of Tehran an alternative. Not to warn them away from Islam or criticize the Muslim way of life if that's what they preferred, but only to let them know there was a choice and they deserved the right to make it for themselves, without threats or harassment. Was our work in Tehran over? Again, only God knew the answer.

We returned home and went to bed, each in her own room, with soft pillows and clean sheets. Lying alone in the dark, my mind raced with thoughts of the dear sisters we had left behind. I could see their faces, smell the ward, feel the close, unhealthy atmosphere of the place—and I missed it so much! I cried myself to sleep, only to be tormented by nightmares of the *basiji* bursting through our front door.

| | |

The morning couldn't come soon enough. First on our schedule was a visit to the doctor to begin treatment for the long list of health problems prison life had brought us or made worse: Maryam's damaged ear and ulcer, my aching back, headaches, tooth problems, and kidney troubles. We had complete physicals and received all the medicines we had been denied for so many months.

Our physical problems could be clearly identified and treated. Our hearts and minds were a different story. Although we had been released, our apostasy case was still pending. We had no doubt that we were being watched and all our phone calls and other communications were monitored. By now, we could spot the intelligence police at a distance whenever we went out. Our release had made news around the world. We were in the spotlight and our old friends were afraid to share it with us. We were worried for their safety in contacting us. Even when we did meet with old friends, who greeted us warmly, it was stressful to talk with them because they had no idea what we had been through and how hard it was to go on as before.

We spent far more time with our new friends—fellow prisoners who had also been released, and those still awaiting their fate behind the walls of Evin. One of our first visits was to Silva Harotonian, who now lived with her mother. She understood how we felt. She, too, had thrown all her old clothes and possessions away. She, too, was still awaiting trial and being shadowed by the security police. She and her mother were also under house arrest and forbidden from traveling outside the country.

For two years before our arrest, Maryam and I had hosted two home churches and given away New Testaments. For nine months in Evin Prison, we had spent every day praising Jesus and proclaiming His gospel. Now our evangelism work was stopped dead in its tracks. Iranians wanting to know more about Christianity dared not contact us. People who once attended our home churches wouldn't come near us. It was like we were in quarantine or had leprosy. We sympathized with their dilemma and spent most of our time at home to avoid raising suspicions of the *basiji* against our Christian friends. Any contact with us could put them in danger. The good news was that we heard indirectly of many cases where news of our arrest and our defiance had led others to Christ. When people learned we were willing to die rather than deny our faith, they wanted to know what it was that was worth that kind of sacrifice. Some we had spoken to in the past who hadn't been interested in Christianity now read the Bible eagerly and asked probing questions about it. We praised the Lord for that.

As our elderly apartment manager explained to me, "After learning about your arrest and your refusal to renounce your faith, I wanted to know what about Christianity could be so powerful that you would sacrifice your lives rather than renounce it. This made me think that if Jesus was not the truth, you would not have been able to resist these harsh conditions. I became very interested in finding and reading a copy of the Bible for myself."

Maryam and I had promised Mr. Ramezani we would contact him. We also wanted to ask him about getting the letters that had been sent to us in prison. Not wanting to use our own phones, we called him from a public phone a few weeks after our release. He was delighted to hear from us and admitted he didn't think that once we were free we would ever call him, since he was a high official in the government. He said that even though, at his suggestion, our judge had ruled we could have our letters, the prison office had overruled him and destroyed them all. Thousands of them.

To our amazement, he invited us to his house for lunch. He said the mysterious man who had dreamed about us, foretold our freedom, and sent him to Evin to visit us in the first place wanted to meet us. We hesitated to visit the home of a powerful man in the Iranian prison system, particularly since we knew we were being watched constantly. Yet we remembered that our mystery man had seen Jesus in a dream and was instructed by Him to come to our aid. Now he wanted to see us. We were so curious, we simply had to accept Mr. Ramezani's invitation.

Our first surprise was how modest his house was. The powerful bureaucrats in Iran live in ostentatious luxury. This house was small and unpretentious. Our host, simply dressed, greeted us at the door and introduced his attractive young wife and their two children. His wife was preparing the meal, and he was helping. Here was a man whose name struck fear in the hearts of all the guards and officials at Evin Prison cooking lunch for us in his own home. Only God could have worked out anything so fantastic. His wife was sweet-natured and calm, with a slim figure and a beautiful smile. After talking with her for a few minutes, we deduced that her husband had helped many other prisoners deal with unfair conditions. How he managed to do that and hold on to his position was another mystery.

Soon afterward, our benefactor arrived from his home in a provincial city. He had come to Tehran just to have lunch with us. He asked us about our conversion to Christianity and listened to our testimonies with rapt attention. He then shared some of his own beliefs and said he had spent years in prison for his opposition to Islam. He said he and like-minded people had meetings together, and he invited us to join them. As much as we would have liked to, we decided that for everyone's safety and for the sake of Mr. Ramezani's family and position, we would not accept his invitation. Our friend was not at all offended by our decision. Rather, he encouraged us to hold fast to our beliefs.

As we gave our testimonies, we noticed that Mrs. Ramezani was quietly crying. Our stories made a powerful impression on her. She asked us to pray for her, and we promised to do so. Mr. Ramezani and his guest encouraged us to keep in touch in order to support one another and exchange ideas.

On the way home, Maryam and I decided we should not maintain contact with Mr. Ramezani or his friend. It was just too risky for them. True, Mr. Ramezani had somehow persevered and survived in spite of the help he had given others. We simply didn't feel peaceful about accepting his offer to stay in touch. A few weeks later, we heard he had been transferred to a job in the provinces. There was no way to know whether our visit had anything to do with his reassignment.

Hearing that all our letters had been destroyed made us even more anxious to get our laptops, books, identity papers, and other personal property back. Silva, who had already gone through the process, explained what we had to do. We wrote a letter to the Revolutionary Court and delivered it in person to the clerk. He told us that the court would tell our lawyer where our things were and how to get them back. He recommended we not pursue the matter ourselves, because some court officials were very angry that we were out of prison. We were world figures in the news now. Our story, and the inability of the regime to control it, infuriated them.

Eventually, the court told Mr. Aghasi that our property was at the police station. We went to the station with Mr. Aghasi and were sent downstairs to speak to a bureaucratic drone named Mr. Yazdi, who was in charge of the storage section. When our lawyer showed him the letter from the court, Mr. Yazdi exploded in anger.

"Who told you to bring a lawyer down here? We don't deal with lawyers! There's no reason for you ladies to bring one with you!"

More likely, he was concerned that Mr. Aghasi knew the law and wouldn't allow him to take advantage of us as he usually did with ex-prisoners trying to get their property back. He finally calmed down, and we convinced him we weren't there to make trouble, but that the court had instructed us to come to him for our property. He asked for a list of items, and we gave it to him.

"I'll look for them and call you when they're available," he said brusquely. "Next time come by yourselves. Do not bring your lawyer to this place again."

A few days later, we got a call that our property was ready for pickup. This time, Mr. Yazdi acted like a different man, extremely friendly and polite. He had everything except our identity papers, which we had to come back for in another week. During our wait, we happened to see the officer who had taken us into custody the day we were arrested.

"Have you been in prison all this time for believing in Jesus Christ?" he asked.

"Yes, we have," I said. "You should know this, since it's your job to frame innocent citizens of this country."

"How did you get released?" he asked with genuine interest. We explained that our case had attracted international publicity and this put pressure on the regime to set us free. The whole matter was in the Lord's hands; these were the tools He used to carry out His will.

"You have no idea what goes on around here," the officer said. "They lock people up for having a couple of CDs or a bottle of whiskey. They must have kept you in prison on phony charges, too. I can't wait to leave this job. I'm only doing my conscription service. You must be famous now after all that has happened to you."

"Yes," Maryam said, "Mr. Rasti has a unique talent for framing his fellow citizens. But in so doing, he helped us spread the message of Jesus among the neediest people—the prisoners of Evin—and gave us worldwide publicity we never could have gotten on our own."

The young officer could only shake his head as he walked away. I like to imagine he has thought about that conversation since then. We certainly have.

CHAPTER 26

THE DAY WILL COME

MARYAM

As we waited for a ruling from the court, several of our friends got news about their own charges. Some were better than expected, others worse. Either way, at least for them the waiting was over.

Setare was sentenced to five years, along with her brother. When she called to confirm the news, she sounded almost lighthearted, laughing and hopeful for the future. She was a strong girl who could stand up to prison life as long as she knew the end was in sight. Arefeh, who had been arrested at a post-election demonstration where her cousin was beaten, was sentenced to four years. She was devastated when she called to give us the news. She couldn't believe she would be locked up for four years for one day of protesting. The judge said it was for her *intention* to act further against the regime. She was convinced he was punishing her for being from a *mujahideen* family, even though she herself was not a member. Her lawyer had already appealed her sentence, and Marziyeh and I tried to cheer her up with the hope that the appeal would be granted. Unfortunately, at best it would reduce her sentence by only a year, and three years was still terribly unjust.

One of the best stories was from our friend Fereshteh, who had suffered with multiple sclerosis in Ward 209 and was under the threat of life imprisonment or death. Her sentence was set at two years because of her medical problems. Her husband had never given up trying to persuade the judge to consider her illness, and finally his work brought this wonderful news. Furthermore, since she had already been in prison for a year, she had only one more year to go.

Mahtab, Sousan, and Rozita had all been freed, though their cases were still pending. Learning of their freedom was the best news we'd heard since our own release. We visited them all, which reinforced our belief that no one understood us as well as people who had shared our experience. Mahtab told us about going every week with her father-in-law to visit her fiancé, who was still in prison in another city. She and her fiancé remained very much in love; her support for him was incredible.

Sousan lived with her two daughters. She was battling depression, but remained as dedicated as ever to fighting the regime any way she could. We encouraged her to concentrate on her children and make sure they got a good education.

Rozita could not have been more joyful at being reunited with her three sons, and they were so happy to have their mother back. It was a joy to see the family content—though a shadow remained over them because her case was still awaiting a verdict.

| | |

Our friends still in Evin were in our thoughts every day. They called to give us the latest news, and we tried to keep their spirits up. The smallest gift or expression of kindness is vastly more meaningful inside prison than on the outside. We remembered how wonderful it had been to receive new clothes, and so we decided to send some to our friends to celebrate Nowruz, the Iranian New Year.

A couple of months after our release, as the New Year's holiday approached, Marziyeh and I went to the market and bought a whole armload of clothes and gave them to relatives of the prisoners to deliver for us. In return, we got a series of phone calls from friends to thank us for the gifts and for not forgetting them. The coming of Nowruz marked a full year since we had been arrested; we had observed the holiday at Evin just after we arrived.

As time went on, our biggest concern was our friend Shirin Alam Hooli. She called to say she'd been interrogated in Ward 209 yet again. Two people questioned her this time. They said if she would give them a list of her friends, maybe they could cancel her execution decree. When she refused, they told her that she was under their control and had two choices: cooperate or die. They ordered her to make a video interview to be broadcast on television. She refused to do that, too. Then they said, "This is the last time we will see you. We will have nothing more to do with you." That statement confused and frightened her.

The stress of her interrogation had aggravated her physical problems. Headaches and nosebleeds were more frequent, and her eyesight began to fail more rapidly; she couldn't see well enough to knit anymore. When we told her she should go to the doctor, she said she had told the authorities she needed new glasses, but they had ignored her.

Shirin called later to say that her brother, Esa, had learned that her sentence would be life in prison. "But I can't stand it," she declared, sounding uncharacteristically forlorn. "I would rather be executed. All the political prisoners have been moved together in Room 6; they argue politics constantly. I have no patience for these discussions anymore. They're useless and I'm tired of them." She was reaching the end of her endurance.

A letter she wrote to her judge and the interrogators somehow found its way onto the Internet. Her powerful words sparked protests around the world, which lifted her hopes a little. We tried to encourage her by saying we thought her decree would be changed.

"I think I will be freed soon," she said. "When I told the other girls that, they laughed. But I won't stay in here forever."

The commutation of her sentence to life in prison, plus the worldwide response to her letter, made us hopeful that in time her prison term might be reduced even more. Then we got a call from Esa that was like a knife to the heart.

He called my cell phone, so agitated and distraught he could scarcely speak. "Please help me! Please help me!" he begged over and over. "I have nobody else! I'm devastated! For God's sake help me!"

"What is it? What's happened?"

"They're going to execute Shirin!"

"What are you talking about? She told us you said the decree was changed by the judge and her sentence had been commuted!"

"That never happened, but I didn't have the heart to tell her. I told a lie instead."

Marziyeh and I agreed that we had to see Esa and get the whole story. To keep the police from overhearing us, we picked him up in Haft-e-Tir Square and drove around while we talked.

"Judge Salavati has confirmed the death decree in the appeals court," he said, frantic with fear. "The written copy of his decision will be sent to Evin. Shirin will have it in a few days."

Judge Salavati, known as "the killing judge," was famous for sentencing prisoners to death. He looked the part, too, with heavy black eyebrows, his big, square face frozen in a fearsome scowl.

What could we do? We met with Silva and some other women to formulate a plan. One woman wrote to Mr. Dolatabadi, the head of the judiciary who had come to see us near the end of our sentence. She claimed to be Shirin's mother and begged him for mercy. We knew the judges liked it when people begged. We prepared a summary of Shirin's life and the facts in her case to distribute to human rights organizations. Others started a blog about Shirin to get publicity and support. The final appeal would be heard in one month: that was all the time we had to save our dearest friend's life.

Esa told Shirin what we were doing. The first time Marziyeh and I talked with her after she learned the truth about her sentence, we could scarcely speak. We didn't know what to say at first, and she was furious with her brother for lying to her. Finally we started joking with each other about Shirin going over to "the other side."

"Promise me that once you arrive there, you'll get in touch and tell me what it's like," I said, fighting back tears.

"Definitely," Shirin answered. "I'll come scare you every night. As soon as my soul leaves my body, I'll fly to your house because it's the closest to Evin Prison. You know how I always wanted to see your house, and now I will."

We talked about somber things, but made them sound like a game. "Promise me that when I die you'll be waiting for my body outside Evin," she admonished. "If you do, I promise to tell you a very important secret."

"We'll be the first people there," I assured her.

We talked regularly after that, keeping Shirin up to date on our efforts to help her. We told her to write a letter explaining that she had been tortured and drugged, and that her old video "confession" was nothing but a string of lies. We begged her to pray to Jesus to help her. He could perform a miracle and spare her life. The thought of this made her happy and she promised to pray. We prayed together over the phone. There's no doubt she loved Jesus in her heart, though she would never say so. She was very glad to hear that many Christians were praying for her. We asked our friends still in Evin to keep a close watch on her and comfort her as much as they could.

| | |

Marziyeh

After the Nowruz holidays, we received word that our court appearance on charges of apostasy would be held on April 13, 2010, at 9:00 a.m. To our surprise, the hearing would be in the provincial court of justice, where we had not been before. This was where many heavy sentences were handed down, including executions.

Maryam and I knew there was a chance we might be sent to prison again. We passed the word to our friends on the inside that we might be rejoining them soon. We also packed suitcases to take to court with us, just in case.

On the appointed morning, we arrived at the courthouse. Leaving our luggage in the car, we stepped inside an enormous building with a seemingly endless maze of hallways and security forces everywhere. Finally, we found the right bureau and waited for Mr. Aghasi. After a few minutes, he came limping into the room. He had some kind of pain in his legs and could barely walk. When we told him we had our luggage in the car, we all laughed to break the tension. He warned us that there were security cameras everywhere, so it would be better if we didn't look happy. He still thought that part of the reason the judge had refused to see us on an earlier trip was because we didn't look like we were afraid of him. Mr. Aghasi explained that we would appear today before a five-judge panel that would make the final ruling on our apostasy charge.

We waited for an hour until our names were called. When we walked into the courtroom, a huge room filled with empty chairs, it took our breath away. Up front was a long desk on a raised platform with the center chair raised higher than the rest. In this highest seat presided the chief judge, a fat middle-aged man with gray hair and beard. On either side were two younger associate judges. A veiled woman sat at a table in front of them. Two other men sat in the corner. Our instinct was to take seats in the middle of the room, but Mr. Aghasi directed us to a table directly in front of the judges. Maryam and I were so used to laughing in order to calm ourselves down that it was hard to resist, yet we maintained control. Our polite greeting to the panel was met with stony silence. We sat down with Mr. Aghasi at the table.

For ten minutes, no one said a word. We couldn't tell whether the judges were reading something in front of them or staring down at us. Or maybe sleeping. We were thinking that if every judge asked us only a few questions each, we would be there for hours. At last, the chief judge intoned a prayer to Allah and ordered the charges against us to be read. The veiled woman stood and read the indictment in a loud voice. It was a long statement charging us with apostasy, promoting Christianity, and possessing Bibles and illegal CDs. It accused us of being apostates who must be dealt with according to Islamic law and asked the court to hand down the "maximum possible punishment for promoting Christianity." As everyone in the room knew, the maximum possible punishment was execution.

The chief judge trained his eyes on us. "Miss Rostampour, do you accept these accusations?"

"No."

"Miss Amirizadeh, do you accept these accusations?"

"No."

"Mr. Aghasi, write down your clients' defense and hand it to the court."

We watched as our lawyer started writing the words that would determine our future. By now he knew better than to try to shade the truth or minimize our Christian faith in any way. He wrote that we had never insulted Islam or the beliefs of others. He wrote that the Bibles and CDs belonged to us and that we had never engaged in promotional activities against the government.

While Mr. Aghasi was writing, one of the associate judges shuffled a stack of papers.

"Miss Rostampour?" he said.

"Yes?"

"I have a few questions for you."

Before he could say another word, the chief judge cut him off. "Ask your questions later!"

"All right," the younger judge answered. "I just wanted to satisfy my curiosity."

Another associate judge had an angry look on his face and a tone in his voice to match. "I have a few questions too!"

Mr. Aghasi stood and handed his written defense to the chief judge, who glanced at the page and turned his attention to us. "Does each of you accept the defense your lawyer has given?"

We said we did.

The angry young judge interjected, "At least let the lawyer read their defense so we can all hear it."

By this time, all four associate judges had sour expressions on their faces. They had come armed with stacks of questions. Evidently, the chief judge had no intention of allowing them to ask any. He called us to the bench and leaned over to speak to us.

"Sign this statement and these forms saying you were in court, and you are free to go home." They were not acquittal documents, only papers saying we had appeared before the panel.

Almost exploding with anger, one of the younger justices barked, "Don't think it will always be so simple. We've let you off the hook this time. But if you ever step into this courtroom again, you will surely be sentenced to death."

After we signed, the chief justice said that our lawyer would be informed of the final disposition of our case. Outside the courtroom, Mr. Aghasi could barely contain his joy. I thought he might go skipping down the corridor, leg pain and all.

"This means you will be acquitted," he said. "That other judge made such a mess of things. Finally your case will be resolved and you will be truly free. I never imagined it would be this easy."

For the first time since our arrest, we did indeed feel truly free. Although we still didn't have an official ruling, our lawyer had no doubt that this was our final court appearance. An indescribable burden was lifted from our shoulders. The pressure was off.

| | |

After a lot of thought, discussion, and prayer, we had decided that once all the legal matters were put to rest we would leave Iran. Though we had been physically released from Evin Prison, we were still held captive by a regime that monitored our every move and could arrest us again at any time. Even without charges pending against us, the *basiji* would never be far away. Christians and anyone curious about Christianity would endanger themselves merely by talking to us, much less visiting us or meeting us somewhere. Some of our friends ignored us in the street out of fear. They were captive in Iran, just as we still were. The whole country knew us by sight; it would be impossible to evangelize quietly, as we had in the past. If religious extremists took matters into their own hands, the government would probably secretly reward them for killing us.

Furthermore, after what had happened, we knew that if we gave the regime the slightest excuse for arresting us, our lives would be in grave danger at the hands of the courts. Iran was our home, our motherland; yet if we had to decide between our faith and our country, we would choose Christ.

Practically speaking, until our case was settled we were still under undeclared house arrest. At that time, we didn't want to leave Iran even if we could, because the government could have announced our "escape" and branded us as fugitives: "See? We told you those Christian girls were up to no good!"

A formal acquittal would be a victory for Christ and a defeat for the regime. We wanted to see them squirm, humbled before an international audience by reversing a shameful death sentence for people who stood firm on their principles. Now that we had our acquittal in official form, it was time to go.

Our friends from Evin called to hear the news and to celebrate with us. We also kept up with Shirin Alam Hooli's case. Our greatest hope was that she would be rescued before we left. Four different activist groups were now publicizing her case and trying to bring pressure on the court to show leniency and compassion.

| | |

MARYAM

At breakfast some days later, Marziyeh's cell phone rang. She listened without speaking—she didn't have to say a word; her face told the story: Shirin Alam Hooli had been executed before dawn that morning. Sousan said she had heard it through the *mujahideen* grapevine.

Impossible! Even the sadistic animals of the Iranian court system would not execute a woman without a final decree from the court, would they?

While Marziyeh began tracing the story on the Internet, I took a taxi to Evin Prison. There was no commotion or scene of any kind outside the gate, only the usual two sentries. I went to an Internet café to see what I could learn online, but found no mention of Shirin anywhere. While I was there, Marziyeh called.

"It's true. Shirin is dead."

She had been killed many times by this savage regime. Now, by the grace of God, at least she was at peace. She was twenty-eight years old.

Marziyeh met me at the prison gate. Shirin's brother and another friend were there too. No one needed to speak. Our eyes told the story. Everyone was crying. We cried until the tears wouldn't come anymore. Then we sat on the curb to wait for Shirin's body to be released.

Eventually, we pieced together the story of her last hours. It was as if she knew the end had come. On Saturday night, she had taken a bath and put on the new clothes we'd sent her for New Year's. Everyone thought she looked prettier and happier than she had in a long time. She'd gone to visit the prisoners in Room 2. She was laughing and drinking tea when a guard came and took her away, locking the door behind her. Shirin spent her last night in solitary confinement. None of her friends knew she was being taken away to execution. No one had a chance to say good-bye. She was alone with her thoughts until the next morning, when she had a noose tightened around her neck. Who could have kicked the chair out from under that quiet, tenderhearted, artistic girl? Who could have been cold-hearted enough to look into those serene eyes as the light in them went out forever?

Shirin was one of five Kurds hanged together on Sunday, May 9, 2010, all convicted of belonging to the PKK, the Kurdistan Workers Party, which leads the struggle to form a Kurdish state from parts of Iran, Turkey, and Iraq. At the last moment, when their blindfolds were removed, they sang a Kurdish song until the instant the ropes silenced their voices.

We waited for her body, hoping to see her beautiful face once more. We had promised her we would be there. At last, her brother learned that her body and those of four other Kurds had already been taken to a cemetery. We would have to go there for the body, but here at the prison we could pick up Shirin's belongings. Marziyeh went inside to retrieve them.

The first item in one of the bags was a blue T-shirt she'd often worn with a necklace we gave her. We cried and hugged her clothes as we went through them, pretending they were Shirin. Who could have imagined that so soon after we'd last seen her we would be here and she would be dead? We heard her voice and saw her face before us, recalling images of her over the months wearing these different clothes. They still carried her scent. It was almost too much to endure.

Why, God? Why is there so much injustice in the world? How can You keep silent in the face of such evil as this? How many more brave young girls must die at the hands of this cruel, evil, cowardly regime?

The Lord sees the evil that people do to one another, and it makes Him sad. Sometimes, from our lowly, earthly perspective, it's impossible to see all of God's perfect plan. But He loves Shirin and suffered the same, and worse, to bring her forgiveness.

A guard at the cemetery said that, yes, the bodies of the executed prisoners were there, but no one could see them without written permission from the court. Because it was too late to get permission, we went home. Our apartment was a very bare place since we had thrown away so many of our belongings. The rooms felt cold and sad. Neither of us could sleep; Marziyeh and I spent the night on the living room floor crying in each other's arms.

The next morning, we went back to the main gate at Evin Prison, where a large crowd had gathered. News had spread that the regime refused to release any of the bodies of the Kurds who had been executed. Some students had started a petition. The crowd quickly identified us and thanked us for being there. Guards watching the people in front of the prison took special notice of us.

About noon, the relatives of another executed prisoner arrived and said the court had refused to release the bodies because they were afraid of a protest or riot. Instead, they gave cards to the dead prisoners' relatives and told them they could present them at the cemetery and collect the bodies later, when the threat of a riot had passed.

We offered our condolences to the mother and sister of Farzad Kamangar, a well-known and respected Kurdish teacher who was one of the victims.

"Don't cry," they told us. "Farzad and the others have not died. They are always alive and we should be proud of them. If we have lost them, we have you instead. The sisters and brothers of Farzad and Shirin and the others live on."

The lawyer for the executed Kurds had been in prison himself. Now he stood before the crowd, and with tears in his eyes said that the court would notify him when they could pick up the bodies, and he would tell everyone.

Marziyeh and I spent another sleepless night in our apartment. The phones at Evin had been cut off the morning after the executions. As soon as they were back on, our friends called in shock and pain. The news horrified them even more than it did us. We couldn't talk together; all we could do was cry for the whole fifteen minutes of phone time allowed. They had learned of Shirin's fate when a guard came in the morning after and said flatly, "She's dead." Nothing more.

The next morning, Mr. Aghasi called to say that even though he still didn't have written documentation, he had received oral confirmation that we were free and our files were closed. This was laughable because we had been told so many times that nothing is official in the Iranian legal system until it is in writing. Three of the judges had written their approval; the other two were on vacation. We never did receive written confirmation of our acquittal.

We also never received Shirin's body, and never saw her again. The executed Kurds were secretly buried in an unmarked mass grave to avoid a public protest or family reaction. We had Shirin's diary, which was smuggled out of Evin and given to us. After making copies, we gave it to a mutual friend to forward to Esa.

| | | |

On May 22, 2010, less than two weeks after Shirin's death, we left Iran, not knowing when or if we would ever be back. As our plane rose through the early morning sky on its way to Turkey, we looked out the window at the lights of Tehran. We had promised our friends in Evin that we would wave as we passed overhead. We were heading to an uncertain future, forced from the land of our birth, leaving a lifetime of memories behind.

Far below, most of the nation was still asleep—our suffering friends in their crowded Evin cells, our Christian brothers and sisters in their homes, and our many secret supporters throughout the country. Our hope for the future is in the Lord and His mercy for our suffering and persecuted people. This unjust and cruel regime cannot last forever. The day will come when God will cause this country to rise from the ashes and give them "the oil of gladness instead of mourning, the garment of praise instead of a faint spirit" (Isaiah 61:3). We pray that the Lord will use the two of us as part of His plan to fulfill this dream.

AFTERWORD

OUR FIRST STOP WAS TURKEY. We had set our sights on living in the United States, but to get there, we had to apply through the United Nations in Turkey. We lived in Antalya for nearly a year, traveling back and forth to the UN office in Ankara and writing the journals of our imprisonment that are the basis for this book. It was very hard to recall and write down the sad experiences we'd had, but we believed we had an obligation to those left behind to tell our story to the world.

We sat through many sessions of intense questioning, first by Turkish authorities and then by people at the UN. Some of our questioners doubted our story, even though it was all over the Internet. They doubted we were Christians, that we had been arrested, and that the Iranian government had backed down and dismissed the charges against us.

The Turkish police were unexpectedly harsh, though not as difficult as the UN officials who questioned us. Our first UN interviews were with Turkish nationals who worked for the UN, but who, like the police, clearly resented the fact that we had "converted" from Islam. Though they could Google our names and see what we had been through, they said we were making up our story and didn't have proper documentation. Later, when we interviewed with American UN officials in Istanbul, we continued to have trouble. One interviewer told Marziyeh she couldn't possibly be a Christian because her baptismal record was from a ministry organization and not from a church.

In God's timing, our visas were approved and we moved to Atlanta, where we established a good relationship with World Relief and began our new lives. It was like being on a different planet. We knew very little English, and everything about daily life was strange for us. We started right away trying to find a way to complete this book about what had happened to us. We wanted to tell the world about being captive in Iran ourselves, but even more so, about a whole nation being held captive.

As this book is published, we are each working on a degree at a community college. We look forward to sharing our story and being part of the American Dream!

As we reviewed our notes and gathered more information, we were reminded that every instance of oppression in the world is unique, and no single solution serves for all. We still don't know all the details about our release. What we do know is that it took a delicate balance between public pressure and private negotiation that only the Lord could have achieved.

If anyone had told us five years ago that by now we would have spent more than nine months in an Iranian prison, been threatened with death, had our story told around the world, written a book (in English, no less), and moved to Atlanta, Georgia, we would have said they were crazy. But we had no idea what the Lord had in mind for us. For all the heartache we have experienced on this journey, we wouldn't have missed it for anything. It has been our honor to serve Christ in this way, to take up our cross and follow Him faithfully anywhere He leads us. And it has been our honor to share this story with you.

NOTES

CHAPTER 2: THE GUILTY GIRLS
1. John 14:6

CHAPTER 5: NEW FRIENDS, OLD QUESTIONS
1. Matthew 7:7

CHAPTER 13: BLINDFOLDED AND BLESSED IN WARD 209
1. From the Constitution of the Islamic Republic of Iran, translated into English, http://www.iranonline.com/iran/iran-info/government/constitution-3.html.
2. "International Covenant on Civil and Political Rights," Office of the United Nations High Commissioner for Human Rights, http://www2.ohchr.org /english/law/ccpr.htm.
3. "Prisoners of Conscience/Medical concern," Amnesty International, UA 95/09, Iran, April 8, 2009, http://www.amnesty.org/fr/library/asset/MDE13/030/2009 /fr/6878ab7e-f6de-4948-9a1b-92ad7e06ca3f/mde130302009eng.pdf.

CHAPTER 15: A LESSON IN FAITH
1. See Revelation 22:13.
2. See Matthew 16:24.

CHAPTER 24: WAITING ON THE LORD
1. Luke 23:34

HOW THIS BOOK CAME TO BE

MARZIYEH AMIRIZADEH AND MARYAM ROSTAMPOUR are two courageous young women. After they were freed from Evin Prison, it would have been both easy and understandable if they had gone to a safe, quiet place to rebuild their lives away from public view. Instead, they began writing their experiences with the hope of sharing them with others.

Leaving their homeland of Iran, they first went to Turkey to apply for residence in the United States. Throughout the long application process, they clung to their dream of coming to America, and their belief that the Lord would use their experience, and their story, for good.

For eight months, they wrote, recalling every friendship, every court appearance, every emotion, every key event of their prison experience. It was very painful to revisit the terrible things that had happened—the shocking injustices, the abuses of the system, the stories of torture and execution of women who had become treasured friends. Sometimes they wrote in tears, barely able to continue, yet they kept going out of a sense of responsibility to the women left behind and with faith that somewhere, somehow, they would share their stories with the world. As difficult as it was to write about what they had seen and experienced, they eventually filled 1,900 handwritten pages with the history of their ministry and their time in Evin Prison.

When I first met Maryam and Marziyeh, I was impressed by their intensity and their sense of calling. They were *compelled* to tell of the Lord's power in their lives, and of the injustices they had suffered at the hands of the Iranian regime. They were tireless in their quest to make every story accurate, to fill every sentence with meaning and purpose.

The three of us wrestled with the translations, working to articulate thoughts and emotions that would have been challenging enough to express in their native Farsi, yet here we were trying to say them in English, with an entirely different alphabet, different grammatical structure, and countless cultural references. For example, "let's touch base" makes no sense if you don't know baseball, and how do you explain that we chop *down* a tree before we chop it *up*? Or that we sit *at* a desk, *in* a chair, and *on* a couch?)

A native English speaker has no idea how treacherous the language can be until he tries to explain why some words are considered off-color while others meaning exactly the same thing are not. Moreover, deeply rooted denominational differences among Christians that are widely understood and respected in America are unknown in Iran; they are strange and bewildering to people who have always been an oppressed minority, and to whom any sort of Christian message or experience is a blessing. On top of everything else, the original translations from Farsi were done in London, requiring various adjustments along the way for American readers, who, for example, think of a "lift" as a ride in someone's car, rather than the British word for *elevator*.

Moreover, there were thoughts and experiences for which no words in any language could do justice. They were so deep, so visceral, so immediate that they were almost beyond description. Yet that was our job. And over the months we worked together, these two brave young women never wavered at the task, never faltered in their dedication and enthusiasm, never let up in their quest for accuracy, even as they looked up hundreds of words in the English/Farsi dictionary on their iPad, carefully copying the definitions by hand in order to learn them.

From start to finish, the process of writing and editing this book based on Maryam's and Marziyeh's journals took almost exactly a year. We spent more time retelling the story than they did living it. For me, every word has been a privilege, every day's work a joy. Marziyeh and Maryam are gifted writers who have become treasured friends. Their story has transformed my life. If, by God's grace, we've done our work well, it will transform yours too.

John Perry
Nashville

ACKNOWLEDGMENTS

THIS BOOK IS A MIRACLE. There's no other way to explain it. Otherwise, how could two Iranian women who are still learning English have written it less than three years after arriving in America?

An opportunity like this could only have come from the Lord. We give thanks to our Savior, Jesus Christ, who carried us safely through all our hardships, brought us to freedom in America, and gave us the chance to share with the world our stories and the stories of other Iranian women.

God has brought many people into our path to make this book possible.

First was Calvin Edwards, who has become our good friend as well as our agent, and who guided us through the many decisions and steps it took to bring this project to life.

We're also grateful to Jan Long Harris and her wonderful team at Tyndale Momentum: senior acquisitions editor Sarah Atkinson, senior communications manager Sharon Leavitt, and our project editor, Dave Lindstedt.

We owe a special debt of thanks to our collaborator, John Perry, who so patiently worked with us to tell an emotional and complex story so beautifully—in what to us was a foreign language. Praise God for these faithful men and women who have helped us realize the dream of sharing our faith and our journey with you.

ABOUT THE AUTHORS

MARYAM ROSTAMPOUR AND MARZIYEH AMIRIZADEH were born into Muslim families in Iran—Maryam in the city of Kermanshah, and Marziyeh in Rafsanjan. They met while studying Christian theology in Turkey in 2005, and realized they had become Christians at about the same time six years earlier. Deciding to join forces, they returned to Iran and began a program of mission outreach. Over the next two years, they handed out twenty thousand New Testaments in Tehran and other cities. They started two house churches in their apartment, one for young people and another for prostitutes. They extended their ministry with mission trips to India, South Korea, and Turkey.

In March 2009, Maryam and Marziyeh were arrested in Tehran for promoting Christianity—a capital crime in Iran—and imprisoned for 259 days in the city's notorious Evin Prison. The official charges against them were apostasy, anti-government activity, and blasphemy, for which they were subject to execution by hanging. As many around the world prayed for their freedom, international pressure on the Iranian government came from organizations such as Amnesty International, the United Nations, and the Vatican.

Eventually, Maryam and Marziyeh were released from prison and cleared of all charges. They consider it an honor to have experienced a little of Christ's suffering by being imprisoned in His name. After their release, they immigrated to the United States and now live near Atlanta.

| | |

JOHN PERRY has written or collaborated on more than thirty books, including *Lady of Arlington*, a biography of Mary Custis (Mrs. Robert E. Lee) nominated for the Lincoln Prize, and is coauthor of the *New York Times* bestselling novel *Letters to God*. Among his recent collaborations is *Miracle for Jen* by Linda Barrick, from Tyndale House Publishers. John lives in Nashville.